LANGUAGES AND DIALECTS
IN THE U.S.

Languages and Dialects in the U.S. is a concise introduction to language varieties and dialects in the U.S. for students with little to no background in linguistics. This edited collection of fourteen chapters offers students detailed insight into the languages they speak and hear around them, framed within the context of language contact, with the goal of promoting students' appreciation of linguistic and cultural diversity. The book begins with "setting the stage" chapters, introducing the concepts of language contact and diversity and the sociocultural context of the languages and dialects featured in the book. The remaining chapters are each devoted to a particular U.S. dialect or variety of American English, exploring the language's sociolinguistic context, history, and salient grammatical features, with problem sets and suggested further readings to reinforce students' understanding of basic concepts and new linguistic terminology. The languages and dialects covered include three Native American languages (Navajo, Shoshoni, and Mandan), African American English, Chicano English, Jamaican Patwa, Southwest Spanish, Dominican Spanish, Chinese varieties, Haitian Creole, Cajun French, Louisiana Creole, and vernacular (or nonstandard) varieties of English.

By presenting students with both the linguistic and sociocultural and political foundations of these particular language varieties, *Languages and Dialects in the U.S.* argues for linguistic and cultural diversity in the U.S., ideal for students in introductory courses in linguistics, sociolinguistics, language and society, language and culture, and language variation and change.

Marianna Di Paolo is Associate Professor of Anthropology at the University of Utah.

Arthur K. Spears is Presidential Professor of Anthropology and Linguistics at The City University of New York.

LANGUAGES AND DIALECTS IN THE U.S.

Focus on Diversity and Linguistics

Edited by
Marianna Di Paolo and Arthur K. Spears

Routledge
Taylor & Francis Group

NEW YORK AND LONDON

First published 2014
by Routledge
711 Third Avenue, New York, NY 10017

And by Routledge
2 Park Square, Milton Park, Abingdon, Oxon OX14 4RN

Routledge is an imprint of the Taylor & Francis Group, an informa business

Library of Congress Cataloging-in-Publication Data
  Languages and dialects in the U.S. : focus on diversity and linguistics /
  edited by Marianna Di Paolo and Arthur K. Spears.
      pages cm.
  Includes bibliographical references and index.
  1. Dialectology–Research–United States.   2. United States–Languages.
  3. Language and languages–Variation.   I. Di Paolo, Marianna.   II. Spears,
  Arthur K. (Arthur Kean), 1943–
  P367.5.U6L37 2013
  427'.973–dc23   2013025931

ISBN: 978-0-415-72857-7 (hbk)
ISBN: 978-0-415-72860-7 (pbk)
ISBN: 978-1-315-85160-0 (ebk)

Typeset in Bembo
by Apex CoVantage, LLC

Printed in Great Britain by TJ International Ltd, Padstow, Cornwall

CONTENTS

List of Tables   *vii*
Preface   *xi*
Acknowledgments   *xv*

PART I
Setting the Stage   **1**

Introduction   3
Marianna Di Paolo and Arthur K. Spears

1 Language Contact   9
   Arthur K. Spears and Marianna Di Paolo

2 Thinking about Diversity   21
   Arthur K. Spears

PART II
Indigenous U.S. Language Varieties   **35**

3 Navajo   37
   Keren Rice

4 Shoshoni   53
   Dirk Elzinga and Marianna Di Paolo

  5 Mandan   69
     Mauricio J. Mixco

PART III
English and Other U.S. Language Varieties   **83**

  6 Vernacular Dialects of English   85
     Walt Wolfram

  7 African American English   101
     Arthur K. Spears

  8 Chicano English   115
     Carmen Fought

  9 Jamaican Creole   126
     Peter L. Patrick

 10 Southwest Spanish   137
     MaryEllen Garcia

 11 Dominican Spanish   151
     Barbara E. Bullock and Almeida Jacqueline Toribio

 12 Chinese   163
     Lauren Hall-Lew and Amy Wing-mei Wong

 13 Haitian Creole   180
     Arthur K. Spears

 14 Cajun French and Louisiana Creole   196
     Michael D. Picone

Contributors   *215*
Index   *221*

TABLES

3.1	Comparing words in the Navajo and Apache languages	38
3.2	Navajo consonant system	39
3.3	Navajo vowels	40
3.4	Navajo diphthongs	40
3.5	Summary of verb morpheme identification and ordering of morphemes	45
4.1	Shoshoni vowels	58
4.2	Demonstratives and demonstrative pronouns (objective forms)	59
4.3	Shoshoni phrases	62
4.4	Shoshoni locatives	62
4.5	Shoshoni noncoronal stops and continuants	63
4.6	Shoshoni coronal stops and continuants	64
4.7	Additional Shoshoni data on coronal stops and continuants	64
4.8	Shoshoni [s] and [ʃ]	65
4.9	Data on Shoshoni stops and continuants	65
4.10	Summary of morphophonological analysis	66
5.1	Mandan and Hidatsa in the Siouan-Catawba language family	71
5.2	The Mississippi Valley subbranch of Siouan	71
5.3	Mandan vowel length data	74
5.4	Mandan vowel nasalization data	74
5.5	Mandan vowel nasalization exercise	74
5.6	Mandan phonology data	75
5.7	Mandan subject agreement data	76
5.8	Subject agreement exercise	76
5.9	Additional subject agreement exercise	76
5.10	Additional Mandan subject agreement data	77
5.11	Mandan subject and object agreement morphemes	77

5.12 Mandan verb stem exercise 77
5.13 Mandan verb stem data 77
5.14 Mandan data on inflection for tense 78
5.15 Mandan data on inflection for Negation-A 78
5.16 Mandan data on inflection for Negation-B 79
5.17 Mandan mystery suffixes data 80
5.18 More Mandan mystery suffixes data 80
6.1 List A: Sentence pairs for *a*-prefixing 88
6.2 Comparing intuitions for different speaker groups 91
6.3 Grammaticality and social acceptability exercise 93
6.4 Restructured past tense *be* 96
6.5 An alternative regularization of past tense *be* 97
6.6 Devoicing in vernacular dialects 99
6.7 Consonant cluster simplification 100
7.1 Example sentences with *be done* 110
7.2 Clause sequence in *be done* sentences 111
7.3 Word set #1: Postvocalic word-final /l/ in a
   Midwestern variety of AAE 113
7.4 Word set #2: Postvocalic word-final /l/ in a
   Midwestern variety of AAE 113
7.5 Word set #3: Postvocalic word-final /l/ in a
   Midwestern variety of AAE 113
8.1 Data from Rosanna (a nonnative speaker of English whose
   first language is Spanish; age 56) 122
8.2 Joaquín (older-generation native CHE speaker; age 45) 124
8.3 Chuck (younger-generation native CHE speaker; age 17) 124
9.1 English vowels and word classes with Jamaican
   Creole equivalents 132
10.1 Categories of traditional Pachuco Caló 146
10.2 Beginning-level reducing hiatus data 147
10.3 Intermediate-level reducing hiatus data 148
11.1 Data from regional dialects of Dominican Spanish 158
11.2 Dominican hypercorrection data 159
11.3 /s/-deletion data from Dominican Spanish 159
11.4 Hypercorrect forms in Dominican Spanish 159
11.5 Double plural marking data 160
12.1 English words borrowed into Cantonese 175
12.2 English words containing /l/ borrowed into Cantonese 175
12.3 Additional English words containing /l/ borrowed
   into Cantonese 176
12.4 Data on Mandarin Chinese classifiers 176
12.5 Additional data on Mandarin Chinese classifiers 177
13.1 Some Haitian words of French origin 185
13.2 Comparison of words in three Haitian varieties and in French 189

13.3	Some Haitian possessive adjective suffixes, Port de Paix dialect	190
13.4	Some nouns and possessive suffixes, Port de Paix dialect	191
13.5	Verbs requiring the presence or absence of *te* under certain conditions, Port de Paix dialect	192
13.6	The meanings of two verbs	194
14.1	French nouns	207
14.2	Codeswitched (English) nouns	207
14.3	Tense, mood, and aspect	210

PREFACE

Marianna Di Paolo and Arthur K. Spears

This textbook is the outgrowth of an idea first discussed at a meeting of the Committee on Ethnic Diversity in Linguistics (CEDL) of the Linguistic Society of America (LSA). CEDL's charge is not only to research ethnic diversity in the field of linguistics in the U.S. but also to find ways to increase diversity among those studying linguistics. Proceeds from the sale of this textbook will go to support CEDL's work.

The first goal of this book is to interest a broad, diverse range of students in linguistics by providing course work that discusses in some detail the languages that they speak or that they hear around them. The second goal is to get students to understand the systematic, rule-governed nature of all language varieties by means of hands-on introductory exercises on the grammars of a sampling of language varieties spoken in the U.S., including those lacking in prestige or suffering from stigma.

This textbook can be used as a main text or one of several texts in introductory linguistics courses and other introductory courses dealing with sociolinguistics, language in the U.S., language in society, language and culture, and language diversity. It is strongly recommended that students in courses using this textbook have taken or be taking concurrently an introductory linguistics course. The introductory chapters are on language contact and diversity. Part II consists of three chapters on American Indian languages representing three different large language families. A chapter on U.S. English vernaculars begins Part III since it covers vernacular Englishes as a group—and issues related to vernaculars generally, not just English ones. Chapters on specific varieties of American English and on other languages spoken in the U.S. follow. Since all of the language-variety chapters stand alone, instructors may want to start with the language varieties most familiar to students in their classes and then go on to less familiar varieties.

These specific-language chapters have exercises ranging from phonology, morphology, and syntax to semantics, sometimes combining two of these core areas of linguistics in one problem. By having problem sets in the language chapters, we can also back up our claims about all language varieties being rule-governed and systematic, each with its own grammar. Students can see firsthand that the language variety under consideration is not just a "lot of slang," "defective," "corrupt," or a "broken version" of some other (standard) language variety. The chapters allow students to begin to understand that each and every language variety can furnish a window into the workings of the human mind and human social interaction.

There is no other textbook like this one. Perhaps the closest book to this one, though quite different in purpose, is *Language Diversity in the USA,* edited by Kim Potowski, which takes a sociology-of-language approach to U.S. language diversity. It contains more in-depth treatments of demographics, along with other discussions (e.g., of history and language use) of the type that appear in this book's chapters. However, it has no material on language structure and offers no problem sets.

The word *ethnic* is in CEDL's name, but its members have actually been concerned with all types of diversity and, more specifically, increasing the representation in our field of members of groups with little or no presence within the current community of linguists. These groups are those that have historically suffered discrimination and limited access to college. Included are groups of color, for example, African Americans, Asians, Caribbean-language-heritage groups, Native Americans, Pacific Islanders, Roma (also known as Gypsies), a number of Spanish-language-heritage groups, and others. (See the chapter "Thinking about Diversity" for more on these issues.) Also included is the working class, who often speak vernacular (i.e., nonstandard) language varieties and who often face greater challenges in gaining a college education than do members of more affluent groups. Though CEDL is concerned with diversity in a broad sense, in practice we have focused in this textbook on groups who have more members and/or about whom the contributors have more expertise. Thus, our focus in practice has been on marginalized ethnic groups and the working class.

We believe that more students from diverse backgrounds would be attracted to the field of linguistics if instructors in introductory courses made more use of course materials based on data from the language varieties of these groups. The thinking is that students would also feel more comfortable in their learning situations and have more appreciative views of their instructors if validations of their cultural backgrounds and special problems were given explicit recognition in the classroom and in teaching materials. This textbook, of course, also serves more traditional students by introducing them to the same information and challenging them to think about their views on all types of language varieties.

CEDL's members believe that many instructors of linguistics courses would be more than willing to use materials that make crucial use of the students' vernaculars (their everyday language with close family members and peers) and the students' speech communities, but they may not have the time or resources to create them. To make such materials readily available and to encourage the creation and dissemination of more materials of this type, CEDL sponsored a workshop at the 2003 Annual Meeting of the LSA, "Practical Approaches to Incorporating Linguistic Diversity into Linguistics Courses." This book incorporates two of the five presentations made at that workshop, Garcia's and Wolfram's.

Often, in introductory textbooks, there are no exercises on marginalized language varieties, or very few. (American Indian languages fare best in this regard.) And the exercises on English deal only with standard English. Discussions of vernacular English varieties are typically left for later in the book when sociolinguistics is discussed. CEDL members questioned whether our professed respect for and serious study of nonmainstream language varieties will be taken seriously if these varieties are normally shunted to the last part of the textbook, reserved for topics that most instructors consider optional. Introductory sociolinguistics textbooks are also found wanting. They typically offer some descriptions of vernacular varieties but do not present students with data-rich problem sets to work through.

For this book, we started by deciding to present chapters discussing nonstandard (or vernacular) language varieties, focusing on those of the larger language minorities in the U.S. such as African American English, Southwest Spanish, American Indian languages, and Jamaican Creole (Patwa). The basic rationale for including all of these chapters in this text is that they will give more weight to linguists' assertion that we value and treasure all language varieties, not just those enjoying power and prestige.

Some students have acquired negative views about their native or home language varieties, often through what they have been taught in school and have heard through the mass media. They erroneously believe that their languages are somehow inferior, unsystematic, or defective. This popular view of vernacular varieties is in direct contradiction to what empirical linguistic research has demonstrated. Some of these important findings are summarized in a resolution adopted unanimously by the LSA at its Annual Meeting in 1997, which asserts that "all human language systems—spoken, signed, and written—are fundamentally regular" and that characterizations of socially disfavored varieties as "slang, mutant, defective, ungrammatical, or broken English are incorrect and demeaning." We trust that after working through this book's exercises, students will share this view.

ACKNOWLEDGMENTS

We take this opportunity to acknowledge the support we have received in preparing this book. We thank The City College of The City University of New York's Office of the President, Gregory H. Williams, and the Department of Anthropology at the University of Utah for supporting our work. Also, we thank Penny Eckert for suggesting the idea of this book at a CEDL meeting, MaryEllen Garcia for sticking with it for so many years, and Walt Wolfram, Tracey Weldon, and Geoffrey Nunberg for their input and advice on early drafts. (Wolfram also contributed a chapter.) Finally, we would like to recognize the hard work of our assistants in helping to bring this book project to its conclusion; they are Jeff Chapple, Charles Townsend, and Deborah Wager.

PART I

Setting the Stage

INTRODUCTION

Marianna Di Paolo and Arthur K. Spears

This introduction, like the entire book, is written primarily for students but also for instructors. Instructors will already be familiar with basic information presented in this and the other chapters, but we hope that this chapter in particular will assist them by presenting a brief look at the relationship of fundamental linguistic ideas to this book's goal of increasing diversity in the corps of linguists. **Linguists**, as you probably already know, are language scientists, conducting empirical research on *all* the world's language varieties—their grammatical structures and their roles and functioning in society and culture. (Important terms are in bold when they are defined.) The work of linguists is to describe the workings of language, not to prescribe what someone thinks language ought to be. Our work, in other words, is **descriptive**, not **prescriptive**, and this applies not only to grammar but also to what is said, even taboo words and messages. The chapter on diversity provides a more detailed discussion of the idea of diversity, so here we will limit ourselves to some basic comments on it.

This textbook is considered a beginning. We hope that it will be expanded in the future to include more language varieties, illustrating the scope of our concern. Consequently, if you, as a student, are not represented by a language chapter, we hope that at least your language background (for example, bilingualism), if not one of the languages you speak, is mentioned in these pages.

The Structure of the Book

This textbook is intended to be used as either a supplement to an introductory textbook covering core areas of linguistics, with additional chapters on historical linguistics and bilingualism or sociolinguistics, or as the main text of a course on linguistic diversity in the U.S., following or taken concurrently with an introductory linguistics course that has included linguistic analysis.

As linguists, we care about the lives of the speakers of the languages we study, the socioeconomic conditions that allow these languages and their speakers to survive and thrive. A number of the language varieties that chapters are devoted to are endangered, notably, but not solely, American Indian languages. Other language varieties included in this volume, such as Southwest Spanish or African American English, are greatly misunderstood and often given little respect. In many cases the varieties were shaped in a multilingual community and continue to reflect that rich heritage. These concerns have led us to provide in each chapter remarks on sociolinguistics—that is, the condition of the language variety in culture and society along with the ways that condition affects and is affected by sociolinguistic variation. Each language chapter also has sources for further reading. The issues confronting that group and their language variety determined the topics selected for discussion.

SOCIOLINGUISTIC VARIATION

Sociolinguistic variation refers to the many instances in language, reflecting sociocultural patterns, in which there are two or more ways to say the same thing, for example, *talking* vs. *talkin'*.

The culmination of each chapter is the set of exercises, which lead the beginning-level student to some understanding of language in general and of that language variety in particular. By working through a tiny area of each language variety's grammar, students can actually "experience" the grammar of these language varieties and gain some idea of why linguists find them fascinating.

We assume that beginning-level students will have some knowledge of a particular core area of linguistics before working through problem sets in that area. For example, before beginning a problem set on the phonology of Dominican Spanish, we recommend that the students read about phonology in their primary textbook and that the instructor review the basic concepts in phonology pertinent to the data in the problem. The students will then get the maximum benefit from working through the phonology exercises on Dominican Spanish.

Beginning with this introduction, Part I of the book sets the stage for the chapters on particular language varieties. In Chapter 1, "Language Contact," Arthur K. Spears and Marianna Di Paolo present issues related to bilingual and multilingual societies that have shaped and may continue to shape many of the language varieties described in the language chapters. There are many basic facts about multilingualism of which most students are unaware, for example, that most of the world's peoples by far live and have lived in multilingual communities, no doubt since the earliest days of human language. Consequently, in an important sense, multilingualism is the "natural" human condition. With multilingualism, there is always language contact, within one speaker (the bilingual, for example) and/or within one community. Many students may subscribe to the erroneous belief that multilingualism has a negative effect on a speaker's cognitive abilities; in fact, more recent research indicates that the multilingual speaker has a cognitive advantage.

The chapter on language contact also clarifies that multilingualism has been a key factor in the history of languages; it is not simply a currently widespread situation globally. For example, multilingualism was present in the communities in which African American English and Jamaican Creole (Patwa) were created, via influences from several languages in contact—as a result of multilingualism. By developing a clearer idea of what multilingualism and language contact are about, to take two concepts treated in the chapter, students can begin to understand how important they are and see them as resources, not obstacles.

The language contact chapter ties into Spears's chapter on diversity in a number of ways. As noted, understanding linguistic situations in communities helps students to understand groups in whose lives these linguistic situations are more prominent. Some of these groups are speakers of stigmatized language varieties, and they suffer various kinds of discrimination. The language contact chapter seeks to increase understanding and respect for largely stigmatized varieties, while the chapter on diversity seeks to increase understanding and respect for the speaker communities of these language varieties.

However, greater understanding and respect for speaker communities also require consideration of history, society, and culture as they relate to diversity in the U.S. Generally, language varieties are stigmatized because their speakers suffer from stigma and discrimination. Such speakers' histories and contributions to society often go unrecognized, not only because of a lack of knowledge, but also because students and others buy into myths and stereotypes. The chapter on diversity draws on anthropology—the holistic, comparative, and historical study of humankind—to refute some of the myths and stereotypes that contribute the most to a lack of interest in or a rejection of increasing diversity in our national life. In addition, the chapter on diversity contextualizes issues of opportunity, inequality, internal oppression, bias, and discrimination—for instructors as well as students. It argues that linguistics can speak to students about their own languages in the context of their own lives.

Part II presents chapters on a selection of American Indian languages representing three large language families. We wanted to honor, so to speak, the indigenous language varieties covered in this book (Navajo, Shoshoni, and Mandan) by placing them before nonindigenous varieties, that is, in Part II. We start with the most spoken and least endangered one, Navajo (although it is endangered to some extent), and end with Mandan, which has only a handful of speakers and is most endangered. The problem sets on American Indian languages highlight the fact that languages are often complex in different ways.

The first of these chapters is by Keren Rice on Navajo, an Athabaskan language and the U.S. indigenous language with the greatest number of speakers. The chapter provides a short introduction to the Navajo people and the language's linguistic affiliation, followed by problem sets on Navajo phonology, morphology, syntax, and verb semantics (classificatory verbs), and then ends with problem sets based on the work of the Navajo Code Talkers from World War II.

The Shoshoni chapter, by Dirk Elzinga and Marianna Di Paolo, situates this Great Basin language as a member of the Uto-Aztecan language family. It includes a sketch of Sacagawea, perhaps the most famous Shoshoni speaker, and her linguistic role in the Lewis and Clark Expedition. It concludes with problem sets on Shoshoni phonology, morphophonology, and syntax.

Next is Mauricio J. Mixco's chapter on Mandan, an indigenous language of North Dakota, which begins with background information on the Mandan and their language, including a short grammatical sketch to facilitate solving the problems. The problem sets have Mandan phonology problems and an extensive set of morphology problems.

Nonindigenous language varieties follow in Part III. It presents chapters on U.S. vernacular varieties of English and other languages spoken in the U.S. Our selection is based on an attempt, within the confines of a single volume, to cover as many different types of varieties as possible that have an easily available linguistic literature. We decided to order the chapters on nonindigenous varieties by their relatedness, including lexical relatedness. Thus, Jamaican Creole "Patwa" is grouped with English varieties because it is "English-related." The bulk of its vocabulary came from English. Jamaican is not English and is not mutually intelligible with English. We hasten to point out also that Jamaican has its own grammar. In the same way, Haitian Creole is grouped with the Cajun variety of French and Louisiana Creole.

We then arranged these nonindigenous language-variety groups approximately by the number of speakers in the U.S., starting with languages having the highest number of speakers. Thus, English varieties and the English-related creole language, Jamaican, are followed by Spanish varieties, then Chinese, and so on. (Note that *Chinese* actually refers to a group of related languages, all treated in one chapter.)

Like chapters 3–5 in Part II, chapters 6–14 in Part III each begin with a brief discussion of the history and social context of the language variety, followed by a description of some of its salient linguistic features, and end with problem sets or exercises. The first of these chapters is Walt Wolfram's "Vernacular Dialects of English." It is presented first since it treats English vernaculars generally and thus serves as a useful starting point for considering English varieties. It gives students hands-on experience with data illustrating the highly patterned nature of vernacular varieties of U.S. English and guides students through an understanding of the difference between grammaticality and social acceptability. It includes problem sets on the phonology, morphology, and syntax of Southern American English (focusing on the English of Appalachia and the Outer Banks of North Carolina) and the syntax and semantics of African American English.

Next is Spears's chapter "African American English." This U.S. variety, actually a group of varieties, has been widely studied by linguists and is sometimes widely misunderstood by the general population. The chapter discusses the various terms such as Ebonics that are also used to label African American English, the variety's origin and development, its present-day use, and some of its grammatical characteristics. The problem set deals with phonology (syllable-final /l/) and also the semantics and pragmatics of a disapproval marker, *be done*.

Carmen Fought's chapter, "Chicano English," tackles the question of what Chicano English is, its role in the Mexican American speech communities from which it arose, and its relationship to both English and Spanish. Based on data collected in Los Angeles, Fought's problem sets lead students to understand the phonological differences between the English of nonnative speakers whose native language is Spanish and the English of true native speakers of Chicano English, who may not know any Spanish at all.

Chapter 9 presents an English-related language, Jamaican Creole, which originated in the Caribbean nation of Jamaica but is now also spoken by a sizable community in the U.S.—and in Canada and Great Britain as well. Peter L. Patrick introduces *di Patwa*, the term used by its speakers, by providing a social and linguistic history of Jamaica, concentrating on the development of this creole from its multilingual roots. The problem sets allow students to explore the phonology of the language, its phonological relationship to British English, and its syntax and semantics.

Chapters 10 and 11 are on two Spanish language varieties spoken in the U.S. The first of these is "Southwest Spanish" by MaryEllen Garcia, which begins by defining the variety and providing a linguistic sketch of this regional vernacular compared to Standard Spanish, followed by a section on Pachuco Caló and codeswitching. Garcia has problem sets on phonology, the lexicon as a product of long-term Spanish-English contact, and codeswitching.

The next chapter focuses on Dominican Spanish. In comparison to colonial Southwest Spanish, it is a relatively recent arrival to the U.S. but also one of the oldest vernaculars of Spanish in the Americas. Barbara E. Bullock and Almeida Jacqueline Toribio's chapter situates Dominican Spanish both in its country of origin as well as in vibrant and growing communities in the U.S. They follow a linguistic sketch of Dominican Spanish with problem sets on phonology, morphology, and syntax.

Next we have Lauren Hall-Lew and Amy Wing-mei Wong's chapter on Chinese, which begins with a classification of Chinese homeland dialects and then discusses the varieties of Chinese brought by immigrants to the U.S. beginning in 1830. A short sketch of notable linguistic features of the language is provided as well as a basic description of the writing system. The chapter ends with problem sets on the phonology of words borrowed into Chinese from English, and on noun classifiers.

The final two chapters move the focus to French-related creole languages and a variety of French spoken in the U.S. First we have Spears's chapter on Haitian Creole, the language created in colonial Haiti. Today, Haiti shares the island of Hispaniola with the Dominican Republic. To explain how the new language, Haitian Creole, emerged and is now regarded, the chapter reviews the multi-lingual history of Haiti, the relationship of Haitian to French, and the current languages of Haitians in the U.S. Spears provides problem sets on phonology and morphology as they interact with dialect variation and also problems on the semantics and pragmatics of tense marking.

Michael D. Picone's chapter on Cajun French and Louisiana Creole, which situates them within the complex linguistic history of Louisiana, completes the volume. In it, he distinguishes the two varieties both historically and linguistically. For Cajun French, the problem sets include items on Cajun inflectional morphol-ogy and that of English words used by Cajun speakers while codeswitching. The theme of the interaction of inflectional morphology and codeswitching is carried through in the problem set on Louisiana Creole.

The users of this book might notice that linguists seem to know much less about most of the language varieties discussed in the chapters than we know about Standard English, but that should not be discouraging. We linguists, as sci-entists of language, are excited about learning more about the unknown and helping others to understand what we have discovered. We hope that students using this volume will come to share that excitement and some day help all of us to understand their own language varieties better, whether or not we were able to represent them in this small collection.

1

LANGUAGE CONTACT

Arthur K. Spears and Marianna Di Paolo

Languages have been in contact with one another throughout human history. Different groups of people come into contact due to various circumstances, and the nature of that contact heavily influences the effects on the language(s) spoken by those groups, in cases where they speak different languages or, perhaps, different dialects (Holm 2004; Mufwene 2001; Thomason 2001; Winford 2003). Since at least 5,000 languages are spoken around the world today and since there are only about 250 countries, language contact is a normal part of our existence as human beings.

The chapters in this book deal with languages involved in three types of language contact. Immediately below, we present some brief remarks about the languages considered in this book, and then we discuss the different types of contact. (We do not include in this chapter contact phenomena not relating directly to this book's language chapters. For a more general discussion of language contact, see Thomason 2001 and Winford 2003.)

First, several chapters deal with new languages (creoles formed in the last 350 years or so). Creoles are dealt with in the chapters that discuss Jamaican (Patwa), Haitian Creole, and Louisiana Creole.

NEW LANGUAGES: PIDGINS AND CREOLES

We use the expression **new languages** to refer to cases in which brand-new languages emerge, partially made up of languages that have come into contact but also with their own new, unique grammatical features. This term is mostly used for pidgins or creoles. A ***pidgin*** language results from a relatively abrupt process of new-language formation, typically caused by speakers without a common language having to communicate. The process is abrupt relative to, say, the formation process for the development of French out of Latin. Pidgins come into existence with grammars simpler than those of the languages they are most closely related to and with a reduced range of social contexts in which they are used. The grammar of a pidgin is stable enough that it can be recognized as a speech form in its own right, different from the input languages. A pidgin becomes a creole when a community begins speaking it as a native language. Not all creoles, however, develop from (grammatically stable) pidgins. That is, none of the speech forms leading to the birth of such creoles are stable enough to qualify as a pidgin.

The second group of this book's languages for which language contact phenomena are important are African American English (AAE), Chicano English, Southwest (U.S.) Spanish, Dominican (U.S.) Spanish, and Louisiana, or Cajun, French. These are language varieties whose distinctive nature, compared to other varieties of the same language, stems from their presence over an extended period in a more intense language contact situation.

AAE is described in some current work on contact linguistics as partially restructured grammatically due to language contact. In other work it is described as the result of group second-language acquisition, that is, language shift—dropping one language over time while adopting another. Both ways of describing AAE get at the fact that, in the process of acquiring English, the early African Americans' creole and West African languages significantly influenced the variety of English that they created—AAE. Many of these influences can still be seen in current AAE, which has some grammatical features in common with a number of creole languages. (See the chapters on AAE and the vernacular dialects of English for examples.)

In the case of Chicano English, the contact brought together English and Mexican/Chicano Spanish (see Carmen Fought's and MaryEllen Garcia's chapters). In the case of Southwest Spanish, the contact was between the same languages, but the chapter zeroes in on how the contact affected Spanish (see MaryEllen Garcia's chapter). The chapter on Dominican Spanish presents a different contact situation for this variety of Spanish, which arrived in the U.S. much more recently. Michael D. Picone's chapter looks at how contact with U.S. English has affected Cajun French, which was transported to Louisiana with the forced exile from (Arcadia) Canada in the eighteenth century of the people who came to be known as Cajuns. One of the most obvious contact-related features of these languages is borrowing from the language with which they are in contact. Another salient feature involves both of the languages in the contact situation: codeswitching, switching back and forth between the languages in the contact situation (for example, between Southwest Spanish and English).

The third group of languages affected by language contact phenomena includes indigenous ones such as Mandan, Shoshoni, and Navajo, as well as Louisiana (Cajun) French, which in the U.S. are in danger of dying out under pressure from the economically and politically powerful language English. (Please see the Shoshoni chapter in regard to the spellings *Shoshoni* vs. *Shoshone*.)

Mandan has only a small number of fluent speakers left. While Shoshoni speakers number in the thousands, very few children are currently acquiring the language in the home. However, there are a number of maintenance and revitalization programs, which include teaching Shoshoni as a second language in many tribal community centers and at three public and two tribal schools in Idaho, Utah, and Nevada. Idaho State University as well as the University of Utah have been offering credit-bearing Shoshoni language courses for a number of years.

Navajo has the largest number of speakers of any U.S. indigenous language, but currently very few children have Navajo as their mother tongue. It is still a strong language, but once a language ceases to have young native speakers, measures must be taken to ensure its long-term survival. Fortunately, a number of revitalization programs are already under way for Navajo.

Language versus Dialect

From your other reading in linguistics, you are aware of the distinction between the terms *language* and *dialect*. Dialects show differences in everything from pronunciation and vocabulary to morphology, syntax, and semantics. Although we cannot always determine where one language stops and another begins, even a person without linguistic training recognizes that there are different ways (dialects) of speaking the same way (language)—so to speak. For example, there are different dialects of English in Britain, the U.S., and Australia. A number of chapters in this book focus on dialects of English (vernacular dialects of English, AAE, and Chicano English), Spanish (Southwest Spanish and Dominican Spanish), French (Cajun French and other varieties of French in Louisiana), and Chinese. (The chapter on Chinese presents the rationale for referring to the varieties of Chinese as dialects of one language.)

DIALECT, STANDARD, AND LANGUAGE VARIETY

In some language-study traditions, especially in Europe, a dialect is an unwritten, historically related form of a national standard variety, and the term may carry a negative connotation. **Dialect**, as used by linguists, is simply a particular form of a language, standard or nonstandard. (The **standard** is the dialect described in grammar books and dictionaries and used in education, government, and other mainstream settings.) *Dialect* is used in a totally nonjudgmental sense in linguistics. The term *dialect* focuses more narrowly than the term *language*. Frequently, the term *language variety* or **variety** is used instead of the term *language* or *dialect* to refer to any level of generalization with regard to speech forms.

Everyone speaks a dialect—of some language. Everyone also speaks a language. Again, the use of one term or the other has to do with focusing narrowly or more broadly. We often find a linguistic continuum, such as that in northwestern Europe, where dialects of Dutch, Flemish (in Belgium), and German gradually change into other dialects as one travels farther and farther away from a given point.

Dialects of the same language, for example, dialects of English, are often mutually intelligible but not always. There are various social, cultural, historical, psychological, and also linguistic factors that may interfere with mutual intelligibility. Repeated exposure to a grammatically distant dialect typically increases one's ability to understand it.

In some cases, language varieties that are mutually intelligible may be treated as separate languages. This is the case with some of the Numic languages of the Great Basin, the region of the U.S. east of the Rocky Mountains and west of the Sierra Nevadas. For example, the mutually intelligible varieties Shoshoni and Gosiute have distinct names and have sometimes been treated as separate languages in some official situations, although linguists, and most speakers, lump them together as dialects of one language, Shoshoni. On the other hand, linguists usually treat Shoshoni and Comanche as separate languages while native speakers of Shoshoni say they understand Comanche.

NUMIC LANGUAGES AND LANGUAGE FAMILY

Numic languages are languages of the northernmost branch of the Uto-Aztecan language family such as Shoshoni, Comanche, Northern Paiute, and Ute. Uto-Aztecan languages are still spoken from northern Idaho and Wyoming to Central America. The best-known, and currently largest, language of the family is Nahuatl, the language of the Aztecs. It is spoken in southern Mexico and by some Mexican immigrants in the U.S.

The term *language family* refers to a group of languages with one common ancestor. Their common ancestry is reflected in lexical similarities and, crucially, in systematic (phonological, morphological, and/or syntactic) structural similarities.

In sum, there are no set linguistic criteria for dividing up the world's language varieties into languages and dividing each language into its various dialects. Often linguistic factors are helpful, but just as often we find that political, social, historical, and psychological factors are important too. Because of these considerations, estimates of the languages spoken in the world today range between 5,000 and 7,000; the number depends on whether a particular variety is counted as a separate language or as a dialect of another language.

The unit of analysis for language contact is the speech community. A speech community may be defined narrowly or broadly. It sometimes involves a village, a large city, a nation, or even a multinational region. A speech community may also be defined on the basis of socially salient groups based on, for example, gender, ethnicity, race, and other types of social and personal identities.

SPEECH COMMUNITY AND LANGUAGE USE

Speech community is defined as a community whose members

1. usually share at least one language variety
2. share rules for language use and the evaluation of speech

Language use involves what is also called "communicative practices" or "ways of speaking."

Outcomes of Language Contact

We can speak of language contact in terms of

1. the way it affects and changes a speech community overall and, especially, the way it affects the survival of the languages in contact,
2. the way it affects the languages in contact, and
3. the new languages that it sometimes creates.

Changes in the Speech Community

The most obvious way that language contact can affect and change a speech community is by leading to bilingualism, which may involve two first languages or a first language and a second language. Bilingualism is a question of degree: a person may not speak both languages (or all the languages, in the case of multilingualism) equally well, especially if one of the languages is a second language. Additionally, we have to distinguish between individual bilingualism and societal bilingualism. The latter exists when bilingualism is widespread in the community, a fairly common situation in the world today. Bilingualism on the societal level—a metropolitan community, a state, or a group of states in the U.S., for example—exists where Southwest Spanish, Dominican Spanish, Cajun French, Louisiana Creole, and Shoshoni are spoken.

NATIVE OR FIRST LANGUAGE (L1) AND SECOND LANGUAGE (L2)

A **native or first language**, or **L1**, is acquired during early childhood, usually by growing up in a social environment where that language is spoken in everyday social interaction. On the other hand, a **second language**, or **L2**, is learned later in life, or perhaps in the classroom or through tutoring at any age. Crucial is that an L1 is acquired early in life and naturally, through everyday social interaction as the learner is enculturated, unlike an L2. Speakers may have more than one L1 and more than one L2.

> Thus, in a two-language contact situation, language X (say, Dominican Spanish in New York) may well be some speakers' L1 but an L2 for other speakers.

Societal bilingualism may be stable or transitory. With stable bilingualism, the two languages (or more languages—what we discuss in regard to bilingualism also applies to multilingualism) continue to be spoken in the community instead of one language becoming dominant and eventually triggering the attrition and death of the other language.

The increased use of English was beginning to eclipse Cajun French until recently, when concerted efforts began to promote it, especially in southwestern Louisiana. However, it is still most likely in decline, due to the strong pressure of English. With few speakers, Louisiana Creole is in serious danger of eventually disappearing. It is in much the same situation as the American Indian languages referred to above. Chicano English will probably be with us indefinitely due to the vibrant and growing Chicano communities in the U.S. AAE, an outgrowth of antiblack racial violence and segregation, will no doubt exist as long as an identifiable African American community exists in the U.S. Jamaican (Patwa) remains vibrant in some cities such as New York, due primarily to the continual influx of Jamaican-speaking immigrants. A parallel situation exists with Haitian Creole.

With Spanish as the biggest exception and other exceptions such as Cantonese (Chinese), the languages of immigrants to the U.S. eventually undergo language death, in the sense that there ceases to be an immigrant *community* speaking the language. Over the generations, societal bilingualism in those locales eventually disappears. This has happened with Italian and German, for example. During the course of the second author's (Di Paolo's) life, Abruzzes' Italian has gone from being her only language in her early childhood in a multilingual community in Colorado to being a language that she communicates in for just a few hours a year because most of the fluent speakers she knew have passed away and the remaining bilinguals are more comfortable in English. (Abruzzes' is the name of this dialect, spoken in Abruzzo, a region of Italy. The apostrophe in the spelling represents a reduced vowel.)

Spanish is a special case because, as second- and third-generation descendants of Spanish-speaking immigrants become English monolinguals, they are replaced, so to speak, by new Spanish-speaking immigrants. As a result, Spanish remains a vital language in numerous American communities. Spanish also has a special place in the U.S. because it is a colonial language. Like English, it was the language of the first European settlers in a large part of the U.S. (see the chapter on Southwest Spanish). Colonial languages in the U.S. persist much longer than immigrant languages because they play a special role for members of their speech communities, as Haugen (1956) pointed out over a half century ago.

Societal bilingualism usually atrophies and ultimately disappears in communities where each language does not become functionally distinct. The term **diglossia** is used for societies in which there is bilingualism but in which the languages serve different functions. Under diglossia, there is a high (H) language and a low (L) language, the former used in more public, formal domains such as education, government, and the legal system. The L language, on the other hand, is used in more private, informal social domains involving, for example, the family, friends, and play. While the L language is learned as an L1 (native language), the H language is normally learned at school.

In some diglossic societies, most people, or at least a majority of them, are bilingual in both languages. In other societies, Haiti, for example, there are just a few bilinguals, who speak both Haitian Creole (L) and French (H). The percentage of bilinguals has been estimated as being as low as 5%. Consequently, given that diglossia involves functional differentiation in the languages, in those societies in which there is limited bilingualism, the majority of the population, with little or no access to formal education, is excluded from full participation in public domains, access to which is crucial for furthering and protecting individual and group needs and interests. As noted in the chapter on Haitian, diglossia in Haiti is diminishing due to the officialization of Haitian along with French and its increased use in the H domain.

On a parallel with *bilingualism*, sometimes linguists use the term *bidialectalism* to refer to situations in which two dialects are used. Related to this notion is the fact that many AAE speakers are bidialectal; that is, they speak AAE and some non-AAE variety of English. Likewise, Chicano English or Appalachian English speakers may also be bidialectal, although less is known about their typical linguistic repertoires.

Effects on the Languages' Survival

In some instances, languages survive language contact but not always. Language maintenance occurs when a group whose language is involved in language contact keeps its language over the long run. In some cases, however, there is language shift, whereby a group adopts a new language, ceasing to use its former language. The latter scenario results in language attrition and then language death.

Nettle and Romaine (2000) estimate that half of the world's current languages are in danger of dying out in this century. They argue that language endangerment, like the extinction of species, is largely driven by the destruction of the world's ecosystems as one dominant economic system spreads and, in the case of languages, results in the loss of cultural and linguistic diversity. Hinton and Hale (2001) paint a more optimistic picture, presenting many examples of successful or at least hopeful cases of language revitalization. (Also see Spears and Hinton [2010] and EMELD [n.d.] for more information on the maintenance and revitalization of endangered languages.)

Many American Indian languages in the U.S. have already suffered attrition and death. There are 175 indigenous languages that survive; and most, perhaps all, are endangered. Attrition can lead to the current situation, in which a number of these languages have only one or a few speakers left. Attrition is normally accompanied by a reduction in the grammatical resources of the language and the social contexts of use. For example, with only a few speakers, the language is no longer used for ceremonial purposes.

Linguists are extremely concerned about today's high rate of language attrition and death worldwide. When we lose a language, we lose an irreplaceable resource that provides a unique way of looking at the world and insight into the human mind. We also lose the opportunity to understand the full range of the grammatical abilities of human beings. And the people who lose their ancestral language lose a crucial connection with their cultural past.

Effects on the Languages in Contact

As noted, language contact often leads to bilingualism. One of the effects of bilingualism is codeswitching, the incorporation of material from another language into the one being spoken or the alternation between two (or more) languages during the same communicative event. (See the chapters on Southwest Spanish and Cajun French for examples.) Linguists disagree on exactly how to define codeswitching, but they all agree that it involves the use of material from two languages (or even more) within one communicative event. Codeswitching may be intersentential, with one sentence in one language and another in another language, or intrasentential, within one sentence. Within a sentence, it may involve inserting everything from a single morpheme to entire clauses from another language. Observe this example from Spanish-English codeswitching with English in boldface: *Compré este **LAPTOP DOWNTOWN*** 'I bought this laptop downtown.'

COMMUNICATIVE EVENTS

Examples of **communicative events** are jokes, conversations, sermons, arguments, classroom discussions, and corporate board meetings.

Codeswitching involves switches between language varieties that are different along the full range of grammar—vocabulary, phonology, morphology, and so on. For switching between dialects of the same language, for example, AAE and a non-AAE variety, linguists sometimes use the term *codeshifting*.

Styleshifting, however, involves variation in the use of two or more possible ways of saying the same thing, often in the same dialect and by the same speaker, and possibly in the same speech event. The different ways of saying the same thing are called **variants**. Variants used in styleshifting are usually socially marked; that is, using more of one variant instead of another often has social meaning. Speakers styleshift, often unconsciously, for stylistic purposes, usually for speaking more or less formally, but also for signaling in-group membership.

Styleshifting might involve, for example, using *ain't* instead of *isn't*, as in *He ain't here* vs. *He isn't here*. It quite commonly involves phonological variation. For example, speakers of English use the variants [ɪn] and [ɪŋ], different ways of pronouncing the verbal suffix written *-ing*, as in *work**ing***. Note the following example:

> Yesterday, I was walk*ing* down the street, try*in'* to find the grocery store I had gone to the day before. Suddenly, I start see*ing* a whole bunch of grocery stores, and I'm go*in'*, "Wait a minute. This isn't the street I was on before."

In this passage, two variants of the verbal suffix *-ing* (underlined) are used. All speakers of English do this. In more formal contexts, more *-ing*s are used; more of the informal variant, *-in'*, are used in more informal, often friendly contexts. Moreover, the statistical rates of usage of one or the other variant differ along class, gender, social situation, and other lines, and the rates of use of the variants are predictable if one has sufficient social information on the speakers and the speech situation (for example, formal or informal).

Language contact is sometimes the driving force behind some of the variation used in styleshifting. But it is important to keep in mind that the speech of virtually all speakers of all languages shows this sort of highly patterned and systematic variation. It is called inherent variation because it is a basic component of all native speakers' usage. The chapters on vernacular dialects of English, Chicano English, and Dominican Spanish provide an opportunity to work through data sets illustrating inherent variation.

Borrowing is the term used for cases in which an item from one language, L_m, which provides the model for the item borrowed into a recipient language, L_r, is completely assimilated into L_r to the extent that native speakers of L_r usually do not know that the item is borrowed. Many English words have been borrowed, for example, from French: *perfume*, *déjà vu*, *avenue*, *pork*, *beef*, *détente*, and *laissez-faire*. Borrowing may result from direct contact, where speakers of the relevant languages share a community. Examples of this type are given in the chapters on Southwest Spanish, Navajo, Cajun French, and Chinese.

The term *interference* (the usual term in L2 research), or *language transfer* (the term used in historical linguistics), focuses on cases where aspects of the grammar of one's own native language are applied to items of the target language being learned. As an illustration, if a Spanish-English bilingual controls one language, say his L1, more than his other language, L2, then there may well be transfer into the L2 as the bilingual speaks it. Often transfer has to do with applying the phonology of an L1 to an item from an L2. For example, English (L2) *tennis* might be pronounced [tenis] by an L1 speaker of Spanish instead of [tɛnɪs], as it would usually be pronounced in most native varieties of English. The pronunciation [tenis] reflects the application of Spanish phonology (which has /e/ and /i/ but lacks the phonemes /ɛ/ and /ɪ/) to an English word. (The Chicano English chapter provides problem sets containing more data of this type.)

In other cases, a bilingual might have English as her L1 (native language), but her English reflects the historical influence of Spanish. So, when she uses an English word that appears to have a Spanish pronunciation, it may simply be the way that she, and other members of her speech community, pronounces the English word in her ethnic dialect of English. (This is the case in numerous communities in which much of the population is descended from Spanish speakers.) While ethnic varieties are often disparaged by outsiders (but not linguists!), an ethnic variety of English in the U.S. often plays an important role in a speech community, including reflecting a positive in-group identity.

The process of L2 acquisition invariably involves not only transfer but also variation in learning, leading to the creation by the learner of a new mental grammar of the language. Thus, L2 acquisition by a whole community of speakers of a single L1 may lead to the creation of a new variety of the L2 influenced in part by the L1. For example, L1 Spanish speakers learning English as an L2 eventually led to the speech community's creation of Chicano English. AAE presents a more complex case: historically, Africans who arrived in the U.S. spoke an array of West African languages as well as creole languages of the Caribbean. Influences from both types of these ancestral languages can still be found in AAE today. While language learning under the influence of one or more than one L1 has been referred to as *imperfect* learning, an unfortunate word with negative connotations, the acquisition of an L1 or of an L2 is never perfect. Language acquisition is always a creative process and not merely a process that "copies and pastes" language from one individual or set of individuals into the learner's brain. (Jeff Pynes's insights [personal communication] were valuable in shaping our thoughts on L2 acquisition.)

New Languages

In this section, we turn our attention to new languages that may result from contact. Of these new languages, this book's chapters treat only creoles. Keep in mind that the term *creole*, in lower case, refers to a type of language. Languages are classified as creoles based mainly on sociohistorical criteria, but some types of grammatical features, illustrated in the Jamaican Creole, Haitian Creole, and Louisiana Creole chapters, are widespread in creole languages.

SUPERSTRATE, LEXIFIER, AND SUBSTRATE LANGUAGES

The **superstrate language** is that of the sociopolitically dominant group in the contact situation. It is typically the **lexifier language**, that providing most of the new language's vocabulary. Creole grammars take on grammatical features (including vocabulary) from both the **substrate** (the language[s] of the subordinate groups) and the superstrate but may reflect innovations traceable to neither. Typically, especially in creoles in the Caribbean and West Africa, the superstrate provides most of the vocabulary, and the substrate provides the morphology, syntax, and semantics.

At this point, something should be said about two different types of situations in creole-speaking societies. We will use Caribbean countries as examples. In some countries, we find diglossia; in others, a creole continuum. As noted, diglossia refers to situations in which there is a prestige language variety (standard) used for "high" (H) functions (that is, in government, education, newspapers, etc.) and a nonprestige, low (L) language variety serving "low" functions (that is, talk among friends and family members and in other situations in which formality is not required). In Haiti, there is diglossia.

Jamaica offers an example of a **creole continuum**, a chain of minimally distinct speech varieties stretching from the acrolect (varieties closest to Standard Jamaican English), through the mesolect, to the most basilectal varieties (those furthest from the standard, showing the greatest continuity with their African roots). This is to say that with such continua, we do not find easily distinguishable speech varieties. Indeed, the acrolectal end of the continuum cannot always be easily distinguished from Standard Jamaican English itself. (See the chapter on Jamaican Creole in this book, which provides more details on what a creole continuum is like and the role of variation within it.)

An example of an **intermediate creole** is Bajan (also Barbadian Creole), the creole of Barbados. It is closer grammatically to its lexifier language, English, than the average creole, hence the use of this term to distinguish it from other creoles such as Jamaican, Haitian, and Papiamentu. Intermediate creoles are considered special cases of language shift to an L2, English in this case, in which L2 learning resulted in a language variety clearly different from most monolingual dialects of English. As such, the range of varieties spoken in a society such as Barbados will usually include **partially restructured languages** in terms of their grammatical distance from the lexifier. Thus, the basilectal range of intermediate creole varieties is further from the lexifier than the basilectal range of partially restructured languages such as AAE. This observation underlies the distinction between the two types, but it must be taken provisionally since in-depth studies of partially restructured languages as a group have only recently begun. Consequently, partially restructured languages are seen as cases of language shift (from indigenous and West African languages) to a European-language L2, resulting in a variety more similar to L1 varieties of the target European language than are found with intermediate creoles. No variety of partially restructured languages has enough creole-like grammatical features for linguists to want to classify it as a creole. So, while AAE (especially vernacular varieties) has some creole-like grammatical features, they are not sufficient in number to warrant classifying any of its varieties as a creole, unlike the situation in Barbados.

In summary, all languages and their dialects have been affected by language contact. All too often language contact has led to the extinction or the near extinction of the subordinate language. But sometimes the outcome of language contact is the formation of a new variety, such as Jamaican Creole, or a new dialect of a language, such as Southwest Spanish.

There is increasing respect for languages of the types discussed in this chapter. For example, there are orthographies for many creole languages of the Americas and for many of the American Indian languages, and in some cases they have been officialized in education and/or government. This has happened in Haiti, for example, though there still remains a good deal of work to be done in implementing official policies, especially those calling for these languages' use in education.

Professional organizations such as the Linguistic Society of America and organizations such as UNESCO support as a fundamental right the use of one's own language variety throughout society. (See, for example, EMELD n.d.) Let us hope that more government institutions follow suit.

References

EMELD (Electronic Metastructure for Endangered Languages Data). n.d. http://emeld. org/features/links2.cfm

Haugen, Einar. 1956. *Bilingualism in the Americas: A bibliography and research guide*. Publication of the American Dialect Society 26. Tuscaloosa: University of Alabama Press.

Hinton, Leanne, and Ken Hale, eds. 2001. *The green book of language revitalization in practice*. New York: Academic Press.

Holm, John. 2004. *Languages in contact: The partial restructuring of vernaculars*. Cambridge: Cambridge University Press.

Mufwene, Salikoko S. 2001. *The ecology of language evolution*. Cambridge: Cambridge University Press.

Nettle, Daniel, and Suzanne Romaine. 2000. *Vanishing voices: The extinction of the world's languages*. New York: Oxford University Press.

Spears, Arthur K., and Leanne Hinton. 2010. Language and speakers: An introduction to African American English and Native American languages. In Arthur K. Spears, guest ed., Language, inequality, and endangerment: African Americans and Native Americans, special issue, *Transforming Anthropology* 18.1: 3–14.

Thomason, Sarah G. 2001. *Language contact: An introduction*. Washington, DC: Georgetown University Press.

Winford, Donald. 2003. *An introduction to contact linguistics*. Malden, MA: Blackwell.

2

THINKING ABOUT DIVERSITY

Arthur K. Spears

Human Equality and Language Equality

This introductory textbook unites approaches to language study from the disciplines of anthropology and linguistics. Our approach could be called linguistic anthropology or sociolinguistics, the first considered a subfield of anthropology, the second a subfield of linguistics. Both overlap significantly in terms of content. In this chapter, I begin by drawing on some of the basic concepts relating to diversity from the two disciplines.

First, however, I should enter some words about a comment in the Preface: "We believe that more students from diverse backgrounds would be attracted to . . . linguistics if instructors in introductory courses made more use of course materials based on data from the language varieties of [historically excluded] groups." However, whom do we have in mind when we speak of increasing diversity in linguistics, or increasing *inclusion*, to use the term that is currently gaining ground on *diversity*? Increasing the number of nonwhite linguists is certainly high on our agenda, but it is certainly not the only high priority.

In terms of increasing diversity in linguistics, race may well be the least understood issue, at least based on my classroom experiences in questioning students about their knowledge of the topic. Because of this, the discussion of race below is somewhat longer than those covering other types of social groups, in order to make sure the basics are dealt with. Ethnicity is closely related to race, and it is high on our agenda in terms of raising representation from nonwhite as well as white groups. Linguistics has already made great strides in increasing the participation of women, though there is clearly still work to be done. We do not have sufficient data on socioeconomic class to make firm claims about participation in linguistics by persons from working-class backgrounds, but we suspect that it should be high on our diversity agenda. (Accordingly, several chapters treat language varieties concentrated in the working class.)

Anthropologists stress the biopsychological equality of all human populations. By this we mean simply that all human populations have an equal capacity for developing and acquiring culture, though there are indeed differences in abilities from individual to individual. This principle is stressed in introductory courses because sometimes students have erroneous assumptions. They consider the range of technological accomplishments in societies around the world and the chronology of societies' accomplishments and reach the false conclusion that some peoples have richer cognitive abilities. Negative ideas about other peoples, based on technological accomplishment, also extend to language. It is commonly assumed that the languages of people in technologically simpler societies are somehow simpler. The term *primitive* is often used. Neither of these ideas, about culture in general or language (which is part of culture), is true.

Those who study human history closely know that certain forms of culture—cities, irrigation systems, metalworking, large-scale agriculture, and so on—arise out of a complex interplay of environment, natural resources, demographics, and chance. Culture, in anthropology and other social sciences, refers to the mental, material, and behavioral patterns that characterize a society, briefly, the design for and pattern of living of that society. Culture in this sense is not solely about operas, symphony orchestras, haute couture, and similar institutions. Such institutions are often referred to popularly as "high culture," in reference to affluent, modern societies. So, although large-scale, irrigation-based agriculture appears to have begun first in the Middle East, and modern industrialization first arose in Europe, these events were due to a complex interplay of environment, natural resources, demographics, and chance. They are not the result of any cognitive superiority of the people involved.

Often, too, people sometimes underestimate the technological achievements of particular societies due to a superficial knowledge of history. Remember also that technological achievements are only one kind of human achievement out of many. The histories of many parts of the world are neglected in our schooling, for example, those of sub-Saharan African peoples. As a result, many people assume that nothing of consequence happened there before the arrival of Europeans. They do not know, for example, that when the Portuguese arrived in central West Africa at the shore of the Kingdom of the Kongo in the fifteenth century, they found a society as culturally complex as their own. The Portuguese established formal diplomatic relations with this kingdom, as they would have with any other society of equal standing.

Conquest and empire building are also dependent on many variables, the interplay of which can explain why some peoples forged empires and others did not. Many people are unaware of the past empires of peoples existing today. How many are aware, for example, of the Serbian Empire, Poland's former status as a major power, or the sub-Saharan Ghanaian Empire in Africa, whose beginning is dated around the eighth century AD? How many know that Spaniards were greatly aided in conquering much of Latin America by the decimation of Native American populations lacking resistance to the Old World diseases that the Spaniards brought with them? The Spanish conquest cannot be attributed mainly to extraordinary military prowess or technology.

Linguists stress the equality of all languages. We note in particular that there are no primitive languages and that all languages—and all dialects, or varieties, of those languages—have a grammar. Their grammars are all systematic, governed by strict rules of pronunciation, word formation, and sentence structuring. One language, for example, English, may seem to have a noticeably primitive noun case system, compared to, say, your average Slavic language, which has a complex case system. However, English is complex in other ways. Consider its vowel system, more complex than the systems of most languages.

CASE

Case refers to what are often called inflectional endings on nouns and other items in the noun phrase. Case endings indicate the role of the noun or the entire noun phrase in the sentence. In English we have a sentence such as the following, translated for comparison into Croatian (spoken in Croatia, in the former Yugoslavia):

(1) The   girl   saw   the   girl.
     Ø   djevojka je   vidjela   Ø   djevojku
                        AUX   PAST+PPL
     'The girl saw the girl.'

In English, there is no inflection determined by whether *the girl* is the subject or direct object. In Croatian there is: *djevojka* (subject, or nominative case) and *djevojku* (direct object, or accusative case). (Croatian does not use articles.) Croatian has two numbers (singular and plural), seven cases, and three genders (masculine, feminine, and neuter), so every noun and all of its modifiers have to be inflected, taking into consideration all of these grammatical properties. Added to this, there are subclasses of nouns that do not fit the regular pattern for their gender. To the monolingual English speaker, this appears quite complex.

Linguists often elaborate the principle of all languages being equal by stating that all language varieties are equally adequate for the communicative needs of their speakers. Speakers of some languages have no need to talk about "bipartisan weapons-of-mass-destruction antiproliferation initiatives" because they have none. English speakers (in some countries) do, but we are relatively helpless when it is time to distinguish among a dozen or more types of camels, or dreams, or relatives, or many other entities that other languages handle with precision and subtlety, with one word or a set phrase.

One dialect, or variety, of a language may seem simpler than another, more prestigious dialect of the same language. For example, African American Vernacular English (AAVE, often called Ebonics), may seem simpler than Mainstream Standard English, also called Standard English, Mainstream English, Academic English, General American English, or Network Standard English (normally heard on television and radio). However, there is no basis whatsoever for claiming this. Remember, too, that AAVE is more prestigious than the mainstream standard in some settings, to wit, in most African American churches. The mainstream standard lacks the grammatical mechanisms and associated rhetorical apparatus required for an eloquent traditional African American sermon.

To illustrate, AAVE has tenses that the mainstream standard lacks. For one, AAVE has a remote perfect tense, which indicates that a situation started a long time ago and continues to the present or continues to have relevance to the present. The following sentence, with the Remote Perfect in bold, means, 'He left a long time ago and is still gone': *He **BIN** lef.* (AAVE specialists spell Remote Perfect *been* with capital letters to indicate that it is stressed and to distinguish it from the *been* present in all English dialects.) AAVE also has a highly intricate mood system expressing disapproval, which is absent from the mainstream standard.

MOOD

Mood includes concepts like subjunctive, indicative, and optative, which are usually expressed in verb phrases; it is the grammatical expression of a speaker's attitude toward the situation expressed by a sentence. (See the chapter "African American English" for more details about mood in AAVE.)

Since African Americans are discussed in several places in this chapter and in this book, and there is, surprisingly, quite a bit of confusion and disagreement about who African Americans are, something should be said about this term. It refers basically to the African-descent U.S. population whose ancestors have been here at least about 150 years, and sometimes the U.S.-born-and-raised offspring of recent black immigrants too. The word *recent* (during the past 500 years or so) is required in this discussion because all humans are of African descent. However, even this qualification ignores the fact that Africans have been traveling to Europe and elsewhere continuously throughout human history. Africans (even from sub-Saharan Africa) were settling in Europe, for example, and raising families during the Greek and Roman Empires, the Middle Ages (called the Dark Ages when I was in school), and afterwards, not to mention before. (The Middle Ages were the Golden Age for Arabs.) If one does the genealogical math, one can see that a substantial number of Europeans who immigrated to the U.S. had recent African descent.

Diversity

Given that this book was inspired by the efforts of a group of linguists to increase diversity, it would be appropriate to say something about the concept of diversity. *Diversity*, along with terms such as *ethnicity, race, social class, culture,* and *mores,* needs to be explained. What is this word used to refer to nowadays, and what are some of the meanings it has that we often do not think about? In looking closely at this word and associated ones, students can gain a better idea of how linguists go about studying language, politics, and ideology—and even language change.

The first point to note about *diversity* is that it is a code word often used in the political arena in connection with a policy agenda. In the process of creating a code word, speakers focus more on a certain meaning of the word than others. That is, they privilege certain meanings. Sometimes the privileged meaning can eclipse the others. *Diversity*, or its adjective form, *diverse*, may refer simply to different kinds of anything, not even people necessarily. This was the most common sense in which the word was used, say, forty years ago. It was also used in the sense of 'being of a different kind', but most likely this second sense was much less common (and this sense was listed as the second, normally less used one, in my dictionary).

The privileged meaning of *diversity* nowadays, however, refers to being of a different kind in the sense of belonging to a certain kind of human social group. When a corporation, for example, wants to increase diversity, we can readily assume that the aim is increasing the representation of different types of social groups in the corporation. Social scientists focus their attention on social groups that are significant because thinking in terms of them permits generalizations and predictions about social life. Consequently, social groups of interest are ethnic, racial, often religious, and sometimes sexuality based (lesbian, gay, etc.), to provide some examples. No one talks about right-eye-dominant people or bracelet wearers in social science treatises because these groupings of humans and generalizations pertaining to them do not really increase our understanding of general social life.

However, note that *diversity* as a code word does not refer to all social groups. It singles out those who have been historically underrepresented, disenfranchised, disadvantaged, and/or shut out of important institutional settings such as business and educational ones. Thus, if a college wants to increase diversity in its student body, it will not redouble its efforts to recruit Lutheran, Dutch American, white male Presbyterian, and heterosexual, white, French-ancestry students. Its focus will be on those who, for a number of historical reasons, have had less access to the college and who the college believes are underrepresented. The quest for diversity in colleges and other institutions is in line with the nation's stated goal of equal opportunity for all and is also intended to make up partially for historical exclusion, which has important present effects.

Observe also that for many American English speakers, *diverse* is in the process of splitting into two words, each with its own pronunciation. Pronounced one way, it tends to have one meaning; pronounced differently, it tends to have the code word meaning. [daɪvɨs] (with secondary stress on the first syllable, primary stress on the second) is the pronunciation for the code word sense 'minority'. [dəvɨs] has the other meaning, 'comprising different kinds' or 'of a different kind (that is, any type, not just social group related)'.

Minority

Diverse, then, has come to mean basically the same as the word *minority*. Thus, one can now hear that a certain candidate for a job is "diverse" or hear someone say, "Is she diverse?" (Compare *Is she a minority?*) Note also how *minority* as a code word can refer to women in many Americans' speech, even though women actually constitute a majority percentage-wise. (In some textbooks on ethnicity and gender, *minority* is defined to include women.) Speaking of women as a minority makes clear that the new, code word, social-agenda sense of *minority* unhinges it from numbers and percentages alone.

There is something else that is very curious about the word *minority*. Leave aside for a moment that *minority* may refer to women. Notice that a white person cannot be a minority (except in the sense of women being a minority), but any person of color (nonwhite) is automatically one. But, one might counter, whites indeed are not a minority. That is true, in the U.S. at least. However, whites are indeed a minority in the world. Going further, one notices that whites are always lumped into one group for the majority/minority distinction, but peoples of color are always split into blacks, Latinos, Asians, Native Americans, and so on. Why are whites not ever split up so that specific white groups, for example, Polish Americans, become minorities? If you would like to ponder this question, you might also ponder why such white ethnic groups, say ninety years ago, were more often spoken of as minorities, more so than today. In the contemporary U.S., if a city has 30% whites, 20% blacks, 20% Latinos, 20% Asians, and 10% Native Americans, that city is still said to have a white majority. Why is it not said to have a people-of-color majority? White groups can be as different from each other culturally and socially as groups of color are different from white groups. Surely, white Jewish Russian Americans in San Francisco, for example, are just as different from white Italian Americans in San Francisco as they are different from African American San Franciscans. Thus, cultural similarity cannot be used as a rationale for lumping whites together. Actually, we might even ask why the highly useful terms *people of color* and *person of color* are not used in the mainstream media. Note that using these terms would often make nonwhites a majority. I hope that this discussion of *minority* will go beyond clarifying its meaning to show additionally how our choices of words and phrases and the frequency with which we use them can affect our view of social groups and society.

Clearly, a political agenda is at work in typically treating whites as one group, a (national) majority, when they are spoken of in reference to groups of color. Our language, American English, is shaped to reinforce, reiterate, and reproduce the idea of white—and male—dominance, demographically and in other ways. The shaping of language use is one of the many ways that the ideology of white supremacy—and patriarchy—is buttressed.

Ethnicity

The term *ethnicity* is intended to capture the status of a group of individuals as an identifiable group of people. An **ethnic group** is one whose members share a collective identity, one that may be based on some combination of shared history, language, religion, or culture. Sometimes ethnicity is forced onto people. The members of the ethnic group would just as soon not be members of it, but the rest of society treats them as distinct through various types of official or unofficial discrimination and exclusion. For example, African American ethnicity (and racial identity) has been enforced historically from the outside through many forms of legal and social exclusion. But African Americans have also come to use and value their ethnic (and racial) distinctiveness. They use it as a tool to build solidarity and combat discrimination and exclusion.

Quick question: what is the ethnicity of Pocahontas (the famous stateswoman in the early history of Native American–British contact in North America)? That's right: Native American, or more specifically Powhatan (her tribe) American. What is the ethnicity of Michael Jordan (the world-renowned basketball player)? That's right: African American. What is the ethnicity of Chita Rivera (the famous actress and dancer)? That's right: Latina American, or more specifically Puerto Rican American. Now, what's the ethnicity of President Reagan? President Nixon? Hillary Clinton? It seems that no one knows for sure but their biographers. *White* is a racial term, not an ethnic one. Whites in the U.S. and in other countries are of many ethnicities.

Some people's ethnicity is very prominent, while for others—well, it seems almost perverse even to ask. Their ethnicity is what social scientists call "unmarked." It is seen as the "norm," unremarkable, not worth talking about, neutral. Other kinds of individuals, however, are always tagged—some would say tarred—with an ethnic label. Observe that even the term *white ethnic* does not refer to President Franklin Roosevelt (even though, strictly speaking, he had an ethnicity, more or less: Dutch American). White ethnics are whites who, as a group, have less prestige, power, and resources, in a manner similar to people of color, whose ethnicity is branded on them, so to speak. White ethnics, like people of color, are generally ethnically marked as Polish American, Jewish American, Italian American, and so forth. They *tend* to be groups with a relatively high percentage of working-class members. Nevertheless, white ethnics overall have more access to power and resources than groups of color (Asians, African Americans, etc.) owing to their whiteness. A Polish American, for example, can rather easily lose his or her ethnicity by, for instance, changing his or her name and marrying the WASP boss's daughter or son. (A WASP is a white Anglo-Saxon Protestant.) White ethnicities are much more easily erasable than those of people of color. Ethnicity in practice is applied to groups that are to some extent discriminated against, those who suffer some disadvantage in comparison to ethnically unmarked whites. (For details on disadvantages experienced by white ethnics, see textbooks on ethnicity such as Schaefer 2012.)

Consequently, even though social scientists may say that everyone, strictly speaking, has an ethnicity, in reality ethnicity is more relevant for social groups who are lower in the pecking order. The way we actually talk about ethnicity makes it a concept similar to socioeconomic class. This is because ethnicity on the societal level virtually always involves hierarchies of dominance and access to wealth and power, as does socioeconomic class. We will turn to this kind of social grouping (class), but first some remarks on race.

Race

Several points should be stressed from the outset in talking about race. (Most of the discussions below follow Spears 1999.) First, race is not based on science; race as a concept and racial categories are sociocultural. As we would expect, then, the definition of race and racial categories differs according to society. **Race** in the U.S. is a social group category based *partially* on physical traits. The following discussion explains why it is only partially so.

Racial categorization cannot be separated from **racism**, behaviors that directly or indirectly support the inequality of racial hierarchy. A **racial hierarchy** arranges racial groups from top to bottom. The closer to the top a racial group is, the more access it has to power and wealth. The racial hierarchy is supported most significantly by the power of the state and social institutions. A racial hierarchy always involves prejudice, discrimination, and exploitation of the groups below the top of the racial hierarchy. In other words, racism is prejudice, discrimination, and exploitation with the power of the state and social institutions behind them. Often this statement is shortened to "Racism is prejudice with power behind it."

Since race is sociocultural, one's racial classification may change going from one society to another. As an example, the same person may be white in Puerto Rico or Brazil but black in the U.S. Someone who is black in the U.S. could go to another country and be white, or, if not white, not black. Instead, they might be classified using terms such as *mulatto, métis, indio, zambo, trigueño, mestizo,* and *coloured,* depending on what country they are in, exactly how they look, and what is known about the person's background.

Second, racial terms, as we would expect given what has just been observed, are illogical, fuzzy, contradictory, unilluminating, and confusing even though people use them all the time and believe they know what they are talking about. Not only do they overlap and vary from society to society, but they are often confused with color terms for people. For example, U.S. blacks may be referred to as black (very dark-skinned), as opposed to brown (brown-skinned), as opposed to yellow (light-skinned), or even white (looking like a white person but actually black). But *brown* is also used sometimes to refer to Latinos as a group (whose members may be black, Asian, white, etc.), who are sometimes thought of as constituting a race, other times an ethnic group, other times simply people with a Spanish-language heritage. For example, we sometimes hear of the "browning" of American popular culture, with the increased popularity of salsa, merengue, and other types of music as well as dance from Latin America.

Sometimes, a racial (or racialized) group is physically identical to the dominant population group of a society, for example, the *burakumin* of Japan. They are socially constructed as a group that is polluted, low caste, and alien in species or race (Takezawa 2006: 6), even though history and archaeology have documented the historical origins of their exclusion and the absence of any separate origin.

Think about the bizarre racial system in the U.S., with regard to black and white. The traditional definition of black is anyone with one drop of black blood. Of course, from a scientific standpoint, there is no such thing as "black blood" or "white blood" or any other kind or racial or ethnic blood. What is meant is anyone with (recent, sub-Saharan) African ancestry. When racists first came up with the definition, they did not know that all humans originated in Africa. Moreover, there are "sub-Saharan–looking" (that is, darker-skinned and broader-featured) people in North Africa and "North African–looking" (lighter-skinned and finer-featured) people in sub-Saharan Africa. But, again, our focus here is on the nonsensical nature of racial classification.

Virtually all African Americans are mixed race, and, as noted, some "look" white and pass for white. The descendants of all the African Americans who have passed for white (normally marrying whites) are black—strictly speaking, according to the one-drop rule. Thus, many people who are white are really black. With whites who are actually black producing offspring with whites, eventually there will be no real whites left—according to the definition. Taking U.S. racial classification to its logical conclusion, this is what we conclude.

Following the Hurricane Katrina disaster that hit New Orleans in 2005, some friends and I watched news coverage of New Orleans neighborhoods, one black and one white. When the camera showed the "white" people in the "white" neighborhood, the African American group that I viewed the newscast with burst into laughter. Most of the whites in the New Orleans white neighborhood would never have been considered white in the North, where we grew up. To us, they resembled light-skinned, non-white-looking blacks. In other words, there is even regional variation in the U.S. with regards to what white looks like.

To reiterate, racial terms make reference to physical features but often in a very oblique, illogical, and inconsistent way. Thus, appearance stereotypes come very much into play. So, a woman is said not to "look Latina," for example. An Asian is judged not to "look Asian." A black man is said to "look like he is white." Actually, a black person in the U.S. may look like almost anyone in the world. As I point out in the chapter on African American English, the black people in the all-black, racially segregated African American community I grew up in "looked like" practically all peoples of the world: whites, Arabs, Norwegians, Polynesians, Senegalese, Chinese, Native Americans—or, at least, like most people's stereotypes of what those groups look like. Some of those black people looked "whiter" than actual whites, who lived in their own racially segregated white neighborhoods.

Third, racial categories, in the end, do not tell us anything really interesting about people except how they may be treated due to the racial classification that society has imposed on them. Racial classifications may give us some clue as to what the person looks like, but then again they may be totally misleading. When humans began to get serious about racial categories in the seventeenth century, they based them on highly observable physical traits such as skin color, hair texture, facial features, and head shape and size. However, such features indicate nothing about intelligence or ability to acquire culture.

Consider, for example, the sickle-cell allele, first noted among Africans and African Americans. This allele (i.e., one of two variants of the gene governing the sickle-cell blood trait) provides resistance to malaria when a person inherits only one sickle-cell allele from a parent. However, if the person inherits this allele from both parents (ending up with two of the sickle-cell alleles), he or she falls victim to sickle-cell anemia, a potentially fatal disease. Early in our understanding of this genetic trait, it seemed to be linked to race. Subsequent research, however, showed that it also occurs in Greece, Turkey, Yemen, India, and Burma—in areas of endemic malaria—inhabited by different "races." Thus, there is good reason to research human populations in terms of their biological traits, but they must be interesting biological traits that indicate something about human adaptation and evolution according to the environment and other factors. Such factors are most often unrelated to ones that have been used in pseudoscientific racial categories. There is no way to support race categories scientifically using the physical traits that these categories have been based on. Scientists often use the term *population* when they seek to identify a human group based on meaningful physical traits such as the sickle-cell trait or blood type. (See any introduction to general, four-field anthropology for more information about genetic polymorphism, resulting from genetic variation.)

In certain cases, all the members of an ethnic group are classified as being of the same race. As an example, all individuals who are ethnically African American are also black, in the racial sense that this term is used in the U.S. Note, however, that not all blacks in the U.S. are African Americans. There is actually a large number of ethnic groups in the U.S. who are considered black racially: Nigerian Americans, Senegalese Americans, and even others whose ancestors (that is, recent ancestors—all human ancestry goes back to Africa) are not from Africa, for example, Fijian Americans, as well as many other groups. Some members of groups whose (recent) ancestry is not African may prefer not to be classified racially as black. However, societies have their racial classification terminologies, and they are applied to individuals regardless of those individuals' wishes.

Fourth, race categories are sociocultural constructs invented and adopted in societies at certain points in history as support for political and economic goals. Race is used to place groups in a hierarchy that determines their access to wealth and power. For example, during the seventeenth century, in the early days of the English colonies in America, racial thinking was not institutionalized with respect to the organization and running of society. The living condition of the average white indentured servant was not appreciably better that that of slaves (or black indentured servants, whose existence is often overlooked). The relations among blacks, whites, and Native Americans living in European settlements were fluid and included cohabitation and the production of mixed-race children. Social relations were governed principally by wealth. Bacon's Rebellion in 1676, in Virginia, is seen by many historians as a key event triggering **racialization** in North America, the process whereby racial categorization and racism came to be essential features of U.S. society.

Though the rebellion was caused by a number of factors, one of the key features of the rebellion itself was the uniting of the poor—of all races—against the wealthy (almost all white) landowning class. The rebellion was eventually put down, but an important outcome of the rebellion, after the old order was restored, was the initiation of laws and other official mechanisms for institutionalizing the higher status of poor whites over the population of color and the strengthening of the link between slavery and being black. There were, of course, other reasons for this strengthened linkage, including the facts that blacks did not have relatives in Native American–controlled areas to escape to and that they did not have local knowledge to aid their escape. Native Americans did. One of the key functions of racial hierarchy in U.S. history has been to provide whites without wealth the psychological compensation of knowing that there are lower-ranked racial groups to whom they can feel superior. Also, the history of U.S. labor organizing is full of cases where racial animosity in white workers was stirred up in order to prevent them from uniting with workers of color to improve the lot of white and nonwhite workers alike. This is one of the many ways in which racism hurts not only people of color but whites also. Nevertheless, racism hurts people of color more than whites without wealth—and of course more than whites with wealth.

Socioeconomic Class

The institutionalization of the racial hierarchy goes a long way toward explaining differences in access to quality education, income, and wealth between whites and people of color in the U.S. Racial hierarchies mimic class hierarchies. Socioeconomic class is basically about wealth and power. (See any introductory anthropology textbook for more discussions on class and the other types of social groups discussed in this chapter.) **Class** is based mainly on occupation, education, income, and wealth. How these four criteria interact and are specified to create class categories is quite complex and controversial. Like gender inequality and racial hierarchy, class is a recent human invention. "[M]ost societies that depend primarily on agriculture or herding have social classes. Agriculture and herding developed within the past 10,000 years, so we may assume that most food collectors in the distant past lacked social classes" (Ember et al. 2002: 321). Early food-collecting societies showed gender equality also, with women often engaging in different types of activities but nevertheless having equal status in the overall fabric of the community. The beginning and evolution of gender inequality are linked to the rise of cities and military institutions, for which the rise of agriculture, herding, and private property was essential.

From differences in wealth and power stem differences in lifestyles, attitudes, and aspirations, which are usually strongly related to class. Along with less access to wealth, the working class (and, to a lesser extent, the middle class) has less access to quality education. This decreased access to education is one of the ways in which the class hierarchy is maintained. Generally, the better one's education, the better one's chances of achieving upward class mobility or at least of maintaining the class status one already has.

An important phenomenon that social scientists have frequently observed in studying social hierarchies is **internalized oppression**. This is the internalization by lower-status groups of negative ideas spread throughout society about them. Working-class students, for example, may end up believing that they are not very intelligent compared to students who have attended elite schools. They are just as intelligent; it is the lower-quality education that society has provided them with that has led to an incorrect conclusion. The problem is not their intelligence or lack of it but access to quality education. Groups who are lower in these hierarchies (based on class, race, ethnicity, etc.) are kept in their place in the hierarchy over time. Thus, most children of working-class parents end up in the working class. The mechanisms that almost shut off upward social mobility include not only educational access but also the images and ideas that are disseminated by textbooks, films, television, and many other media and institutions. Groups lower in these hierarchies are presented in less positive ways than are groups higher in these hierarchies. A result, for example, is the dearth of television programs and movies that present the working class as admirable and worthy of respect. The scarcity of positive images reinforces the great number of negative images.

Conclusion

We, the editors of this textbook, and the members of the Linguistic Society of America's Committee on Ethnic Diversity (actually concerned with various kinds of diversity) have taken a small step that we hope will have big consequences:

presenting positive discussions and respect-promoting exercises on the languages of groups who have not always been accorded what they deserve and who to some extent may have internalized negative views of their own languages. We present these chapters also for students who are not members of these groups, for their educational enrichment also.

References

Ember, Carol R., Melvin Ember, and Peter N. Peregrine. 2002. *Anthropology*. 10th ed. Upper Saddle River, NJ: Prentice Hall.

Schaefer, Richard T. 2012. *Race and ethnicity in the United States*. 7th ed. Upper Saddle River, NJ: Pearson Prentice Hall.

Spears, Arthur K. 1999. Race and ideology: An introduction. In Arthur K. Spears, ed., *Race and ideology: Language, symbolism, and popular culture*, 11–58. Detroit: Wayne State University Press.

Takezawa, Yasuko. 2006. Race should be discussed and understood across the globe. *Anthropology Newsletter* 47.3 (March): 6, 7.

PART II

Indigenous U.S. Language Varieties

3

NAVAJO

Keren Rice

Introduction

Navajo, or Diné bizaad ('Navajo language'), is the language of the Navajo people, or Diné, 'the People'. The Navajo homeland is bounded by four sacred mountains: Sierra Blanca Peak to the east, San Francisco Peaks to the west, Mount Taylor to the south, and Hesperus Peak in the north. The language is spoken primarily in the Navajo Nation, encompassing portions of northeastern Arizona, northwestern New Mexico, and southeastern Utah, and covering over 25,000 square miles.

According to the 2010 U.S. Census, 332,129 individuals claimed Navajo ethnicity. The most recent information we have on speakers is based on the 2000 U.S. Census as reported in the *American Community Survey* of 2007: there were 170,717 speakers of Navajo, of which 2.9% were monolingual. The same source notes that there were 200,560 speakers of all other Native American languages put together.

Although Navajo is a member of the Athabaskan language family, the word *Navajo* comes from Tewa, a language of the Kiowa-Tanoan family spoken in New Mexico. The Tewa word, *navahuu*, means cultivated lands or great planted fields. The word *Navajo* first appears in writing in 1626, where the term *Apaches de Nabajó* was used to describe this particular group of people, referring to the type of land that they inhabited.

History

The Athabaskan language family stretches from Alaska and parts of Canada, to northern California and parts of Oregon, to the Southwest of the U.S. Navajo is very closely related to the different Apache languages (Jicarilla Apache, Western Apache, Mescalero Apache, Plains Apache, and Lipan), and these languages together constitute the Apachean branch of the Athabaskan family. Navajo is not related at all to other languages spoken in the same geographic area such as Ute,

TABLE 3.1 Comparing words in the Navajo and Apache languages (Hoijer 1938)

	Navajo	Western Apache	Chiricahua Apache	Mescalero Apache	Jicarilla Apache	Lipan	Plains Apache
'you sg.'	ni	^{n}di	^{n}dí	^{n}dí	ni	^{n}di	di–
'two'	naaki	naaki	naaki	naaki	naaki	naaki	ndaachi'
'bone'	-ts'in	-ts'in	-ts'į'	-ts'ine	-ts'in	-ts'įh	-ts'į
'water'	tó	tóo	tó	tú	kó	kó	kóo
'earth'	ni'	ni'	nii	nii	nii	nii'	nǫǫ

Note: The acute accent represents a high tone, and the hook under a vowel represents nasalization of the vowel.

Zuni, or Hopi. The close relationship between Navajo and the Apache languages can be seen by comparing words in these different languages (see Table 3.1).

While there are some differences between these words, they are very similar to each other and show the close relationship between these languages.

Social Context

In 1930, 71% of Navajos were monolingual Navajo speaking, and the Navajo Nation was largely monolingual Navajo speaking until around World War II. In a 1992 study, it was found that 54.3% of Navajo preschoolers were monolingual English speakers, while only 17.7% were monolingual Navajo; the rest were Navajo-English bilingual speakers (reported in Hinton and Hale 2001). Although many indigenous languages of North America are not being transmitted to children, Navajo was long thought to be the most secure of them, but these figures suggest that, despite a large number of speakers, the language is not being passed on. The consequence, if this continues, is that it may not be very long before Navajo is not used as a language of everyday conversation.

Navajo has been important in bilingual education in the U.S. in the past 50 years. Rough Rock Demonstration School began in 1966, following research showing that education is most effective if it involves the native language. Children were taught in Navajo at the Rough Rock school, and it became a model for schooling in many parts of the world. There is also Navajo immersion at some schools, and Navajo has been taught at a number of colleges and universities in the Southwest for some time. The book *Diné Bizaad: Speak, Read, Write Navajo*, by Irvy W. Goossen (1995), is a popular textbook for learning the language. The book *Dine Bizaad Binahoo'aah: Rediscovering the Navajo Language*, by Evangeline Parsons Yazzie and Margaret Speas (2008), is an excellent overview of the language.

The writing system for Navajo was first developed in the late nineteenth century, and in the early twentieth century missionaries produced Bible translations and religious texts in Navajo as well as dictionaries and grammars. The orthography was standardized in the 1930s.

Some Linguistic Features

Navajo has a large sound system. The consonant inventory, using the International Phonetic Alphabet (IPA), is given in Table 3.2. Note that while phonetic transcription is used here, elsewhere in the chapter orthography is used. In the table, orthographic equivalents are given in parentheses when they differ from the IPA symbols.

The consonants written with a raised comma after them are called ejectives or glottalized consonants. They are produced with constriction at the glottis; they are similar to a consonant followed directly by a glottal stop. Notice that lateral is assumed to be a place of articulation.

It is very important to keep in mind that each cell in this table is filled by what functions structurally as a single sound from the standpoint of Navajo phonology, regardless of whether one, two, or three characters are used to write this sound.

The vowels of Navajo are shown in Table 3.3. Please note that a hook under the vowel represents nasalization of the vowel.

There are also several sequences identified as diphthongs in Navajo, as shown in Table 3.4. Like the vowels, these come in short and long pairs, with length indicated in the orthography by the doubling of the glide portion of the diphthong.

TABLE 3.2 Navajo consonant system (Young and Morgan 1987 and many other sources)

	Labial	Dental	Lateral	Alveolar	Alveo-palatal	Velar	Glottal
Voiceless unaspirated stops and affricates	p (b)	t (d)	tɬ (dl)	ts (dz)	tʃ (j)	k (g)	
Voiceless aspirated stops and affricates		tʰ (t)	tɬʰ (tɬ)	tsʰ (ts)	tʃʰ (ch)	kʰ (k)	
Voiceless ejective stops and affricates		t'	tɬ'	ts'	tʃ' (ch')	k'	ʔ (')
Voiceless fricatives			ɬ	s	ʃ (sh)	x (h)	h
Voiced fricatives			l	z	ʒ (zh)	ɣ (gh)	
Nasals	m	n					
Glides	w				j (y)		

TABLE 3.3 Navajo vowels

Short vowels		Long vowels		Short nasalized vowels		Long nasalized vowels	
i	o	ii	oo	į	ǫ	įį	ǫǫ
e	a	ee	aa	ę	ą	ęę	ąą

TABLE 3.4 Navajo diphthongs

Short diphthongs		Long diphthongs	
ei	oi	eii	oii
ai, ąi, ao		aii, ąii, aoo	

In addition, Navajo has tones. An acute accent above a vowel marks high tone. Vowels without any tone marking have low tone. Some minimal pairs for tone are given in (1).

(1) a. 'anii'   'face'   'aníí'   'nostril'
     b. nilį   'she/he is'   nílį   'you (sg.) are'
     c. taa'   'in the water, inside of the water' táá'   'three'

Not only is Navajo famous for its complex consonant system; it is also well known for some of its phonological processes, its intricate verb word (that is, verb morphology), and several semantic systems. All of these, as well as other properties of the language, are introduced through the problems in this chapter.

Further Reading

Navajo is probably the best described of all the native languages of North America. There is an outstanding grammar and dictionary of Navajo, usually known as Young and Morgan (1987), as well as a volume called an analytic lexicon of Navajo (Young and Morgan 1992). Almost all of the information about Navajo in this chapter is drawn from these two resources. The book *Dine Bizaad Binahoo'aah: Rediscovering the Navajo Language*, by Evangeline Parsons Yazzie and Margaret Speas, is a wonderful source about the language. An additional book of great value is Leonard Faltz's 1998 *The Navajo Verb: A Grammar for Students and Scholars* as well as the references given earlier. An excellent bibliography on Navajo linguistics is available at the following address: http://www.swarthmore.edu/SocSci/tfernal1/navbib.htm.

More information on Navajo education is available in the articles on Navajo in Hinton and Hale (2001).

If you are interested in mystery novels, you might enjoy reading the books by Tony Hillerman that are set in the Southwest. Navajo people, and the Navajo language, figure prominently in his work.

Problem Sets

Phonology

The following questions aim at understanding various aspects of the consonant system of Navajo. (Refer to Tables 3.2–3.4 as you answer the questions.)

1. **Allophones versus Phonemes**
    Consider the sounds [x], [xʷ], and [xʲ]. These are illustrated in the words in (2). IPA is used for the sounds under consideration here.

    (2)   a.   xai   'winter'
              xah   'quickly, rapidly, speedily'
              xaa   'what?, how?'
          b.   xʷoʃ   'thorn'
              xʷó   'he, she, they, his, hers, theirs'
              xʷódah   'up, up high, up above'
          c.   xʲeeł   'pack, package, bundle, burden, load'
              xʲis   'pus'
              xʲił   'date, day (set for an event)'

    a. Are these three sounds allophones of one phoneme, or do they form separate phonemes of Navajo?
    b. Provide evidence for your answer to (a).
    c. Can you predict which of the above will occur in the following words? If yes, give the symbol; if no, explain.
        i.   [ ]aadʒin   'there is a black patch of it'
        ii. [ ]oɣan   'hogan, home, type of dwelling'
    d. The following words contain voiced velar fricatives, [ɣ], [ɣʷ], and [ɣʲ]. Based on what you have seen about the voiceless velar fricative, can you predict how the voiced velar fricative would likely be pronounced in the following words? If yes, give the form; if no, explain why not.
        i.   'a[ ]aa'   'wool'
        ii. bi[ ]e'   'his/her son'
        iii. bi[ ]oo'   'his/her/its teeth'

2. **Voicing Alternations**
    Consider the following alternations in consonant quality. The hyphen represents a morpheme boundary. Ignore any changes in vowels and tones.

    (3)   [s z]   séí   'sand'   bi-zéí   'his/her/its sand'
          [ʃ ʒ]   ʃéé'   'saliva'   bi-ʒéé'   'his/her/its saliva'
          [x ɣ]   xai   'winter'   díí-ɣaaí 'this winter'

    a. Describe the distribution of the voiced and voiceless fricatives in the forms in (3).

b.   Are the voiceless and voiced fricative pairs at the same place of articulation allophones or distinct phonemes based on the above data? Explain your answer.

c.   Suppose you know that the following word begins with an alveolar fricative.

   [ ]aad   'word, language'

   Can you predict the voicing of the fricative? If so, give the form; if not, explain why not.

   What would you predict that the form that means 'his/her word' would be?

3.   Syllables in Navajo

Now consider the shape of syllables in Navajo by answering the following questions. Recall that each cell in the consonant table is filled with what is considered as one sound in Navajo phonology. For instance, in Navajo [ts] is a single consonant, an affricate, rather than a sequence of consonants.

a.   Based on the Navajo data that you have seen so far in all of the exercises, how many consonants can appear maximally in the onset of a syllable in Navajo?

   one   two   three

b.   How many consonants can appear maximally in the coda of a syllable in Navajo?

   zero   one   two   three

c.   Based on your answers to the above, and ignoring the possibilities for the nucleus of the syllable, the maximum syllable in Navajo is (circle only one):

   CV   CVC   CCVC   CVCC   CCV   CCVCC

4.   Borrowings

Some nouns have been borrowed into Navajo from other languages. The words below have been borrowed from Spanish (Sp.) or English (Eng.) into Navajo. Orthography is used here rather than transcription. (Periods are used to mark syllables in the words. Notice that the syllabification from the source languages carries over into Navajo, and stress in the source language is realized as vowel length in Navajo.)

(4) | Source (language) | Navajo | Gloss |
      | -------------------- | -------------- | ------------ |
      | A.me.ri.ca.no (Sp.) | bi.la.gáa.na | 'white man' |
      | to.ro (Sp.) | dóo.la | 'bull' |
      | num.ber (Eng.) | nóom.ba | 'number' |
      | car.bu.re.tor (Eng.) | gáá.bo.lei.ta | 'carburetor' |

a.   Each of the words in the source language has the consonant /r/ in it. Examine how /r/ is borrowed from the source language into Navajo. (Hint: Begin by underlining each r in the source word and then looking for what each one of the *r*'s corresponds to in the Navajo word.) Describe how /r/ is borrowed into Navajo, making reference to syllable structure.

b. Suppose that the following English words were borrowed into Navajo. For each, show what you think the Navajo form would be by filling in either an *l* or Ø for the English /r/'s.

English	"Navajo"
butter	butte___
partner	pa___tne___
ready	___eady

Morphology

5. Numbers

Here are some numbers in Navajo. (From this point on, orthography rather than IPA is used unless specifically noted.)

(5)

ła'	'one'	tseebíí	'eight'
naaki	'two'	náhást'éí	'nine'
tą́ą́'	'three'	neeznáá	'ten'
dį́į́'	'four'	ła'ts'áadah	'eleven'
'ashdla'	'five'	naakits'áadah	'twelve'
hastą́ą́h	'six'	naadiin	'twenty'
tsosts'id	'seven'	naadiintáá'	'twenty-three'

a. Based on *ła'ts'áadah* and *naakits'áadah*, describe the pattern for producing the numbers 'eleven' and 'twelve'.

b. Assuming that all of the numbers from 'eleven' through 'nineteen' are formed in the same way, give the forms that you predict for 'fourteen' and 'nineteen'.

c. What do you think that the following number is?

   táádiin

d. Describe the pattern for predicting the tens.

e. Describe the morpheme order of *naadiintáá'* 'twenty-three'.

f. How do you think you would say 'forty-two'?

g. Take a guess at what the following might mean, paying attention to the meaning of the parts. (There are sometimes small differences in how the numbers are pronounced on their own and how they are pronounced in combination with other numbers.) The first one is done.

neeznádiin   100
naakidi neeznádiin
tseebíí neeznádiin ła'ts'áadah

6.   Verb Structure: Morpheme identification and Ordering of Morphemes

The verb of Navajo is complex and has been the object of much study in Navajo linguistics. The verb is like a sentence in English, containing information about the subject, the object, aspect, and adverbial notions as well as the main meaning of the verb.

Some examples of verbs are given in (6)–(9), written in Navajo orthography. Actual surface forms differ slightly from the forms given here.

(6)	hasmááś	'I come rolling up out.'
	hanimááś	'You (sg.) come rolling up out.'
	hamááś	'She/he/it comes rolling up out.'
(7)	hasts'ǫǫd	'I stretch my neck up out.'
	hanits'ǫǫd	'You (sg.) stretch your neck up out.'
	hats'ǫǫd	'She/he/it stretches his, her, its neck up out.'
(8)	hashdlóósh	'I creep up out on all fours.' (*sh* = /ʃ/)
	hanidlóósh	'You (sg.) creep up out on all fours.'
	hadlóósh	'She/he/it creeps up out on all fours.'
(9)	hashłé	'I take it up out (e.g., a belt from a box).'
	hanilé	'You (sg.) take it up out (e.g. a belt from a box).'

(Ignore the variation between [ł] and [l] in these forms.)

a.   Identify each of the following morphemes in the data above by listing all of the allomorphs after the appropriate gloss.

Stems:	Subjects:	Adverb:
'roll'	first person singular subject	'up out'
_____	_____	_____
'stretch neck'	second person singular subject	
_____	_____	
'creep on all fours'	third person singular subject	
_____	_____	

b.   Note that the first person singular subject has two forms. Identify these. Based on (6)–(9), state the underlying form of the first person singular subject. Justify your choice of form.

The following data illustrate some additional adverbs.

(10)	'adasmááś	'I roll down from a height.'
	ch'ésmááś	'I roll out horizontally.'
	yisdásmaas	'I roll to safety.'

(11)   'adashdlóósh   'I creep down from a height on hands and knees, come down on all fours.'

 ch'éshdlóósh   'I creep out horizontally on hands and knees.'

 yisdáshdlóósh   'I creep to safety on hands and knees, escape by creeping to safety on all fours.'

c. Identify the Navajo adverbs in (10) and (11) by filling them in below.

Navajo	Gloss
_____	'down from a height'
_____	'out horizontally'
_____	'to safety'

d. Taking all the data into account, state the order of morphemes in the Navajo verb.

e. Suppose that you find a new verb stem of the form *'eeł* 'float, go by boat'. How do you predict you would say the following?

 I float to safety by boat.

 You (sg.) float down from a height.

 She/he floats out horizontally.

Now add the following forms:

(12)   yisdánismááś   'I roll you (sg.) to safety.'

 yisdáyilé   'He/she carries it to safety.' (rope, belt, snake, pair of gloves or shoes)

 yisdáshilé   'He/she carries me to safety.' (stretched out and limp like a rope)

f. Identify the morphemes with the following meanings.

 first person singular object   _____

 second person singular object   _____

 third person singular object   _____

g. Now copy your previous responses into the following Table 3.5.

TABLE 3.5 Summary of verb morpheme identification and ordering of morphemes

Verbs		Subjects		Direct objects		Adverbs	
Navajo	Gloss	Navajo	Gloss	Navajo	Gloss	Navajo	Gloss
___	___	___	___	___	___	___	___
___	___	___	___	___	___	___	___
___	___	___	___	___	___	___	___
___	___	___	___	___	___	___	___

h. Revise the order of the morphemes given in (d) by adding the direct objects.
i. How do you predict you would say the following?

I float you down from a height.
I roll you out horizontally.
She/he takes it (ropelike object) up out.

The verbs below show another prefix. This prefix is usually called inceptive and means 'start'.

(13) dismáás   'I start to roll along.'
      dimáás   'She/he starts to roll along.'

j. Based on the following forms, state where this morpheme belongs in the order of morphemes.

(14) yidilé   'She/he starts to handle it (ropelike object).'
      hanidismaas   'I start to roll you (sg.) up out.'

k. How would you say the following?

I start to float you to safety.
He starts to roll you up out.

Syntax

7. Word Order

WORD ORDER

Word order refers to the linear order of the main elements of a phrase or clause. The main elements of a sentence, which is a type of clause, are the Subject, Object, and Verb. SOV word order means that those elements are in the order Subject-Object-Verb, the most common word order in the languages of the world. While Old English had SOV word order, Modern English has SVO order.

Here are some Navajo sentences. Some further abbreviations are needed:

Poss: possessor   O: object   S: subject

Details of the morphology of the verb are ignored, as the focus here is on word order. Do not try to account for pronominal forms of any sort.

(15) tsee'é   sido
      skillet   3S is hot
      'The skillet is hot.'

(16) shi'éétsoh   bik'idah'asdáhí   bikáa'gi   siłtsooz
1sg.Poss coat chair   3O on   3S be located [cloth O]
'My coat is lying on the chair.'

(17) 'ashkii   at'ééd   yich'á'   yáłti'
boy   girl   3O to   3S talk
'The boy is talking to the girl.'

(18) 'ashkii   'at'ééd   yiníł'į́
boy   girl   3S sees 3DO
'The boy sees the girl.'

(19) dzaanééz   bééghashii   yishhash
mule   cow   3S bit
'The mule bit the cow.'

(20) ashkii   mósí   shich'á'   nayìiłt'e'
boy   cat   1O to   3S dropped down
'The boy dropped the cat down to me.'

a. Write a set of basic phrase structure rules to account for word order in Navajo.

b. The sentences below have more complex noun phrases. Revise the phrase structure rules to account for them.

(21) mósí   tsídii   léi'   yich'į'   'ahootah
cat   bird   certain   3O at   3S sprang
'The cat sprang at a bird.'

(22) dine   t'óó'ahayói   'áłahdaazlį́į́'
people many   assembled
'Many people assembled.'

(23) 'ashiiké   t'óó diigis   léi'   tółiikaní   ła'   'iidoolííł
boys   foolish   certain   wine   some   3S will make
'Certain foolish boys will make some wine.'

c. The following sentences have adverbs. Revise the phrase structure rules to include these adverbs.

(24) tsin   bigaan   shił   yaa   'ádzaa
tree 3Poss limb 1sg.O with   down   3 did
'The tree limb bent down with me.'

(25) na'niłkaadí   t'ááchaałda   'alghał
herder   ravenously   3S eat meat
'The herder is ravenously eating (meat).'

Finally, one way of making negatives is shown in (26).

(26)   shizhé'é   béégaashii   doo   nayiisnii'   da
       1sg.Poss father   cow   negative   3S buy   negative
       'My father did not buy a cow.'

d.   Provide the glosses for words that are not glossed in the sentence below.

(27)   shizhé'é   Kinłání góó   doo   deeyáa   da
                     Flagstaff to   3S go
       'My father is not going to Flagstaff.'

e.   Revise your phrase structure rules to accommodate the negative.

8.   *Wh-* Questions

Here are some *wh-* questions in Navajo.

(28)   a.   'ashkii ha'át'íísh yiyiiłtsą́   'What did the boy see?'
            _____   _____ _____

       b.   ha'át'íísh 'ashkii yiyiiłtsą́   'What did the boy see?'
            _____   _____   _____

(29)   a.   Mary hádą́ą́'sh óltadéé́ nádzá   'When did Mary return from
                 _____   _____ _____   school?'

       b.   hádą́ą́'sh Mary óltadéé́ nádzá   'When did Mary return from
            _____   _____ _____   school?'

a.   Provide the English glosses for all the Navajo words in these sentences by fill-
     ing in the blanks.
b.   List the Navajo question words and their English glosses. These are sometimes
     called *wh-* words in English. Based on the Navajo forms here, what might you
     call them in Navajo?

     Two different ways of forming questions are illustrated here.

c.   Describe each of the strategies of question formation, taking into account the
     phrase structure rules you created. (Think of *ha'át'íísh* as a direct object and
     hádą́ą́'sh as an adverb.)

Semantics

9.   Classificatory Verbs

Navajo has a well-known category of verbs known as classificatory verbs.
All have the basic meaning that an object is located in a position. Here are a few
examples. The terms usually used to describe each of these verb classes are given
in parentheses if such a term exists.

CLASSIFICATORY VERBS

Classificatory verbs are a subset of a wider category of words known as *classifiers*. A classifier is a word that refers to some (usually physical) characteristic of a noun that it is associated with. In the case of these Navajo verbs, speakers choose which of the location verbs to use depending on the physical attributes of the nouns. (For more on classifiers, please see the chapter on Chinese.)

(30)   siką́   objects contained within another container (open container)

silá   ropelike objects, objects that come in pairs (slender flexible object)

siyį́   large load, bundle (load, pack, burden)

sitį́   animates in reclining, prone positions (animate object)

sitą́   sticklike, flat stiff objects (slender stiff object)

sitłéé'   moist, mushy consistency (mushy matter)

siłtsooz paperlike, clothing, blankets (flat flexible object)

shijaa'   plural objects (profusion of small objects)

si'ą́   default (single solid, roundish object)

sidá   animates, usually humans, in sitting position

Here are a few examples used in sentences.

(31)   atoo' siką́   'The soup is there.'
(32)   chéch'il bináá' si'ą́   'An acorn is there.'
(33)   tsé shijaa'   'The rock pile, pebbles are there.'
(34)   hooghan shijaa'   'There is a group of homes.'
(35)   shimá bikee' silá   'My mother's shoes are there.'
(36)   hashk'aan sitą́   'The banana is there.'
(37)   tóóshchíín   łeets'aa'   nímazí   bii'   sitłéé'
       hot cereal   dish   round   3O in   mushy object is
       'There is hot cereal in the bowl.'
(38)   gish sitą́   'There is a cane.'

a.   Here are some nouns. Indicate which class you think each one belongs in by providing the classificatory verb.

   dishes in a dishpan   single coin
   shoestring   a number of coins
   pencil   a five-dollar bill
   open blanket   load of firewood

b. The following sentences come in pairs, with the usual classificatory verb
used to express the location of an object found in the first of the set, and
an unusual classificatory verb that shows an extension of meaning found in
the second. What do you think the likely meaning is of the second one in
each set?

   i.   a.   'asdzą́ą́   sidá
            woman   3S sit
            'The woman is sitting.'
       b.   'asdzą́ą́   sitłéé'

   ii. a.   nahasht'e'ii   sitį́
            kangaroo rat 3S lie
       b.   nahasht'e'ii   si'ą́

  iii. a.   gish   sitą́
            cane   sticklike object is located
       b.   łééchąą'í   sitą́
            dog

Navajo Code-Talking

10. Deciphering the Code

During World War II, the Navajo Code Talkers were active on the Pacific
front, serving in the Marines. The Navajo language was used as a code; it
was chosen because it was a language of considerable complexity, and few
non-Navajos understood the language. See http://www.history.navy.mil/faqs/
faq12-1.htm and http://www.navajocodetalkers.org for more discussion and
fuller examples.

The code consisted of two parts. First, Navajo words were used for various
things. The writing system used here is the one that was used at the time for the
code. Here are a few examples of words.

(39)

English word	Navajo word	Literal translation
Alaska	beh-hga	'with winter'
dive-bomber	gini	'chicken hawk'
fighter plane	da-he-tih-hi	'hummingbird'
battleship	lo-tso	'whale'
barrier	bih-chan-ni-ah	'in the way'
cable	besh-lkoh	'wire rope'
gasoline	chidi-bi-toh	'gasoline' (car-its-water)
pyrotechnic	coh-na-chanh	'fancy fire'

The second part is more what one usually thinks of as a code. Some of the code is given here.

(40)

Navajo word	Literal translation	Navajo word	Literal translation
wol-la-chee	'ant'	be-tas-tni	'mirror'
be-la-sana	'apple'	tsah	'needle'
na-hash-chid	'badger'	tlo-chin	'onion'
moasi	'cat'	ne-zhoni	'pretty'
chindi	'devil'	gah	'rabbit'
dzeh	'elk'	dibeh	'sheep'
chuo	'fir'	klesh	'snake'
jeha	'gum'	a-who	'tooth'
cha	'hat'	shi-da	'uncle'
lin	'horse'	a-keh-di-glini	'victor'
tkin	'ice'	gloe-ih	'weasel'
yes-hes	'itch'	tsah-as-zih	'yucca'
jad-ho-loni	'kettle'	besh-do-tliz	'zinc'
dibeh-yazzie	'lamb'		

Using the correspondences in the table above and taking into consideration how we often spell our words when using relatively low-quality channels of communication such as over telephones, decipher the following words written in code:

tsah be-la-sana a-keh-di-glini tsah-ah-zih
gloe-ih wol-la-chee a-who dzeh gah
dibeh-yazzie tkin tsah jeha shi-da yeh-hes klesh a-who tkin moasi dibeh

References

Faltz, Leonard. 1998. *The Navajo verb: A grammar for students and scholars.* Albuquerque: University of New Mexico Press.

Goossen, Irvy W. 1995. *Diné Bizaad: Speak, read, write Navajo.* Flagstaff, AZ: Salina Bookshelf.

Hinton, Leanne, and Ken Hale, eds. 2001. *The green book of language revitalization in practice.* San Diego: Academic Press.

Hoijer, Harry 1938. The Southern Athapaskan languages. *American Anthropologist* 40, 1, 75-87.

Parsons Yazzie, Evangeline, and Margaret Speas. 2008. *Dine Bizaad Binahoo'aah: Rediscovering the Navajo language.* Flagstaff, AZ: Salina Bookshelf.

U.S. Census Bureau. 2007 (2000). *American Community Survey.* Washington, DC: U.S. Department of Commerce.

U.S. Census Bureau. 2012 (2010). *Profile America: Facts for features*, American Indian and Alaska Native Heritage Month, November 2012. Washington, DC: U.S. Department of Commerce.

Young, Robert W., and William Morgan Sr. 1987. *The Navajo language: A grammar and colloquial dictionary*. Rev. ed. Albuquerque: University of New Mexico Press.

Young, Robert W., and William Morgan Sr. 1992. *Analytical lexicon of Navajo*. With Sally Midgette. Albuquerque: University of New Mexico Press.

4

SHOSHONI

Dirk Elzinga and Marianna Di Paolo

Introduction

Shoshoni is a member of the Numic branch of the Uto-Aztecan language family. Prehistorically, the Shoshones ranged across the Great Basin from central Nevada through western Utah, southeastern Idaho, and western and central Wyoming. Currently, they reside in a number of reservations and "colonies" as well as larger urban centers in roughly the same area. According to the 1990 U.S. Census, Shoshoni is spoken by 2,284 people of a total tribal population estimated at about 7,000. However, Gould and Loether (2002) believe that the U.S. Census Bureau greatly underestimates the number of speakers; they estimate that there are actually 5,000 Shoshoni speakers in Nevada, Idaho, Utah, California, and Wyoming.

Although we will use the spelling *Shoshoni* to refer to the language and *Shoshone* for the people, the spelling *Shoshone* is used by others for both without any difference in meaning. We prefer the former spelling for the language because the two most widely used orthographies of the language spell the word with a final -*i*. The people themselves normally refer to themselves in Shoshoni as *newe* 'people'. (Please see Gould and Loether 2002 for more discussion on this and related issues.) However, the names of the tribes generally contain the word *Shoshone*, for example, the Ely Shoshone Tribe in Ely, Nevada; the Shoshone-Bannock Tribe in Fort Hall, Idaho; the Shoshone-Paiute Tribes of the Duck Valley Indian Reservation, straddling the border between Nevada and Idaho; and the Eastern Shoshone Tribe in Wind River, Wyoming. Likewise, in keeping with the most common orthographies used for the language, we use the spelling *Gosiute* for one of the major dialects of Shoshoni, while we respect the tribes' use of the spelling *Goshute* as in the Confederated Tribes of the Goshutes, located in western Utah and eastern Nevada.

History

Other more distantly related members of the Uto-Aztecan family include Hopi, Tarahumara, and Nahuatl. Some 2,000 years ago, speakers of the Numic languages began to radiate, fanlike, into the Great Basin (a large, arid region of the western U.S. extending roughly from the Sierra Nevada to the Rocky Mountains; it has no natural outlet to the sea) from a small territorial apex in southern California. Numic is divided into three wedge-like language zones: Western, Central, and Southern Numic. Each wedge contains at least one language in California and the other(s) in the Basin. Shoshoni is one of the three Central Numic languages. The other two are Tümpisa or Panamint Shoshoni (in California) and Comanche (now in the southern Great Plains). Linguists have shown that Shoshoni is closely related to Comanche and Panamint, and native speakers of Shoshoni report that they can understand at least some Comanche.

There are three major dialect divisions of Shoshoni: Western Shoshoni, Gosiute, and Northern Shoshoni, though in practice these divisions are not clearly defined geographically. Geographic variation in the language is better characterized by the notion of a dialect continuum: neighboring groups of speakers differ minimally from each other, but the farther a community is from another, the more likely it is that the speech of the two communities will differ substantially.

DIALECT CONTINUUM

Dialects of a language are very often differentiated from each other by obvious bundles of features of pronunciation, grammar, and vocabulary. A **dialect continuum** describes a situation where the differences between varieties of a language in close geographic proximity are either minor or few in number. As a result, there is mutual intelligibility between neighboring groups. But because the differences accumulate with geographic distance, there are substantial differences between language communities that are far apart, especially ones that are on either end of the geographic dialect continuum.

Many place-names in the Great Basin attest to the widespread historical presence of Shoshones throughout the region. These place-names include Tonopah ('mountain mahogany water') in Nevada, Ibapah ('chalky white clay water') in Utah, Tooele ('black bear') in Utah, Oquirrh Mountains ('wood place') in Utah, Pocatello (Pocatello was a prominent Shoshoni chief) in Idaho, and Fort Washakie (Washakie was also a prominent Shoshoni chief) in Wyoming.

Probably the best-known speaker of Shoshoni was Sacagawea, also spelled Sacajawea, the only woman to accompany the Lewis and Clark Expedition of 1805–6, honored recently by appearing with her infant son, Jean Baptiste Charbonneau (also known as Pompey or Pompy), on the one-dollar coin. (The following primary and secondary sources informed this discussion of Sacagawea: Lewis (2001), Fisher (1812), Criswell (1940), Clark and Edmonds (1979), "Sacagawea's Baby" (n.d.), Smithsonian National Museum of Natural History (n.d.).)

The Lewis and Clark Expedition was, in large part, a scientific journey, commissioned by Thomas Jefferson to bring back knowledge of the unexplored (by European Americans) northwestern portion of the newly acquired Louisiana Purchase. Besides the samples and records of the flora and fauna, and the maps of the region, the Expedition also returned with information about the people of the region whom they encountered along their routes and records, usually wordlists, of the languages they spoke.

Starting in St. Louis at the then western edge of the settled U.S., the Expedition wintered over at the Mandan-Hidatsa villages before pushing on for the long journey to the Pacific coast. (See also the chapter on Mandan.) There Captain Lewis and Captain Clark hired a French-Canadian trapper named Toussaint Charbonneau as an interpreter, who spoke some of the indigenous languages of the area. One of Charbonneau's two young Shoshone wives, Sacagawea, accompanied him on the journey because the Expedition leaders believed that her knowledge of her native language would serve them well in their anticipated negotiations with the Lemhi Shoshone for the purchase of horses needed to cross the mountains. (In the Expedition journals, the Shoshone were usually referred to as the Snake Indians, a name based on their signed name in Plains Sign Language.) As a 12-year old, Sacagawea, a Lemhi herself, had been captured in a raid by members of the Hidatsa (referred to in the journals of the Expedition as the Minnatarees, Mandan for 'they came to the water'). Later she was sold to Charbonneau.

Neighboring tribes along the Expedition route spoke many languages, some of them as mutually incomprehensible and as unrelated as English and Arabic. Long before Europeans arrived in the West, a tradition of multilingualism developed in the transition zones from one speech community to another, aided by sign languages used as **lingua francas**, that is, languages used as a means of communication among people whose native languages are not mutually intelligible.

Serendipitously, Shoshoni was spoken over a very large area of the Expedition route—from the Wind River in western Wyoming to the Boise River in western Idaho, an even larger area than today—a fact that Lewis and Clark may not have known when they planned their journey. Because of Shoshoni's geographic expanse, it had many language neighbors, and consequently the possibility of many bilingual translators for those other languages, making Sacagawea's ability to speak Shoshoni a much more valuable commodity than could have been imagined. (Two of these neighboring languages, Bannock and Northern Paiute, are Western Numic languages, and even today there are speakers of these languages who also speak Shoshoni.) The westernmost speaker of Shoshoni encountered by the Expedition was probably a Shoshoni woman, a prisoner of the Chopunnish living at the mouth of the Walla Walla River in Washington, who with Sacagawea served as part of the translation chain between the Expedition leaders and her captors.

At least at the beginning of the Expedition, neither Sacagawea nor Charbonneau spoke English. Some of the original members of the Expedition spoke to Charbonneau in French, who then served as a link in a translation chain. When Sacagawea also participated in the chain, she communicated with her husband in Hidatsa. Then the chain would minimally have been English>French>Hidatsa> Shoshoni. In the Pacific Northwest the Expedition journals reported a much longer translation chain of about a dozen languages from English to the local indigenous language and, of course, back again. Getting an e-mail to Australia today takes far less time than getting a sentence through a 12-language translation chain!

Although Sacagawea's initial role was to serve as an interpreter, she turned out to be valuable to the Expedition in a number of other ways, especially as a guide, upon reaching her original homeland, and as a woman of that region who was skilled in gathering and preparing edible roots, which helped them through periods of great hunger. The Expedition journals make it clear that she was an exceptional team member, and although not paid for her work, many times she proved herself more valuable than Charbonneau. Many believe she lived out her last years at the Shoshone reservation at Wind River, Wyoming.

Finally, the controversies associated with the name of this Lemhi Shoshone heroine are linguistically and culturally instructive. First, there are a number of reasons for the variant spellings of her name. One is that neither Shoshoni nor Hidatsa was a written language at that time. (They both now have orthographies.) The second is that the journalists of the Expedition are notorious for their nonstandard and variable spellings even of everyday English words. In Clark's Journal, at least on April 7, 1805, her name is recorded as Sah-kah-gar-wea, according to a history cited by LewisandClarkTrail.com ("Lewis and Clark History" (n.d.)). (Clark often wrote *r* in English words in which no *r* occurs in the standard orthography. This suggests that he spoke an *r*-less variety of English and so could not use his own pronunciation as a guide to using the grapheme *r* in spelling words.) As to the meaning of her name, the Shoshoni translation is usually given as 'boat launcher', but as the Mandan chapter explains, the Hidatsa believe it means 'bird woman' in their language. Others (John McLaughlin, personal communication) wonder whether the first morpheme of her name might be Shoshoni *saya* or *saiya*, 'mudhen', which would in part explain the Hidatsa analysis. It is, of course, possible that after she was captured her Shoshoni name was reinterpreted by the Hidatsa. From a twenty-first-century, Eurocentric perspective, that seems more likely than it would for a woman of her strength of character to have kept a name given to her by her captors after she returned to her own people.

Social Context

All present-day Shoshoni speakers are also fluent in English. In many locations, children are no longer acquiring Shoshoni as a first language and therefore speak only English. If this trend continues, the language will be in danger of becoming extinct.

Largely lost already to most of the living speakers are a familiarity with the old material culture and knowledge of the cultural motivations for traditional behavior. For decades, it has been rare in urban areas for speakers of Shoshoni to hear the language in formal, traditional settings (Miller 1972). However, although most of them are elderly, there are still fluent speakers today who can tell traditional stories, sing traditional songs, pray, conduct healing ceremonies, and speak formally in Shoshoni.

Modern recording methods have allowed us to preserve and so to pass on some of the precious art of using the language and some knowledge of traditional cultural practices. For example, some of the traditional oral culture was captured in recordings made by Wick R. Miller in the 1960s and 1970s of some of the last monolingual speakers of the language. There are also two studies of Shoshoni poetry songs: Vander (1997) and Crum, Crum, and Dayley (2001), the latter with an accompanying CD. Today many Goshute and Shoshone tribes from Wyoming to western Nevada who are engaged in revitalization efforts are documenting their own dialects of the language as well as their tribes' traditional practices.

Our own work on the Wick R. Miller Collection Shoshoni Language Project at the University of Utah is an example of such a preservation and revitalization project. The project, which includes both authors of this chapter and Mauricio J. Mixco (author of the chapter on Mandan), is centered on the 130 Miller tapes, which we have digitized to make them more accessible to tribal members as well as scholars. The roughly 80 hours of Shoshoni on those tapes has now been transcribed and translated by teams of scholars and native speakers in Utah, Nevada, and Idaho. One of the most important goals of this project is to make these materials and the teaching materials based on them easily accessible to the Shoshone and Goshute people to support them in their efforts to institute or to continue their language preservation and revitalization programs. Another very important goal is to create an easily searchable electronic corpus and dictionary that will allow linguists and Shoshoni language scholars to increase our understanding of the Shoshoni language and culture.

Some Linguistic Features

Shoshoni has a six-vowel system as shown in Table 4.1. The orthographic representation of /e^i/ is _ai_, but it is often written as _ai_, without the underlining. The vowel /i/ ranges in pronunciation from a high to a mid central unrounded vowel, depending on the dialect (Di Paolo and Sykes 2010). The high vowel variant [ɨ] is similar to the vowel in _just_ in the phrase _Just a minute_. The mid vowel variant is similar to English [ə]. Regardless of the specific pronunciation it is written _e_ in the two most widely used orthographies.

Vowel length is reported to be phonemic, meaning that each vowel in the table has a long counterpart and that vowel length can make a difference in meaning. Shoshoni also has vowel clusters such as in _oapin_ 'worm' (subject form) or _pia_ 'mother'. (Although Shoshoni scholars use the term _vowel clusters_ for these vowel collocations, they are reminiscent of Spanish vowels in hiatus, as described in the

TABLE 4.1 Shoshoni vowels

i	ɨ (*e*)	u
eⁱ (*ai*)		o
	a	

Southwest Spanish chapter, and may prove to be the same phenomenon.) Another special characteristic of Shoshoni vowels is that in some contexts, the otherwise voiced vowels can become voiceless, as in *tekkah* 'eat', in which the final vowel is usually voiceless.

VOICELESS VOWELS

It may seem unusual to think about vowels being voiceless, since vowels are the most sonorous segments. However, in many languages a vowel can be devoiced for phonetic or phonological reasons. As an example, many English speakers have a **voiceless vowel** in the first syllable of the word *potato*, especially in a casual, conversational style: [pə̥'tʰeɪrə]. Shoshoni voiceless vowels also occur in very specific phonological contexts. In the practical orthography for Shoshoni developed by Wick Miller, short, unstressed vowels are voiceless when followed by *h*.

Shoshoni has both single and geminate consonants. While the single consonants have a wide distribution, the geminate consonants /pp, ttθ, tt, kk, kkʷ/ occur only in word-medial position, as is the case with geminate consonants in most of the languages in which they occur. The problem sets will illustrate some of the many phonological processes that act on Shoshoni consonants.

Shoshoni is an agglutinating language, meaning that morpheme boundaries are easy to find and that grammatical morphemes typically have only single functions. (See the Mandan and the Navajo chapters for more on agglutinating morphology.) This morphological characteristic is especially obvious in the verbs, as can be seen in the words in (1).

(1) a. pa-   ma-   ka   -nnu
         WATER.   HAND.   eat SLOW.
         INSTRUMENTAL   INSTRUMENTAL   COMPLETION
         'watered'
     b. koitsoih   -teki   -to'i
         wash   begin   FUTURE
         'will start to wash'

Even words that in English can be glossed as 'here', 'there', 'this', and 'that', all of which indicate relative distance from the speaker, are made up of several morphemes in Shoshoni. For example, Table 4.2 shows that the morphological structure of the locative demonstrative *sikka* 'this-OBJ' is made up of three morphemes, *s-i-kka*.

DEICTIC WORDS AND LOCATIVES

Deictic words, also called **locatives**, are words that point to a location relative to the speaker—near or far. Demonstrative pronouns in English are examples of deictic words: *this, these* (near); *that, those* (far). In some languages, deictic words may also take the listener's location into account.

As you can see, the English glosses, for example, 'that yonder', simplify the complex meanings of the Shoshoni demonstrative words because English does not normally divide up locations as carefully as Shoshoni does.

TABLE 4.2 Demonstratives and demonstrative pronouns (objective forms)

	'Definite or continuing topic'	*Relative distance from the speaker*	*'Singular demonstrative or third person pronoun'*	*English gloss*
A.	s–	i– 'the speaker is touching the object'	-kka	'this'
B.	s–	ai– 'close enough for the speaker to touch but not touching'	-kka	'this'
C.	s–	o– 'middle distance from the speaker'	-kka	'that'
D.	s–	a– 'far away from the speaker but visible'	-kka	'that (yonder)'
E.	s–	u– 'out of the speaker's sight'	-kka	'that (not visible)'

The word order of Shoshoni sentences is Subject-Object-Verb (SOV), as the sentences in (2) illustrate. (For a definition of *word order*, please see the Navajo chapter.) SOV is the most common word order in the world's languages, so it is not surprising that other unrelated languages such as Mandan and Navajo also have that word order. (Please note: In the sentences below, there is some indication that many of the Shoshoni words are made up of more than one morpheme, but for the sake of clearly showing the word order we have simplified the morphology of the individual words. Please see the preceding discussion of the structure of three of the words: *pamakannu, koitsoihtekito'i,* and *sikka.*)

(2) a. Andy   punkunii   pamakannu.
               horses-OBJ   water-PAST
         'Andy watered the horses.'

     b. Ne   hunanna   puinnu.
         I   badger-OBJ   see-PAST
         'I saw a badger.'

     c. Ne   pii   sikka   ne   mapaiankannu.
         my   mother   this-OBJ   me   made-for-PAST
         'My mother made this for me.'

     d. Ne   kentu   kahni   tukkanku   tsippiha   puinnu.
         I   yesterday   house   under   squirrel-OBJ   see-PAST.
         'I saw a squirrel under the house yesterday.'

     e. Ne   ekise   awe   koitsoihtekito'i.
         I   soon   dish-OBJ   wash-start-FUTURE.
         'I will start to wash dishes pretty soon.'

Note: These four example sentences are taken from Crum and Dayley (1993: 1–3), although here we have modified the glosses. Our sentence (2a) is their (3), (2b) is their (1), (2c) is their (13), (2d) is their (5), and (2e) is their (6).

The problem sets below will allow you to explore more of the linguistic structure of Shoshoni.

Further Reading

For an endangered language, Shoshoni is relatively well documented. Tape-recorded collections such as Miller's have allowed linguists and native Shoshoni-speaking scholars to produce a fair amount of scholarly material on Shoshoni and its speakers. Each of the four available grammars differs from the others in scope and purpose: Miller (1996) is a grammatical sketch of Gosiute; Crum and Dayley (1993) is a comprehensive reference grammar of Western Shoshoni written by a native speaker (Crum) together with a linguist (Dayley); Gould and Loether (2002), also a collaboration between a native speaker (Gould) and a linguist (Loether), is a language textbook and pedagogical grammar of the Fort Hall variety of Western Shoshoni; McLaughlin (2012) contains additional grammatical information not found elsewhere, which was gleaned from a close analysis of oral narratives, and aims for a more pan-dialectal coverage than the other grammatical descriptions currently available. Also available are collections of texts (Miller 1972; Crum and Dayley 1997), collections of songs (Vander 1997; Crum, Crum, and Dayley 2001), and a number of print dictionaries (for example, Miller 1972; Tidzump 1970; Crum and Dayley 1993, 1997; Crum, Crum, and Dayley 2001), and one online dictionary in the Fort Hall orthography (Gould and Loether n.d.). In addition, Miller and others have published sociocultural studies such as Miller (1970) and Hage and Miller (1976).

Although a number of Shoshone and Goshute communities throughout the Great Basin are engaged in language programs, much of the revitalization activity in recent years has been initiated by or in collaboration with the Wick R. Miller Shoshoni Project, directed by Marianna Di Paolo. The project has been engaged in materials preservation and digitization; and in the archiving, development, and dissemination of materials to members of Shoshoni-speaking tribal communities. The materials include digital recordings and electronic dictionaries, curricular materials for all age groups, children's books, claymation films, and other materials from the original Wick R. Miller Collection and materials developed in collaboration with community members in recent years. The project also provides Shoshoni-language teacher education workshops and since 2009 the summer Shoshone/ Goshute Youth Language Apprenticeship Program for high school students and young people who have attended the high school program in previous summers.

(Note: The Wick R. Miller Collection Shoshoni Language Project at the University of Utah was funded first by NSF # 0418351 *Preserving and Enhancing Accessibility of Gosiute/Shoshoni Materials in the Wick R. Miller Collection* [Mauricio J. Mixco, Principal Investigator, and Marianna Di Paolo, co–Investigator, 2004–07]; and by grants from Barrick Gold of North America, Inc. *The Wick R. Miller Collection: Returning to the Community*, to Marianna Di Paolo [Principal Investigator, 2007–].)

Problem Sets

These problem sets are largely based on data and/or exercises from Wick R. Miller's courses at the University of Utah, from Crum and Dayley (1993), and from Elzinga (1999).

Syntax: Basic Word Order

1. a. What is the word order of the adjectives, possessive adjectives, nouns, and postposition/prepositions in the following phrases in Shoshoni? (Note: The data are written in the Miller orthography.)

TABLE 4.3 Shoshoni phrases

ne papi	'my older brother'
en papi	'your older brother'
ne pia	'my mother'
en pia	'your mother'
en punku	'your horse'
onten punku	'brown horse'
tosa punku	'white horse'
tuu" punku	'black horse'
tuu" paa	'black water'
tuu" weta	'black bear'
pia pa	'on (the) mother'
huu" pa	'on (the) stick'
peyen pa	'on (the) duck'
en punku pa	'on your horse'

b. How would you say 'on my horse' and 'on (the) black horse' in Shoshoni? (Note: In these phrases, English 'the' is not overtly expressed in Shoshoni.)

2. a. How do we know that the Shoshoni speaker of sentence (1c) is touching the thing that her mother made for her?

b. If the speaker of sentence (3c) wanted to say 'My mother made that (yonder) for me', how would she say it?

3. Consider the following sentence:

Ikkih   ma   tsatteki.
here   it   put
'Put it here.'

If *ikkih* is a locative adverb meaning 'here (speaker is touching the location)' and *ukkuh* is a locative adverb meaning 'over there, out of sight', what do the remaining locative adverbs in this list mean? (For this exercise, ignore the final vowel.)

TABLE 4.4 Shoshoni locatives

Shoshoni	*English gloss*
ikkih	'here (speaker is touching the location)'
aikkih	_____
akkuh	_____
okkuh	_____
ukkuh	'over there, out of sight'

Phonology

The data in the following problem are drawn from the Gosiute dialect of Shoshoni. It is important to complete each part of the problem before proceeding to the next. Please note that Shoshoni [tθ] should be considered a single stop consonant in the phonology of the language even though it consists phonetically of two sounds.

Noncoronal Stops and Continuants: Examine the forms in Table 4.5 and answer the questions that follow. (Coronal consonants are made by using the tip of the tongue. Noncoronals are those consonants that are not made with the tip of the tongue.)

TABLE 4.5 Shoshoni noncoronal stops and continuants

[paː]	'water'	[kaː]	'rat'
[peɣ ʷi]	'swell'	[kuna]	'firewood; fire'
[puinnu]	'saw'	[kiniː]	'hawk, falcon'
[punu]	'navel'	[kaɣu]	'grandmother (mother's mother); grandchild (woman's daughter's child)'
[pia]	'mother'	[iɣi]	'young'
[potto]	'grinding stone'	[kʷinaː]	'eagle; large bird'
[koβa]	'carry in the arms; hug'	[kʷasi]	'tail; tail feather'
[taiβo]	'European American'	[kʷitti]	'shoot'
[tojaβi]	'mountain'	[iɣʷi]	'smell something'
[hiβiði]	'drinking'	[niːɣʷi]	'say, tell'
[muβi]	'nose'	[teɣʷahni]	'chief; boss; leader'

4. a. Are the noncoronal voiceless stop/voiced continuant [p/β] pair allophones of one phoneme, or do they form separate phonemes in Shoshoni? Provide evidence for your answer by describing the distribution of the pairs of allophones.

    b. Now use the data to answer question (a) about each of the following two other noncoronal voiceless stop/voiced continuant pairs: [k/ɣ] and [kʷ/ɣʷ]. (Some words in the table may contain more than one sound relevant to this question.)

    c. Give the underlying form for each of the following words:
    [pia]
    [koβa]
    [kaɣu]
    [niːɣʷi]

Coronal Stops and Continuants: Now that you have established a generalization for the distribution of noncoronal voiceless stops and the corresponding voiced continuants, consider the forms in Table 4.6.

TABLE 4.6 Shoshoni coronal stops and continuants

[tθakkɨna]	'sew (singular object)'	[moðo]	'beard, mustache; whiskers'
[tθɨɣɨ]	'brush rabbit'	[muði]	'sharp (of a point)'
[eʒikko]	'sling shot'	[iði]	'unpleasant odor or taste'
[iʒappɨ]	'coyote'	[paði]	'older sister'
[hiβiʒoː]	'old lady'		
[piʒi]	'breast'		

5. a. Are the three coronal sounds [tθ], [ʒ], and [ð] allophones of one phoneme, or do they form separate phonemes of Shoshoni? (Remember that the vowel [ɨ] is a high central unrounded vowel.)
   b. Provide evidence for your answer to (a) by stating the generalization governing the distribution of the three sounds.
   c. Provide underlying forms for the following words:
      [iði]
      [tθakkɨna]
      [iʒappɨ]
      [paði]

Now consider the forms in Table 4.7 and answer the questions that follow.

TABLE 4.7 Additional Shoshoni data on coronal stops and continuants

[tojaβi]	'mountain'	[kʷaharɨ]	'antelope'
[tiyohih]	'send'	[seði]	'this'
[teɣʷahni]	'chief; boss; leader'	[piði]	'arrive'
[karɨri]	'sitting (singular subject)'	[hanniðui]	'will use'
[poro]	'digging stick'	[hiβiði]	'drinking'
[pɨra]	'arm'		

6. a. In these data, are the three sounds [t], [r], and [ð] allophones of one phoneme, or do they form separate phonemes of Shoshoni?
   b. Provide evidence for your answer to (a) by stating the generalization governing the distribution of the three sounds.

c. Given your response to (b), provide the underlying forms for the following words:

[hanniðui]
[pɨɾa]
[teɣʷahni]
[seðɨ]

[s] and [ʃ]: Consider the data in Table 4.8, and answer the questions that follow.

TABLE 4.8 Shoshoni [s] and [ʃ]

[kasa]	'wing'	[suwai]	'want, think'
[kosojo]	'bushy hair'	[kʷeʃi]	'tail'
[kʷasu]	'dress, shirt'	[meʃo]	'cricket'
[pɨːsi]	'fur, down'	[wiʃu]	'string'
[saija]	'mudhen'	[eʃi]	'gray'

7. a. Are [s] and [ʃ] allophones of one phoneme? Explain your answer.
    b. Give the underlying form for each word in the table above.

Morphophonology: More on Stops and Continuants

(Review the responses to (1)–(5) with your instructor before working on this section.)

Use the data in Table 4.9 to answer the questions that follow.

TABLE 4.9 Data on Shoshoni stops and continuants

Underlying form	Phonetic form	Gloss
nɨ papi	nɨ βaβi	'my older brother'
in papi	im baβi	'your older brother'
pia	pia	'mother'
nɨ pia	nɨ βia	'my mother'
in pia	im bia	'your mother'
pakuitanu	paɣuiðanu	'shattered'
tsi" pakuitanu	tsippaɣuiðanu	'shattered (by a) pointed instrument'
ma pakuitanu	maβaɣuiðanu	'shattered (by) hand'
tsi" patanu	tsippaðanu	'spread (by a) pointed instrument'

(Continued)

TABLE 4.9 *Continued*

Underlying form	Phonetic form	Gloss
ma patanu	maβaðanu	'spread (by) hand'
punku	puŋgu	'horse'
ontɨn punku	ondɨm buŋgu	'brown horse'
tosa punku	tosa βuŋgu	'white horse'
tu:" punku	tu: ppuŋgu	'black horse'
ɨn punku	ɨm buŋgu	'your horse'
ɨn tu:" punku	ɨn du: ppuŋgu	'your black horse'
pa:	pa:	'water'
tu:" pa:	tu: ppa:	'black water'
ontɨn pa:	ondɨm ba:	'whisky'
taipo	taiβo	'European American'
tu:" taipo	tu: ttaiβo	'African American'
pia pai	piaβai	'to have (a) mother'
pia pa	piaβa	'on (the) mother'
hu:" pai	hu:ppai	'to have (a) stick'
hu:" pa	hu:ppa	'on (the) stick'
pɨyɨn pai	pɨyɨmbai	'to have (a) duck'
pɨyɨn pa	pɨyɨmba	'on (the) duck'

8. a. Fill in the blanks in Table 4.10 by listing all the allomorphs (the phonetic forms) corresponding to the gloss given in the leftmost column. Include the entire word or phrase in which the morpheme occurs to facilitate your analysis for the remainder of the questions in this section. The fourth row is already completed for you. (Note: In this data set some underlying forms have as many as four allomorphs, and some have fewer.)

TABLE 4.10 Summary of morphophonological analysis

Gloss	Underlying form	Allomorph 1	Allomorph 2	Allomorph 3	Allomorph 4
my					
your					
older brother					
mother	pia	pia	ɨm bia	nɨ βia	
		pia-βai			
		pia-βa			
horse					
duck					
brown					
white					
stick					
water					
black					
European American					

Gloss	Underlying form	Allomorph 1	Allomorph 2	Allomorph 3	Allomorph 4
to have (a/the)					
on (a/the)					
hand					
pointed instrument					
shattered (by)					
spread (by)					

b. Wick R. Miller, a noted linguist and one of the creators of the Miller orthography for Shoshoni, arbitrarily selected the symbol /"/ to account for certain phonological facts of Shoshoni. Examine the underlying and phonetic forms in which /hu:", tu:", tsi"/ occur and explain the phonological meaning of this symbol.

c. The data show just one underlying nasal consonant at the end of syllables, /n/. List all the nasal consonants that appear in the phonetic forms in syllable-final position. Then state the generalization that accounts for the phonetic realization of this underlying nasal.

d. All stops in Shoshoni are voiceless underlyingly. State the generalization that accounts for the voicing of underlying voiceless stops.

e. Considering what you have discovered about stops and continuants in all of the problems sets above, do phonological processes that affect consonants within words in Shoshoni also affect consonants between words? Give some examples (from any of the problem sets) that support your response.

References

Clark, Ella E., and Margot Edmonds. 1979. *Sacagawea of the Lewis and Clark Expedition.* Berkeley: University of California Press.

Criswell, Elijah Harry. 1940. *Lewis and Clark: Linguistic pioneers.* Columbia: University of Missouri Press.

Crum, Beverly, Earl Crum, and Jon P. Dayley. 2001. *Newe Hupia: Shoshoni poetry songs.* Logan: Utah State University Press.

Crum, Beverly, and Jon P. Dayley. 1993. *Western Shoshoni grammar.* Occasional Papers and Monographs in Cultural Anthropology and Linguistics 1. Boise, ID: Boise State University, Department of Anthropology.

Crum, Beverly, and Jon P. Dayley. 1997. *Shoshoni texts.* Occasional Papers and Monographs in Cultural Anthropology and Linguistics 2. Boise, ID: Boise State University, Department of Anthropology.

Di Paolo, Marianna, and Robert D. Sykes. 2010. Acoustic evidence for a vowel shift in Shoshoni. Presented at the Society for the Study of Indigenous Languages Annual Meeting, Baltimore, MD, January 2010.

Elzinga, Dirk. 1999. The consonants of Gosiute. PhD diss., University of Arizona.

Fisher, William, ed. 1812. *New travels among the Indians of North America: Being a compilation, taken partly from the communications already published, of Lewis and Clark, to the President of the United States, and partly from other authors who travelled among the various tribes of Indians . . . with a dictionary of the tongue [Cree]*. Philadelphia: J. Sharan.

Gould, Drusilla, and Christopher Loether. 2002. *An introduction to the Shoshoni language*. Salt Lake City: University of Utah Press.

Gould, Drusilla, and Christopher Loether. n.d. *Shoshoni on-line dictionary*. http://shoshoni dictionary.com/shoshonidictionary.asp

Hage, Per, and Wick R. Miller. 1976. 'Eagle' = 'bird': A note on the structure and evolution of Shoshoni ethnoornithological nomenclature. *American Ethnologist* 3.3: 481–488.

Karttunen, Frances. 1994. *Between worlds: Interpreters, guides, and survivors*. New Brunswick, NJ: Rutgers University Press.

Lewis, Meriwether, 1774–1809 (2001). *Original journals of the Lewis and Clark Expedition*. Vol. 1, Parts 1–2. Ed. Reuben Gold Thwaites. Scituate, MA: Digital Scanning. Electronic resource. http://site.ebrary.com/lib/utah/Doc?id=10015046

"Lewis and Clark History: Sacagawea ~ Sacajawea ~ Sakakawea." LewisAndClarkTrail. com. http://lewisandclarktrail.com/sacajawea.htm

McLaughlin, John E. 2012. *Shoshoni grammar*. Languages of the World/Materials, no. 488. Munich: LinCom Europa.

Miller, Wick R. 1970. Western Shoshoni dialects. In Earl H. Swanson Jr., ed., *Languages and cultures of western North America: Essays in honor of Sven S. Liljeblad*, 17–36. Pocatello: Idaho State University.

Miller, Wick R. 1972. *Newe Natekwinappeh: Shoshoni stories and dictionary*. University of Utah Anthropological Papers 94. Salt Lake City: University of Utah Press.

Miller, Wick R. 1996. Sketch of Shoshone, a Uto-Aztecan language. In William C. Sturtevant, ed., *Handbook of American Indians*, vol. 17, 693–720, Ives Goddard, ed., *Languages*. Washington, DC: Smithsonian Institution.

"Sacagawea's Baby—Jean Baptiste Charbonneau." n.d. Retrieved from LewisAndClark Trail.com. http://lewisandclarktrail.com/sacagaweasbaby.htm

Smithsonian National Museum of Natural History. n.d. "Lewis & Clark: Mapping the West." http://www.mnh.si.edu/education/lc/lcmapping/

Tidzump, M. 1970. *Shoshone thesaurus*. Grand Forks, ND: Summer Institute of Linguistics, University of North Dakota.

Vander, Judith. 1997. *Shoshone Ghost Dance religion: Poetry songs and Great Basin context*. Urbana: University of Illinois Press.

5

MANDAN

Mauricio J. Mixco

Introduction

The Mandan were among the earliest of the extant indigenous peoples to have settled along the Missouri River in the Northern Plains of present-day North Dakota. Today there are some two hundred people, on and off of the Fort Berthold Reservation, who claim some Mandan ancestry. Most Mandans now also partially descend from other indigenous groups, Hispanics, African Americans (members of the nineteenth-century U.S. military stationed on the Upper Missouri), or a variety of European explorers, trappers, traders, and settlers who have been active in the region's history since first contact. The Mandan language is the sole member of its own (Mandan) branch of the Siouan family within the larger Siouan-Catawba language family.

History

Once in a position of wealth, power, and cultural achievement in their palisaded, earth lodge villages, these erstwhile bison hunters, horticulturalists, and traders were decimated by epidemics after first European contact with an expedition led by Sire de Verendrye in 1738. In 1837, a mere 33 years after the Mandan chief, Big White, welcomed Lewis and Clark's Corps of Discovery to his villages with trust and hospitality during the expedition's first winter on the Great Plains, thousands of Mandans died of smallpox, leaving a mere 200 survivors. They had also suffered population attrition in battles with mounted Uto-Aztecan-, Siouan-, and Algonquian-speaking nomads, including the Comanche, Assiniboine, Lakota, Arapaho, and Cheyenne, among others. Of the original 13 Mandan clans, only 2 divisions remained, the Three-Clans and the Four-Clans, which soon merged with comparable clans in the Hidatsa tribe. The Hidatsa were close allies and neighbors of the Mandan but distant linguistic relatives (see Table 5.1; Will and Spinden 1906; Parks 1991, 3:11).

In 1845 remnants of the Mandan, Hidatsa, and Arikara tribes came to share Like-A-Fishhook Village (named after a bend in the Missouri River north of the Knife River confluence near the town of Stanton, in present-day North Dakota). The Hidatsa remained relatively viable due to a fortuitous absence during the worst of the epidemics. A vast reservation in North Dakota and Wyoming was promised to the three tribes by the Fort Laramie Treaty of 1851. However, it was progressively reduced until a presidential executive order established the present Fort Berthold Reservation in 1891, now located entirely within the central part of western North Dakota. Since the Indian Reorganization Act of 1934, the three tribes have been joined together administratively in the Three Affiliated Tribes Nation.

Bismarck, North Dakota's capital, has a twin city, Mandan, on the western bank of the Missouri River; its name recalls the location of early Mandan villages (e.g., Slant Village) at the confluence of the Heart and Missouri Rivers. Today most Mandans live near the Twin Buttes subagency in the southern half of the reservation, near the hamlet of Halliday. (A subagency is a secondary administrative center away from the main tribal headquarters, which in this case is located near New Town in the northwestern corner of the reservation.) Other Mandan settlements are scattered throughout predominantly Hidatsa settlements, at Mandaree, Drags Wolf Village, New Town, and Parshall on the western and northern shores of Lake Sakakawea, frequently pronounced Sacajawea. (Note that the alternative spelling and pronunciation Sacajawea is not in accord with the original Hidatsa name, meaning 'bird woman', from *saka:ka* 'bird', *wia* 'woman', for the young Lemhi Shoshoni mother who served as a key translator for Lewis and Clark's expedition.)

Mandan is an endangered language today. At this writing, it is spoken fluently by only three elderly people and less fluently by one or two younger semispeakers (i.e., partially fluent speakers) on the Fort Berthold Indian Reservation, which brackets the dammed section of the Missouri River, referred to above as Lake Sakakawea. Mandan speakers are trilingual, also speaking Hidatsa (related to Mandan within the Siouan language family; see Table 5.1) and English. They acquired Hidatsa in childhood, either from relatives or at local mission schools where Hidatsa predominated. They also began to acquire English there, later perfecting it through educational, military, or work experiences.

As is the case with many other tribal and minority languages around the world, when a language ceases to be acquired by its youngest generations, it is considered to be on the path to extinction. As fewer and fewer speakers use it, the language atrophies, as a muscle does without exercise. Usually, knowledge of traditional cultural practices, beliefs, and lifeways also ceases to be a part of daily life. As this happens, the specialized vocabulary appropriate for traditional behaviors and thought processes disappears, as does the competence that lies behind the ability to construct complex sentences and employ more elaborate word-building patterns.

In addition to Mandan, Siouan itself contains three branches: (a) Missouri River, (b) Mississippi Valley, and (c) Ohio Valley, as shown in Table 5.1 (Campbell 1997).

TABLE 5.1 Mandan and Hidatsa in the Siouan-Catawba language family

Catawba	Siouan				
			Siouan-Catawba		
*Catawba, *Woccon	Mandan	Missouri River	Mississippi Valley	Southeastern (a.k.a. Ohio Valley)	
	Mandan	Crow	Hidatsa	(see Table 5.2)	*Tutelo, *Saponi, *Moniton, *Ofo-Biloxi

*Extinct language.

TABLE 5.2 The Mississippi Valley subbranch of Siouan

Mississippi Valley		
Dakotan	*Dheghiha*	*Chiwere-Winnebago*
Teton, Santee, Yankton, Yanktonais, Assiniboine, Stoney	Omaha-Ponca, Osage-Kansa, *Quapaw	Winnebago, Chiwere(Iowa-Oto-*Missouri dialects)

*Extinct language.

Despite the Hidatsa people's residing with and being allied to the Mandan, the Hidatsa language itself, as Table 5.1 shows, is most closely related to Crow (southeastern Montana). Both Hidatsa and Crow are in the Missouri River branch. The two other divisions of Siouan are the Mississippi Valley and Southeastern (or Ohio Valley) branches, with extinct members—Tutelo, Saponi, Moniton, and Ofo-Biloxi—in the southeastern part of the U.S., along with the more distantly related and also extinct Catawba and Woccon.

The Mississippi Valley branch (see Table 5.2) is the largest, with three subbranches, each containing a number of languages: the Dakotan subbranch (Teton, Santee, Yankton, Yanktonais, Assiniboine, and Stoney), the Dheghiha (Omaha-Ponca, Osage-Kansa, and *Quapaw), and the Chiwere-Winnebago (Winnebago and Chiwere along with the Iowa-Oto-Missouri dialects). Several Dakotan languages are still spoken in the general vicinity of Mandan. The extinct Catawba (once spoken in the Carolinas along with its sister language, Woccon) was a collateral partner to Siouan in Siouan-Catawba. For Siouan-Catawba, tentative remote relationships with Caddoan and Iroquoian have been postulated (Chafe 1976).

Arikara, the third language on the Fort Berthold Reservation, is most closely related to Caddo, Wichita, Kitsai, and Pawnee, all in the Caddoan language family (previously spoken in the Central and Southern Plains).

Social Context

Mandan is also referred to as *Rʉʔetaː(re)* or *Rʉʔitaː(di)*, after the village and dialect from which it sprang. (The ʉ is a high back nasalized vowel.) Given the number of precontact villages, it is probable that some additional degree of dialect diversity once existed in Mandan. Some linguists believe that a handful of lexical items are still possibly of Rʉptare or Rʉptade, Rʉptaː(di) origin, that is, one of the dialects that did not survive the earliest reservation period. What little is known of earlier varieties comes from the writings of travelers like Maximilian, Prinz zu Wied Neu-Wied (1839–41), George Catlin (1841), and others (see Will and Spinden 1906).

On the Fort Berthold Reservation, social and linguistic contact among the Indian settlements and farms along the Missouri River bottomlands had been frequent and effortless until these were flooded in 1951 by the U.S. Army Corps of Engineers for the purposes of power generation and modern irrigation. This massive government project broke up the Native American language communities, putting great distances between former neighbors and making natural contact virtually impossible, as well as simultaneously eradicating any vestiges of surviving, pre-reservation Mandan dialect variation. The reservoir that resulted from the inundation, Lake Sakakawea, cuts the reservation diagonally in two. People who had once been a short walk, horseback ride, or ferry crossing away from each other were resettled hours apart. The integrity of the Mandan speech community was literally swept away by the flood waters.

Some Linguistic Features

The Mandan verb almost always occurs at the end of its clause or sentence, with the Subject and Object, in that order, usually preceding it (this is often referred to as SOV order); compare the Mandan equivalents for the following English sentences. (For a definition of *word order*, please see the Navajo chapter.) Note that unlike English *pre*positions (e.g., *to, from, in, at*, etc.), Mandan shows *post*positions, usually suffixed to their noun or pronoun. (The use of postpositions rather than prepositions is one of the differences between languages with an SVO order, like English, and SOV languages, like Mandan, Turkish, and Japanese). Furthermore, possession is not marked by independent pronouns (e.g., *my, your, her, our*, etc.) as in English, but by prefixes (such as in *wį-hʉːsi* 'my pants' in (1)). Mandan demonstrative pronouns (English *this, these, that, those*, etc.) must also mark the typical position of the designated item (e.g., *qʔt eː hqk* 'that [standing]', *re rqk* 'this [sitting]', *re wqk* 'this [lying])':

(1)	wį-	hʉːsi	re	wqk	wa-	kitah-	hre-	ʔʃ
	my	pants	this	lie	I	change	cause	

'I'm changing these pants of mine.' (lit. 'I cause my pants lying here to change.')

(2) wrį-   ta: re:ʔh–   hre-   kiʔ,   ʔiwąp-   ta: re:ʔh–   oʔʃ
     water   to   go   cause   when,   down   to   go
     'When one puts it in the water, it goes to the bottom.'
     (What is glossed as 'put' in the free translation is, literally, 'make go'.
     The gloss for the *oʔʃ* morpheme and its allomorph, *ʔʃ*, is left for exercise (10).)

Thus, what would normally be expressed in an English sentence with separate
words and particles is expressed in Mandan by morphemes that tend to be bound
together into longer words made up of the roots and affixes, which are "glued"
together and, therefore, are easy for a linguist to discover and take apart (which is
what *analyze* means). Due to this gluing, linguists call this an *agglutinating* pattern;
thus, Mandan has an *agglutinating* morphology. Another characteristic of agglutinating
morphemes is that they usually (but not always) have a one-to-one relation with their
meanings (i.e., each morpheme usually has one and only one meaning), for example:

(3) ki-   wa-   xoprį-   kre-   ʔʃ
     reflexive   something   holy   plural
     'they become holy' (lit. 'they by themselves become something holy')

(4) ki-   wa-   xoprį-   hre-   kre-   ʔʃ
     reflexive   something   holy   cause   plural
     'they make themselves holy' (lit. 'they make themselves something holy')

Further Reading

There are few published sources on Mandan grammar. Aside from the aforemen-
tioned reports and wordlists, the first published modern description of the language
is by Edward Kennard (1936), an ethnographer who also collected numerous, still
unpublished, narrative texts. More recently, the late Robert C. Hollow has left us an
unpublished University of California-Berkeley doctoral dissertation, *Mandan Dictionary* (1970), from which we have liberally quoted here, in an early generative
phonology framework. It is a great stride beyond the broad phonetic transcription
and rough morphological analysis in Kennard. Richard T. Carter (1991a, 1991b) has
worked on the language most recently, publishing a phonological study as well as a
syntactic analysis of one of the Kennard texts. There is also a grammatical sketch and
an article on Mandan syntax (Mixco 1997a, 1997b).

Problem Sets

Phonology

1. **Vowel Length**
   Examine the data in Table 5.3. Are there any minimal pairs based on vowel
   length? If so, what are they, and what can you conclude to be true of Mandan
   phonology from any such minimal pairs?

TABLE 5.3 Mandan vowel length data

akinjn	'bridge'	ihjʔ	'hair'
raːteoʔʃ	'you stand up'	ihj	'to drink'
nąteoʔʃ	'to be stood up'	hiʔ	'teeth'
ʃiːhoʔʃ	'to be sharp'	mjːh	'woman'
ʃjːhoʔʃ	'to be strong'	mąh	'turnip'
waʔh	'snow'	mąːh	'arrow'

2. Vowel Nasalization

In the data in Table 5.4, examine the distribution of the oral and nasal vowel pairs such as [iː, jː]. (The nasal vowels have a cedilla, also called a 'nasal hook', under the phonetic vowel symbol.)

a. Determine whether pairs of oral and nasal vowels are allophones of different phonemes or allophones of the same phoneme. Provide evidence for your answer. If the sounds in a pair are allophones of the same phoneme, use natural classes to state the contexts in which each sound occurs.

TABLE 5.4 Mandan vowel nasalization data

raːteoʔʃ	'you stand up'	ihjʔ	'hair'
nąteoʔʃ	'to be stood up'	ihj	'to drink'
xtąte	'thunderbird' (mythic)	hiʔ	'teeth'
jːxaː	'to be alone'	mjːh	'woman'
ʃowok	'to be deep, hollow'	ʃjːhoʔʃ	'to be strong'
akinjn	'bridge'	mąːh	'arrow'
ʃiːhoʔʃ	'to be sharp'	waʔh	'snow'
mąh	'turnip'		

b. Provide underlying forms for the following words in Table 5.5, keeping in mind what you discovered in (1) and (2a).

TABLE 5.5 Mandan vowel nasalization exercise

Surface form	English gloss	Underlying form
ihjʔ	'hair'	
jːxaː	'to be alone'	

3. Underlying Representation and Phonological Rules

a. Mandan does not allow certain underlying clusters such as those made up of identical consonants or those including a sonorant consonant (for example, *pp, *tt, *kk, *wr, *pr, *kr) in surface forms. Examine the data in Table 5.6 and then list the consonant clusters that are allowed. (Note that the periods indicate syllable boundaries. Also, /r/ becomes [n] and /w/ becomes [m] before or after nasal vowels. These sounds are not pertinent to the issue at hand.)

b. Given these data, what is one strategy that Mandan uses to break up consonant clusters that are not allowed? (In answering this question, compare the consonant clusters in the underlying forms with the corresponding surface forms.)

TABLE 5.6 Mandan phonology data

Underlying form	Surface form	Gloss
wrį	wį.nį	'water'
kowero	ko.we.ro	'husband'
werok	we.rok	'worm'
wį:h	mį:h	'woman'
ptį:re	ptį:.ne	'bison'
pʃaʃ	pʃaʃ	'sweetgrass'
skųh	skųh	'to be sweet'
apxa	a.pxa	'wing'
oxka	ox.ka	'wild'
pke	pke	'turtle'
psi	psi	'to be black'
akreh	a.ke.reh	'to be pitiful'
kipsą	ki.psą	'painted turtle'
oxtą:re	ox.tą:.ne	'cedar'
kiwą:	ki.mą:	'six'
huprįh	hu.pį.nįh	'soup'
xoprį	xo.pį.nį	'to be holy, sacred'
pʃixare	pʃi.xa.re	'sage'
kʃikʃe	kʃi.kʃe	'lightning'
xtąte	xtą.te	'thunderbird' (mythic)
į:xa:	į:.xa:	'to be alone'
ʃowok	ʃo.wok	'to be deep, hollow'

Morphology

4. **Subject Agreement**
   Analyze the following data in Table 5.7 to determine how subjects of transitive verbs are marked in Mandan, and fill in the blanks in Table 5.8. (Again you may ignore the morpheme -oʔʃ for this exercise.)

VERB TRANSITIVITY

A *transitive verb* is one that allows a direct object; *intransitives* do not.

TABLE 5.7 Mandan subject agreement data

wa-pa:ʔx-oʔʃ	'I set it upright'	pa:ʔx-oʔʃ	'he/she sets it upright'
wa-kiną:-oʔʃ	'I tell her'	nų-pa:ʔx-oʔʃ	'we set it upright'
ra-pa:ʔx-oʔʃ	'you set it upright'	ra-pa:ʔx-nįt-oʔʃ	'you (pl.) set it upright'
ra-kiną:-oʔʃ	'you tell her'	pa:ʔx-kere-oʔʃ	'they set it upright'

TABLE 5.8 Subject agreement exercise

_____	'I'	_____	'we'
_____	'you'	_____	'you' + pl.
_____	'he/she'	_____	'they' (he/she + pl.)

5.   **Subject Agreement**

   a.   In the following data (Table 5.10), determine what morphemes mark the subject and the plural, respectively, and fill in the blanks in Table 5.9. (Hint: Mandan has a **zero [Ø] morpheme** corresponding to English *he, she* and *it*.)

ZERO (Ø) MORPHEME

Zero (Ø) morpheme refers to a morpheme that is unpronounced on the surface; linguists keep track of it by using the zero symbol (Ø).

---

   b.   How do your answers differ from (4)?
   c.   How do these verbs differ from the verbs in (4)?

TABLE 5.9 Additional subject agreement exercise

_____	'I'	_____	'we'
_____	'you'	_____	'you' + pl.
_____	'he/she/it'	_____	'they' (he/she + pl.)

TABLE 5.10 Additional Mandan subject agreement data

mą-waːxweː-oʔʃ	'I'm hiding'	nį-ʃiʔ-oʔʃ	'you are good'
noː-waːxweː-oʔʃ	'we're hiding'	nį-ʃiʔ-nįt-oʔʃ	'you (pl.) are good'
siː-oʔʃ	'it's yellow'	ʃiʔ-oʔʃ	'he/she is good'
siː-kere-oʔʃ	'they're yellow'		

6. **Subject and Object Agreement**
   a. In the following data (Table 5.13), determine which morphemes mark subject and object for these transitive verbs and fill in Table 5.11:

TABLE 5.11 Mandan subject and object agreement morphemes

	Subject		Object
	Singular	*Plural*	
1st	_____	_____	_____
2nd	_____	_____	_____
3rd	_____	_____	_____

   b. List the Mandan verb stem for each of the following in Table 5.12:

TABLE 5.12 Mandan verb stem exercise

Mandan	Gloss
_____	'tell'
_____	'see'
_____	'speak'
_____	'set upright'

TABLE 5.13 Mandan verb stem data

wa-nį-pe-oʔʃ	'I speak to you'	ra-paːʔx-oʔʃ	'you set it upright'
nį-he-oʔʃ	'he/she sees you'	ra-paːʔx-nįt-oʔʃ	'you (pl.) set it upright'
noː-he-oʔʃ	'he/she sees us'	paːʔx-kere-oʔʃ	'they set it upright'
mą-kiną-oʔʃ	'he/she tells me'		
kiną-oʔʃ	'he/she tells him/her'		
nų-nį-kiną-oʔʃ	'we tell you'		

c. Taking all of these data into account, state the order of morphemes for transitive verbs in Mandan. (For the purpose of this exercise please ignore -oʔʃ.)

7. **Inflection for Tense**

a. Using the following data (Table 5.14), determine which morphemes mark tense, and provide a gloss for each one.

TABLE 5.14 Mandan data on inflection for tense

mą-kiną-oʔʃ	'he/she tells me'	mą-kiną-kt-oʔʃ	'he/she will tell me'
nį-he-oʔʃ	'he/she sees you'	nį-he-kt-oʔʃ	'he/she will see you'
nǫ:-he-oʔʃ	'he/she sees us'	nǫ:-he-kt-oʔʃ	'he/she will see us'
wa-nį-he-oʔʃ	'he/she sees you'	wa-nį-he-kt-oʔʃ	'I will see you'
kiną-oʔʃ	'he/she tells him/her'	kiną-s-oʔʃ	'he/she told him/her'
nų-nį-kiną-oʔʃ	'we tell you'	nų-nį-kiną-s-oʔʃ	'we told you'
wa-nį-pe-oʔʃ	'I speak to you'	wa-nį-pe-s-oʔʃ	'I spoke to you'

b. Now add tense to the order of morphemes in the Mandan transitive verb. (You will not be able to include 'plural'.)

8. **Inflection for Negation-A**

In the data in Table 5.15, determine what two units mark negation. These two units together, though physically separate, constitute one morpheme. What type of morpheme is this?

TABLE 5.15 Mandan data on inflection for Negation-A

wa:-mą-kiną-nįx-kt-oʔʃ	'he/she will not tell me'
mą-kiną-kt-oʔʃ	'he/she will tell me'
wa:-nį-he-nįx-kt-oʔʃ	'he/she will not see you'
nį-he-kt-oʔʃ	'he/she will see you'
wa:-nǫ:-he-nįx-kt-oʔʃ	'he/she will not see us'
nǫ:-he-kt-oʔʃ	'he/she will see us'
wa:-kiną-nįx-s-oʔʃ	'he/she didn't tell him/her'
wa:-nų-nį-kiną-nįx-s-oʔʃ	'we didn't tell you'
wa:-wa-nį-pe-nįx-s-oʔʃ	'I didn't speak to you'
wa:-nǫ:-ra-he-nįx-s-oʔʃ	'you didn't see us'
wa:-wa-nį-he-nįx-kt-oʔʃ	'I will not see you'

9. **Inflection for Negative-B**

Determine the marking of negation in the data in Table 5.16 as opposed to those in question (8) above. What type of morpheme is this? Can you predict its occurrence as opposed to the one in (8)?

TABLE 5.16 Mandan data for inflection for Negation-B

wa:-mą:-kiną-xi-oʔʃ	'he/she doesn't tell me'
mą:-kiną-oʔʃ	'he/she tells me'
wa:-nį-he-xi-oʔʃ	'he/she doesn't see you'
nį-he-oʔʃ	'he/she sees you'
wa:-nǫ:-he-xi-oʔʃ	'he/she doesn't see us'
nǫ:-he-oʔʃ	'he/she doesn't see us'
wa:-kiną-xi-oʔʃ	'he/she doesn't tell him/her'
kiną-oʔʃ	'he/she tells him/her'
wa:-nų-nį:-kiną-xi-oʔʃ	'we don't tell you'
nų-nį:-kiną-oʔʃ	'we don't tell you'
wa:-wa-nį-pe-xi-oʔʃ	'I don't speak to you'
wa-nį-pe-oʔʃ	'I speak to you'
wa:-wa-nį-he-xi-oʔʃ	'I don't see you'
wa-nį-he-oʔʃ	'I see you'

10. Mystery Suffixes

Examine the following affirmative and negative imperative sentences (i.e., positive and negative commands), paying special attention to the final *mystery suffixes* (Table 5.17). Unlike the usual agglutinating pattern of Mandan, each of these verb-final morphemes bears more than one element of meaning simultaneously. (We call such elements portmanteau morphemes.)

IMPERATIVE

Imperative refers to an order or command.

PORTMANTEAU MORPHEME

A *portmanteau morpheme* bears more than one meaning. For example, the {-s} verbal morpheme in English has three meanings simultaneously: 'present tense', 'third person', and 'singular'.

The English free translations contain the words *(wo)man, (wo)men, boy(s), girl(s)* to indicate the type of person being addressed in the Mandan verb. Keep in mind that the English gloss is just an approximation of the Mandan meaning and that these English nouns, in and of themselves, do not capture the full meaning of the Mandan final morphemes. To determine the full meaning of the Mandan final morphemes you will need to consider the entire Mandan verb and the entire English sentence.

a. Based on these data, explain how positive imperatives are made in Mandan, making sure to take into account the full meaning of the Mandan final morphemes.
b. Then explain how negative imperatives are made in this language.

TABLE 5.17 Mandan mystery suffixes data

pa:ʔx-ta 'Set it upright, man/boy!'	ka:re pa:ʔx-ta 'Don't set it upright, man/boy!'
pa:ʔx-ną 'Set it upright, woman/girl!'	ka:re pa:ʔx-ną 'Don't set it upright, woman/girl!'
ʃiʔ-nįt-ną 'Be good, women/girls!'	ka:re ʃiʔ-nįt-ną 'Don't be good, women/girls!'
ʃiʔ-nįt-ta 'Be good, men/boys!'	ka:re ʃiʔ-nįt-ta 'Don't be good, men/boys!'
si:-ną 'Be yellow, woman/girl!'	ka:re nǫ:-he-ta 'Don't look at us, man/boy!'
skųh-ta 'Be sweet, man/boy!'	

More Mystery Suffixes

Mandan does not have a separate word that literally means 'please', as English does. Nevertheless, Mandan does have a process to soften commands (positive and negative imperatives, as you saw in (10a and b)) to be the equivalent of a polite request in English.

c. Examine the data in Table 5.18 and then explain how Mandan softens commands.

TABLE 5.18 More Mandan mystery suffixes data

mą-kiną-ną-hak	'Please, tell me, woman/girl!'
mą-kiną-ta-hak	'Please, tell me, man/boy!'
ka:re ʃiʔ-nįt-ną-hak	'Please, don't be good, women/girls!'
ka:re ʃiʔ-nįt-ta-hak	'Please, don't be good, men/boys!'
ka:re pa:ʔx-ta-hak	'Please, don't set it upright, man/boy!'
ka:re pa:ʔx-ną-hak	'Please, don't set it upright, woman/girl!'
ka:re nǫ-he-ta-hak	'Please don't look at us, man/boy!'
kiną-ną-hak	'Please tell him/her, woman/girl!'
skųh-ną-hak	'Please be sweet, woman/girl!'

References

Campbell, Lyle. 1997. *American Indian languages: The historical linguistics of Native America.* Oxford Studies in Anthropological Linguistics. New York: Oxford University Press.

Carter, Richard T. 1991a. Maximilan's Ruptare vocabulary: Philological evidence and Mandan phonology. In Frances Ingemann, ed., *1990 Mid-America Regional Linguistics Conference Papers*, 479–489. Lawrence: Department of Linguistics of the University of Kansas.

Carter, Richard T. 1991b. Old Man Coyote and the wild potato: A trickster tale. In H. Christoph Wolfart, ed., *Linguistic studies presented to John L Finlay*, 27-43. Winnipeg: University of Manitoba.

Catlin, George. 1841. *Letters and notes on the manners, customs and conditions of the American Indians.* 2 vols. London: Published by the author at the Egyptian Hall, Piccadilly.

Chafe, Wallace L. 1976. The Siouan, Iroquoian, and Caddoan languages. In Thomas A. Sebeok, ed., *Native languages of the Americas*, vol. 1, 527–572. New York: Plenum.

Hollow, Robert 1970. Mandan dictionary. PhD diss., University of California, Berkeley.

Kennard, Edward. 1936. Mandan grammar. *International Journal of American Linguistics* 9: 1–43.

Mixco, Mauricio J. 1997a. Mandan switch-reference: A preliminary view. *Anthropological Linguistics* 39.2: 220–298.

Mixco, Mauricio J. 1997b. The morphosyntax of the Mandan simultaneous aspectual suffix. Paper presented at the Seventeenth Annual Siouan-Caddoan Languages Conference, May 16–17, 1997, Wayne State College, Wayne, Nebraska.

Parks, Douglas R. 1991. *Traditional narratives of the Arikara Indians.* Vol. 3, *Stories of Alfred Morsette.* Trans. Douglas R. Parks. Lincoln: University of Nebraska Press.

Wied Neu-Wied, Alexander Phillip Maximilian, Prinz zu. 1839–41. *Reise in das innere Nord-Amerikas in den Jahren 1832–1834.* 2 vols. and atlas. Coblenz: J. Hoelscher.

Will, George F., and H.J. Spinden. 1906. *The Mandans.* Peabody Museum Publications. 3:81–210. Cambridge, MA: Harvard University.

PART III

English and Other U.S. Language Varieties

6

VERNACULAR DIALECTS OF ENGLISH

Walt Wolfram

The General Scope of Vernacular Dialects

The following exercises focus on vernacular (nonstandard) dialects of English on several levels. (See the introductory chapters and the chapter on African American English for definitions of the terms *dialect* and *vernacular*.) First, they involve exercises that rely on "language intuitions." By **language intuitions**, I mean the inner knowledge about language that comes from the fact that speakers of a language have internalized language patterns and therefore can make choices based on that knowledge. This knowledge stands apart from the ability to talk about language in technical terms. Everyone who speaks a language has language intuitions, whereas only linguistically trained professionals typically would have the knowledge to discuss these patterns in technical detail. Second, the exercises examine how judgments of linguistic well-formedness, or "grammaticality," intersect with judgments of social acceptability. For many laypeople, linguistic grammaticality and social acceptability are not distinguished, but it is essential that this distinction be recognized in studying language, particularly in the study of language varieties that have been socially stigmatized.

GRAMMATICALITY

Grammaticality refers to the conformity of a sentence or structure to the rules of the specific patterns of a language variety. For example, a sentence like *The blue box is in the closet* follows the rules for forming a sentence in English, whereas *The box blue is in the closet* is ungrammatical since it does not follow these general rules. This notion applies regardless of the social evaluation of a structure.

Third, patterns are considered based on data sets that have been set up to illustrate the systematic distribution of forms in vernacular dialect grammar. The features included in these exercises range from those that are common to practically all the vernacular language varieties of American English—spoken by the majority of the population—to those figuring in the vernaculars of just a few hundred speakers. Both regional and sociocultural varieties in various combinations are included. For each exercise, the relevant vernacular dialect is given in the introduction to the exercise.

Language Intuitions, Grammaticality, and Social Acceptability

Several exercises follow that illustrate how inner knowledge and judgments about the well-formedness of constructions, or intuitions, can be used in analyzing patterns in a vernacular dialect. *Well-formedness* means that a sentence is grammatical in a specific dialect. By *grammatical* I mean obeying the rules of grammar of a particular language variety that the speaker knows unconsciously. (This knowledge allows the speaker to speak a dialect as a native speaker, that is, following its own grammatical rules.) A sentence that is grammatical in one dialect may not be grammatical in another. One of the exercises also shows how grammaticality is often confused with social acceptability and standardness in making judgments about sentences. *Social acceptability* means that those who hear and use a sentence in a social situation consider it appropriate, not out of place, following the rules of expected social behavior. I can illustrate the difference between social acceptability and grammaticality with the following sentence: *She ain't here.* This sentence is grammatical in many (vernacular) dialects of English: it follows their rules of grammar. However, in some social situations, it would be considered socially unacceptable, for example, if a U.S. president said it during a nationally televised speech in referring to his secretary of state, who at the time was out of town. U.S. presidents in nationally televised speeches are expected to use Standard English. *Ain't* qualifies this example sentence as vernacular, or nonstandard. No doubt, when out hunting with buddies or in other very informal situations, many U.S. presidents (e.g., Lyndon Johnson, Jimmy Carter, Bill Clinton, George W. Bush, and Barack Obama) have used *ain't* because in that social situation, it was perfectly expected and socially acceptable—and grammatical in the dialect spoken.

Sometimes a person may call a sentence ungrammatical when actually it is just socially unacceptable—in some social settings. To illustrate this point, sentences with curse words may be perfectly grammatical but socially unacceptable in some social settings (in church, to cite one case). Another kind of example relates to sentences from dialects associated with socially subordinate groups. Unfortunately, this confusion is one of the by-products of the application of the **Principle of Linguistic Subordination** by nonspecialists (nonlinguists), who typically consider the varieties of socially subordinate groups to be ungrammatical, linguistically unworthy, and unsystematic approximations of the varieties spoken by socially dominant groups (Lippi-Green 2012). Linguists, on the other hand, make a very careful distinction between grammaticality, which characterizes the structure of any language variety, whether the group that speaks it is socially subordinate or dominant, and social acceptability, which is a function of a particular speech community's social evaluation of a linguistic form.

An Exercise in Grammatical Patterning: A-prefixing (Adapted from Wolfram and Schilling-Estes 2006)

In rural dialects of the U.S., some words that end in *-ing* may take an *a-* prefix (usually pronounced with the schwa [ə]) attached to the beginning of the form. Although this pattern is receding somewhat, it is still quite robust among older speakers in many rural Southern communities and is one of the features often associated with **Appalachian Vernacular English.**

APPALACHIAN VERNACULAR ENGLISH

Appalachian Vernacular English is a variety of English typically used by working-class speakers who reside in the Southern Highland region of the U.S., including West Virginia, southeastern Virginia, eastern Tennessee, and western North Carolina.

The language pattern or "rule" for this form allows the *a-* to attach to some words but not to others. In this exercise, you will figure out this pattern by looking at the kinds of *-ing* words *a-* can and cannot attach to. You will do this using your inner feelings, or "gut reactions," about language. These language intuitions tell us where we *can* and *cannot* use certain structures. The task of language scientists is to figure out the structural linguistic reason for these inner feelings and to state the exact patterns that characterize the usage. One of the interesting aspects of the *a-* prefix pattern is that most native speakers of English seem to have fairly strong intuitions about this form, whether or not they use it as a part of their everyday speech (Wolfram 1982). So don't hesitate to rely on your intuitions even if you don't use this form on a regular basis.

I. Look at the sentence pairs in List A in Table 6.1 and decide which sentence in each pair "sounds better" with the *a-* prefix. For example, in the first sentence pair, does it sound better to say *A-building is hard work* or *He was a-building a house*? For each sentence pair, select the sentence that sounds better with the *a-* for yourself and then for at least one other native English speaker (and preferably more than one). Put an "x" on the appropriate line, (a) or (b), for the better-sounding sentence.

TABLE 6.1 List A: Sentence pairs for *a-* prefixing

		Your intuitions	Another speaker's intuitions	
(1)	a.	_____	_____	A-building is hard work.
	b.	_____	_____	She was a-building a house.
(2)	a.	_____	_____	He likes a-hunting.
	b.	_____	_____	He went a-hunting.
(3)	a.	_____	_____	The child was a-charming the adults.
	b.	_____	_____	The child was very a-charming.
(4)	a.	_____	_____	He kept a-shocking the children.
	b.	_____	_____	The story was a-shocking.
(5)	a.	_____	_____	They thought a-fishing was easy.
	b.	_____	_____	They were a-fishing this morning.

Answer the following questions.

1. Based on your and the other speaker's intuitions, do you think that there is some pattern that guided your choice of an answer? You can tell if there is a definite pattern by checking with other people who did the same exercise on their own. In your response, say how many other people you checked with and describe the results of comparing your intuitions for these sentences: how often do you agree?

2. Do you think that the pattern might be related to grammatical categories or "parts of speech"? To answer this, see if there are any grammatical categories where you *cannot* use the *a-* prefix. (Hint: Look at the intuitions for the *-ing* forms in the data that function as verb participles [in progressives] and compare those with the intuitions for the *-ing* forms in the data that operate as nouns [i.e., gerunds] or adjectives.)

II. You have just completed the first step in figuring out the pattern for the *a-* prefix, the part of speech of the *-ing* word. Now let's look at another factor that determines the use of the *a-* prefix. Based on the sentence pairs in List B, determine whether or not the *a-* form can be used after a preposition. Use the same technique you used for List A. Begin by selecting the sentence that "sounds better" for each sentence pair. (You must use your own intuitions for this exercise, but you may also make use of the intuitions of another native speaker of English.) Put an "x" in front of the sentence that sounds better.

List B: A Further detail for *a-* patterning

(6)	a.	_____ They make money by a-building houses.
	b.	_____ They make money a-building houses.
(7)	a.	_____ People can't make enough money a-fishing.
	b.	_____ People can't make enough money from a-fishing.
(8)	a.	_____ People destroy the beauty of the mountains through a-littering.
	b.	_____ People destroy the beauty of the mountains a-littering.

(3) Is *a*-prefixing preferable with or without a preceding preposition?

(4) Why do you think that this is the case in terms of English language structure? (Hint: Think about what sort of grammatical category the *a*- word
must belong to—a noun [gerund], as in *Swimming is fun*, or a verb [progres-
sive], as in *He was swimming*).

III. You have now added another detail for figuring out the pattern for *a*- prefix,
the behavior of *a*- in regard to prepositions. But there is still another part
to the pattern of *a*- prefix use. This time, however, it is related to pronunciation. For the following *-ing* words, try to figure out what it is about the
pronunciation that makes one sentence sound better than the other. For this
exercise, the stressed syllable of each word is marked with the symbol ´. Follow the same procedure as before. Begin by putting an "x" in front of the
sentence that "sounds better" with *a*- for each sentence pair. (Again, you may
choose to supplement your intuitions with those of another native speaker of
English.)

List C: Figuring out a pronunciation pattern for the *a*- prefix

(9) a. _____ She was a-discóvering a trail.
     b. _____ She was a-fóllowing a trail.
(10) a. _____ She was a-repéating the chant.
     b. _____ She was a-hóllering the chant.
(11) a. _____ They were a-fíguring the change.
     b. _____ They were a-forgétting the change.
(12) a. _____ The baby was a-recognízing the mother.
     b. _____ The baby was a-wrécking everything.
(13) a. _____ They were a-décorating the room.
     b. _____ They were a-demánding more time off.

5. Make a general statement about the stressing of *-ing* words that makes one
sentence sound better than the other.

6. Now summarize what you have discovered about *a*-prefixing by stating precisely how the pattern for attaching the *a*- prefix works. Be sure to include
the three different details from your examination of the examples in **Lists
A**, **B**, and **C**.

IV. In **List D**, select which of the sentences are grammatical with the *a*- prefix
by circling the *-ing* form. Then, using the statement of the pattern you gave
in (III), explain why the ungrammatical sentences are ungrammatical.

List D: Applying the *a*- prefix rule

(14) She kept hánding me more work.
(15) The team was remémbering the game.
(16) The team won by pláying great defense.

(17) The team was pláying real hard.
(18) The coach was chárming all of the fans.

Native Speaker Intuitions and African American Vernacular English

Now we're going to look at a form that's used in African American Vernacular English (AAVE), particularly as it is used by young speakers in metropolitan areas. (See the chapter on African American English for the distinction between AAVE and African American Standard English.) The form *be* is used where other dialects might use *am*, *is*, or *are*, except that it has a special meaning. Native speakers of this dialect can tell intuitively where it may be used and where it may not be, just as you could for the *a-* prefix.

I.   **Your intuitions:** Try out your intuitions (whether you're an AAVE speaker or not). In the sentences given here, choose one of the sentences in each pair where *be* seems to fit better by putting an "x" in front of it. Choose only one sentence for each pair. If you're not sure of the answer, simply make your best guess.

(19) a. _____ Sometimes his ears be itching.
     b. _____ His ears be itching right now.
(20) a. _____ Every time I go there he be busy.
     b. _____ I think he be busy today.
(21) a. _____ John be late for school today.
     b. _____ Sometimes John be late for school
(22) a. _____ He be my partner when we play tennis.
     b. _____ The woman in the pictures be my mother.
(23) a. _____ He be sleeping at the moment.
     b. _____ Usually he be sleeping in the afternoon.

7.   Did you feel confident in making your sentence choice based simply on intuitions? Why or why not?

II. **Comparing intuitions for different speaker groups:** Now compare the responses of two groups of speakers to these sentences. One is a group of 38 young African Americans from the city of Baltimore, Maryland, who are mostly native speakers of AAVE; the other is a group of 76 European American adults from the surrounding suburban area who are, for the most part, not familiar with this variety (Wolfram 1982). For each pair the sentence that is grammatical in AAVE is italicized and the percentage of speakers in each group who selected the sentence correctly is given for the respective groups.

You will notice that there is a significant difference in the responses. Responding to the questions in Table 6.2 will help you understand the results of this survey.

TABLE 6.2 Comparing intuitions for different speaker groups

African American (AAVE Speakers) responses, % correct (N = 38)	European American responses, % correct (N = 76)	Sentence pairs
92%	38%	(24) _____ a. *Sometimes his ears be itching.* _____ b. His ears be itching right now.
79%	41%	(25) _____ a. *Everytime I go there he busy.* _____ b. I think he be busy today.
82%	53%	(26) _____ a. John be late for school today. _____ b. *Sometimes John be late for school.*
79%	55%	(27) _____ a. *He be my partner when we play tennis.* _____ b. The woman in the picture be my mother.
87%	36%	(28) _____ a. He be sleeping at the moment. _____ b. *Usually he be sleeping in the afternoon.*

8. Describe how your intuitions differed from the actual correct sentences. Is there a linguistic pattern to your intuitions?
9. Which group of speakers in the survey had more accurate (and, therefore, more systematic) intuitions about the patterning of the form?
10. What does this indicate about dialect knowledge of this AAVE form by speakers of AAVE and speakers of other varieties of English?
11. Which sentence in each pair has a habitual meaning of some type? (The *habitual* aspect [in AAVE] expresses that an event or activity takes place intermittently over time or place, such as a repeated or customary action. For more on the habitual and other types of *aspect*, see the Jamaican Creole chapter.)
12. How is this habitual meaning related to the correct sentences in each pair?
13. a. What kind of knowledge do speakers need to have in order to select the appropriate grammatical option?
    b. Do they need to be able to describe consciously what "habitual *be*" refers to in order to make the right choice?
    c. What does this indicate about the nature of linguistic intuitions?

III. Following the patterns for *be* use: Now that you know how the form *be* is used, predict which of the sentences below follow the rule for *be* use in AAVE dialect and which do *not*. Write (**Y**)es if the sentence follows the pattern of this dialect, rather than standard dialects, and (**N**)o if it does not, and give a linguistic reason for each answer based on what you have learned about *be*.

(29) _____ The students always be talking about linguistics in class.
(30) _____ The students don't be talking right now.
(31) _____ Sometimes the teacher be early for class.
(32) _____ The teacher be making a fool of herself at the moment.
(33) _____ Linguists always be asking silly questions about language.

14. Taking into account what you have learned about *a*-prefixing and AAVE *be*, how does this exercise counter the popular notion that vernacular dialects are little more than violations of basic grammar rules?

Sorting Out Grammaticality and Social Acceptability

The notions of grammaticality and social acceptability are quite different things, as pointed out earlier in this chapter. Grammaticality always relates to particular dialects (or languages). Remember that there are, of course, situations in which it is the standard sentence, grammatical in Standard English, that is not socially acceptable in a particular social situation. Consider this perfectly grammatical standard sentence, which is *not* socially acceptable on a neighborhood basketball court: "Would you be so gracious as to shoot the basketball?"

Several logical combinations of social acceptability and grammaticality judgments exist, as follows:

1. *Grammatical* (in Standard English) and *socially acceptable* (Standard English is acceptable in a classroom setting, for example).
   e.g., *I'm not going to like this class.*
2. *Grammatical* (in Vernacular English) and *socially unacceptable* (Vernacular English is not acceptable in a classroom setting).
   e.g., *I ain't gonna like this here class.*
3. *Ungrammatical* (in any variety of English—see below) and *socially acceptable* (said, for example, by a nonnative speaker, who is excused for the grammatical error).
   e.g., *This allows to get more mileage.* Cf. *This allows you/one to get more mileage.* The sentence is not grammatical in any variety of English because the logical subject of the infinitive *to get* must be expressed immediately following the main verb *allows.*
4. *Ungrammatical* (in Appalachian [Vernacular] English) and **socially unacceptable** (Appalachian English is not acceptable in a classroom setting).
   e.g., *The a-charming person likes this class.*
   (The sentence is ungrammatical because the *a-* prefix cannot attach to an adjective.)
5. *Grammatical* (in a vernacular, here AAVE) and **socially acceptable**.
   e.g., *Every time I go to they house, they be greasing down!* ('Every time I go to their house, they are really eating great food with gusto!' Said at a home social gathering of AAVE speakers).

I. Judge the sentences in Table 6.3 in terms of *social acceptability and grammaticality*. The dialect you are to consider in determining grammaticality is indicated for each sentence in parentheses. Under the "Socially Acceptable" column, a social context is given. Use your judgment and indicate

TABLE 6.3 Grammaticality and social acceptability exercise

	Grammatical?	Socially acceptable?
(34) The instructor handed out the exercise. (SE)	_____	College classroom _____
(35) Prof. Jones be a good instructor. (SE)	_____	Faculty meeting _____
(36) She's a-cooking. (Ap. Eng.)	_____	A group of Ap. Eng. speakers sitting in a home _____
(37) The students kept a-doing the exercise (Ap. Eng.)	_____	College president addressing faculty _____
(38) She always be dribbling up the lef side of the court, don't she? (AAVE)	_____	One spouse to another at a basketball game (both AAE speakers) _____
(39) She be doing her homework right now, been't she? (AAVE)	_____	An African American high school teacher speaking to an African American parent _____
(40) They go to school by a-taking a bus. (Ap. Eng.)	_____	A native of Appalachia, home for a visit after living in California for 20 years _____
(41) The dog in the picture be my dog. (AAVE)	_____	A white high school teacher to an African American student, attempting to show that he likes African American students _____

AAVE, African American Vernacular English; Ap. Eng., Appalachian English; SE, Standard English.

what you think. (The Answer Key provides the author's judgment regarding acceptability.)

15. What might be an explanation for not considering sentence (41) as socially acceptable?
16. What do these sentences say about social acceptability?

Data Sets Using Vernacular Dialects

Linguists studying vernacular dialects use the same kinds of techniques that they would use analyzing any other language system. That is, they look at lots of cases of a given form in natural language use and try to figure out distributional patterns governing language forms in morphology, syntax, and phonology. This is often a long process, in which the linguist notices a form as it is used (or not used) in different linguistic contexts, formulates a hypothesis about its patterning, and then examines as much data as possible in order to confirm or disconfirm the hypothesis. Of course, initial hypotheses often go through a number of revisions before precise statements about patterns are worked out. For the sake of organizational simplicity, this process is often compressed as the data are organized and packaged for convenient student use. However, it is important to appreciate how painstakingly detailed and time-consuming such analysis really is. Hundreds of hours of listening to recorded conversations are typically involved just to collect enough examples of one form in order to conduct a reliable analysis.

Sometimes this process can be circumvented by directly eliciting language intuitions about the grammaticality of particular constructions, as we did in the exercise on habitual *be*, but this process is a bit tricky when applied to vernacular dialects because speakers often get linguistic grammaticality confused with standardness. In other words, they may respond that something that is perfectly grammatical in their vernacular is *not* grammatical simply because they know it does not follow the grammatical rules of the standard dialect. In the final analysis, there is no substitute for listening to hours and hours of conversation in order to determine the linguistic patterning of forms.

In the following we consider a few sample data sets for different forms based on representative vernacular dialects. They are compiled in this format simply for instructive purposes.

Nouns, Quantifiers, and Morphological Patterning

QUANTIFIER

A **quantifier** is a word that indicates a quantity of some type. For example, *ten*, *lots of*, and *some* are quantifiers in sentences such as *She has ten/lots of/ some acres of land.*

Throughout a large area of the rural South, especially in southern Appalachia, there is a set of words that may be used in a plural context without attaching the plural suffix -*s* under some linguistic conditions. Some examples are given in List A, which shows that these sentences are grammatical in this dialect with or without the plural -*s* suffix.

List A: Nouns without plural -s

(42) a. We caught *two hundred pound_* of flounder.
      b. We caught *two hundred pounds* of flounder.
(43) a. How *many bushel_* does he have?
      b. How *many bushels* does he have?
(44) a. There are *two pint_* sitting in the backyard.
      b. There are *two pints* sitting in the backyard.
(45) a. There are *lots of gallon_* of water.
      b. There are *lots of gallons* of water.
(46) a. They have *three acre_* for building.
      b. They have *three acres* for building.

In List B the sentences are grammatical in this dialect only if the nouns have the plural *-s* suffix.

List B: Nouns with plural *-s*

(47) a. We caught *two hundred cats*.
      b. *We caught *two hundred cat_*.
(48) a. How *many dogs* does he have?
      b. *How *many dog_* does he have?
(49) a. They have *lots of ponies* down below.
      b. *They have *lots of pony* down below.
(50) a. They have *three sisters*.
      b. *They have *three sister_*.
(51) a. It's about *six teachers*.
      b. *It's about *six teacher_*.

17. What is the difference in the type of nouns in List A and List B that might explain why some nouns *must* have the *-s* and why others do not need to attach it?
18. In List C the nouns of List A are given again. As they are used in List C, however, the *-s* plural is required. Compare the syntax of the sentences in List A to those of List C, and explain when the *-s* must be attached to the noun.

List C: When the plural suffix *-s* needs to be attached

(52) a. We had *pounds* of flounder that spoiled.
      b. *We had *pound_* of flounder that spoiled.
(53) a. Sometimes people use *bushels* instead of *pounds*.
      b. *Sometimes people use *bushel_* instead of *pound_*.
(54) a. The *pints* of ice cream are in the freezer.
      b. *The *pint_* of ice cream are in the freezer.
(55) a. We had *gallons* of water in the skiff.
      b. *We had *gallon_* of water in the skiff.
(56) a. The best *acres* are owned by the government.
      b. *The best *acre_* are owned by the government.

19. Based on your analysis as stated in your response to (53) and (54) together, determine whether each sentence in List D is grammatical or not in Southern Appalachian English without the plural *-s* suffix. Then, indicate whether each sentence is 'grammatical' or 'ungrammatical' AND give the reason for your answer.

List D: Predicting plural *-s* absence

(57) She had three pound__ of fish left.
(58) She had pound__ of fish left.

(59) Old Mrs. Mayes has ten dog__.
(60) It's forty inch__ to the top.
(61) It's inch__ to the top.
(62) It's lots of inch_ to the top.

Restructuring Past Tense **Be**

In many dialects of English, the conjugated forms of the verb *be* are quite irregular for both the present and past tense. *Be* is the only English verb that changes its form in the past tense according to the person and number of the subject. For the most part (and historically), *was* is used with singular forms (e.g., *I was, she was,* etc.), whereas *were* is used with plural forms (e.g., *we were, they were,* etc.), so that we might say that *was* marks singular and *were* marks plural.

By analogy with other verbs of English, speakers of most vernacular dialects use only one form for the past tense of *be*. Thus, in many vernacular dialects, speakers *regularize* the past tense of *be* as shown in Table 6.4.

I. **An alternative regularization:** A different kind of regularization exists in some coastal dialects along the Mid-Atlantic coast of the U.S., particularly on the Outer Banks of North Carolina and the islands of the Chesapeake Bay (Tangier Island and Smith Island). In the U.S., this pattern is restricted to these coastal dialects, although it is also found among some dialects in the British Isles. This regularization pattern occurs with *were* along with *was*. To see how *were* regularization works in these varieties, look at the conjugation of *were* and *was* in the following sets of sentences.

In Table 6.5, the List A sentences may regularize to *was*, but in the List B sentences, the *were* regularization pattern is used.

TABLE 6.4 Restructured past tense *be*

Singular	*Plural*
Affirmative	
I *was*	We *was*
You *was*	You/y'all/youse/you'uns *was*
He/she/it *was*	They *was*
Negative	
I *wasn't*	We *wasn't*
You *wasn't*	You/y'all/youse/you'uns *wasn't*
He/she/it *wasn't*	They *wasn't*

Note: The forms *y'all* (Southern), *you'uns* (Smoky Mountains and Pittsburgh), and *youse* (Northern) are all vernacular dialect variants for the second person plural form *you* so that distinct singular and plural forms are preserved throughout the paradigm.

TABLE 6.5 An alternative regularization of past tense *be*

List A	
I *was* here	We *was* here
You *was* here	Y'all *was* here
He/she/it *was* here	They *was* here

List B	
I *weren't* here	We *weren't* here
You *weren't* here	Y'all *weren't* here
He/she/it *weren't* here	They *weren't* here

20. Based on the data in List A and List B immediately above, explain the alternative regularization patterns for past tense *be* in these sentences.
21. How does it differ from the Standard English use of *was* and *were*?

II. **Applying the regularization rule:** Use the Mid-Atlantic coastal dialect pattern that you discovered in (20) to change each of the sentences given below to its opposite form; that is, change affirmative sentences to negative ones, and negative sentences to affirmative ones.

(63) Marilyn *weren't* in school yesterday.
(64) The student *was* writing the answer.
(65) We *weren't* there yesterday.
(66) *Was* he there yesterday?
(67) I *was* there yesterday, *weren't* I?

Analyzing Phonological Data

The following are several examples of dialect patterning from phonology. Again, they are arranged in data sets that are convenient for analysis rather than demonstrating the elaborate analytical procedures of extraction, organization, and creation of exploratory hypotheses that lead up to this stage. They represent both regional and social varieties of English, or a combination of these, as is often the case in vernacular varieties. They also represent different levels of complexity in the analysis.

The Pin-Pen *Merger*

In some Southern dialects, as well as other dialects of English now, words like *pin* and *pen* are pronounced the same, usually as [pʰɪn], rather than [pʰɪn] and [pʰɛn] respectively, as in other varieties of English. This pattern of pronunciation is also found in other words. List A has words where the sounds spelled *i* and *e* are pronounced the *same* in these dialects. In other words, in these dialects, the words in each pair are homophones.

List A: *i* and *e* pronounced the *same*

(68) *tin* and *ten*
(69) *kin* and *Ken*
(70) *Lin* and *Len*
(71) *windy* and *Wendy*
(72) *sinned* and *send*

Although *i* and *e* in List A are pronounced the *same*, there are other words in these dialects where the sounds spelled *i* and *e* are pronounced differently. List B has word pairs where the vowels are pronounced *differently*. That is, in this list the words are not homophones but minimal pairs.

List B: *i* and *e* pronounced differently

(73) *lit* and *let*
(74) *pick* and *peck*
(75) *pig* and *peg*
(76) *rip* and *rep*
(77) *litter* and *letter*

22. Based on these examples, state the phonological environment that accounts for this partial merger of [ɪ] and [ɛ].
23. Based on your analysis, predict whether each pair of words in List C would be pronounced the same or differently in these dialects.

List C: Same or different?

(78) *bit* and *bet*   _____
(79) *pit* and *pet*   _____
(80) *bin* and *Ben*   _____
(81) *Nick* and *neck*   _____
(82) *din* and *den*   _____

24. What is the basis for your prediction?
25. Some dialects also pronounce the words *rim* and *rem* the same but not *rip* and *rep*.

   a. Revise the statement you made in (22) to include this pattern.
   b. Create lists for this pattern that are similar to List A and List B. Each list should have at least three pairs of items in it.

Devoicing in Vernacular Dialects (Adapted from Wolfram and Johnson 1982: 94)

A number of vernacular dialects of English have a devoicing process in which /d/ is devoiced so that it sounds like /t/. Phonetically, the /d/ may be produced

TABLE 6.6 Devoicing in vernacular dialects

[sǽlət]	salad	[bǽts]	bats
[sǽlədz]	salads	[rǽbət]	rabbit
[bɛ́d]	bed	[rǽbəts]	rabbits
[bɛ́dz]	beds	[bǽd]	bad
[stúpət]	stupid	[bǽdnəs]	badness
[stúpədnɪs]	stupidness	[rǽpət]	rapid
[bǽt]	bat	[rǽpədz]	rapids
[ʃrɛ́rəd]	shredded	[bǽrəd]	batted

as a glottal stop [ʔ] or an unreleased *t* [t'], but we transcribe it simply as [t] for convenience here.

26. Based on the data in Table 6.6, state the conditions under which /d/ can be devoiced.

Consonant Cluster Simplification (Adapted from Wolfram and Johnson 1982: 139)

In some vernacular varieties of AAE, certain syllable-final (syllable-coda) consonant clusters are reduced or simplified by deleting the final consonant of the cluster. (Note that the term *simplified* here refers to a linguistic process and does not imply a value judgment.) However, not all final consonant clusters can be simplified. The susceptibility of final clusters to reduction is governed by the phonetic structure of the cluster itself. Based on the data below, determine the phonetic conditions under which a cluster may be reduced by answering the following questions.

27. For each word in Table 6.7, fill out the appropriate column with either the final consonant that was deleted or the final consonant that was retained.
28. Excluding from consideration examples (9), (13), and (21) in the "Deleted" and "Retained" columns in Table 6.7, when can the final members of a consonant cluster be deleted? (Hint: Think about phonological environments and natural classes.)
29. What is the difference between the retained consonants in (9), (13), and (21) and the other retained consonants? (Hint: Think again about natural classes.)
30. Summarize what you now know about consonant cluster simplification based on your responses to (28) and (29).
31. Now consider the given pronunciation of (15), *golf.* Using the summary you wrote for (30), explain its pronunciation in this data set.

Conclusion

As we have seen in the preceding exercises, linguistic patterning is no respecter of social status. In fact, the most convincing argument for the linguistic integrity of all language varieties comes from the kind of systematic patterning demonstrated

TABLE 6.7 Consonant cluster simplification

		C deleted	C retained				C deleted	C retained
1. [tɛs]	test	___	___	15. [galf]	golf		___	___
2. [was]	wasp	___	___	16. [gʌlp]	gulp		___	___
3. [dɛs]	desk	___	___	17. [kræŋk]	crank		___	___
4. [lɛf]	left	___	___	18. [koʊl]	cold		___	___
5. [fan]	find	___	___	19. [mæs]	mask		___	___
6. [wal]	wild	___	___	20. [græs]	grasp		___	___
7. [æk]	act	___	___	21. [baks]	box		___	___
8. [læmp]	lamp	___	___	22. [man]	mind		___	___
9. [rægz]	rags	___	___	23. [æp]	apt		___	___
10. [bɛlt]	belt	___	___	24. [seɪv]	saved		___	___
11. [finəʃ]	finished	___	___	25. [beɪð]	bathed		___	___
12. [reɪz]	raised	___	___	26. [fiks]	fixed		___	___
13. [sɪks]	six	___	___	27. [smɛl]	smelled	___	___
14. [gɪf]	gift	___	___	28. [pɛlt]	pelt		___	___

in the types of exercises examined in this chapter. Fundamental principles of linguistic organization can be illustrated as effectively using vernacular dialects as they can using examples of socially favored varieties of a language. Furthermore, the examination of linguistic patterning in vernacular dialects counters one of the great popular myths about language variation: that vernacular dialects are little more than unsystematic deviations from the patterns of standard varieties. As we have seen, nothing could be further from the truth; in fact, sociolinguists and social dialectologists who study vernacular dialects spend their careers describing the kind of systematic patterning revealed in these examples.

These exercises should also illustrate the ways in which legitimate linguistic differences have been misinterpreted and misappropriated on the basis of social privilege and sociopolitical dominance. Learning about the intricate nature of linguistic patterns as applied to vernacular dialects is one of the most effective ways of countering linguistic inequality—one of the most persistent and debilitating forms of social exclusion and discrimination.

References

Lippi-Green, Rosina. 2012. *English with an accent: Language, ideology, and discrimination in the United States.* 2nd ed. New York: Routledge.
Wolfram, Walt. 1982. Language knowledge and other dialects. *American Speech* 57: 3–18.
Wolfram, Walt, and Robert Johnson. 1982. *Phonological analysis: Focus on American English.* Washington, DC: Harcourt, Brace, Jovanovich/Center for Applied Linguistics.
Wolfram, Walt, and Jeffrey Reaser. 2007. Dialects and the Ocracoke Brogue. 8th grade dialect curriculum. http://www.ncsu.edu/linguistics/code/Research%20Sites/ocracoke.htm.
Wolfram, Walt, and Natalie Schilling-Estes. 2006. *American English: Dialects and variation.* 2nd ed. Malden, MA: Blackwell.

7

AFRICAN AMERICAN ENGLISH

Arthur K. Spears

Introduction

African American English, now usually written without a hyphen between *African* and *American*, is also called Ebonics, Black English, and African American Language. Today, linguists normally use the term *African American English* (AAE), and that is the term I use in this chapter. Some linguists use the term *African American Language*, but my view is that this term should refer to African American language as a whole, which includes other English varieties and non-English ones.

The term *African American* itself is somewhat fuzzy. It basically refers to people of known African descent whose families have been in the U.S. for at least 150 years, since around the time slavery was abolished. Since people of African descent have been immigrating continuously to the U.S. throughout its history, it is difficult to establish a strict cutoff point. This loose definition would include, to take one example, Cape Verdean African Americans who began immigrating to the U.S. in significant numbers in the early 1800s.

The Standard and the Vernacular

It is important to distinguish between two basic types of AAE: African American Standard English (AASE) and African American Vernacular English (AAVE). We often think of Standard English as one variety, but there are actually many varieties of it, most geographically based. Important to note also is that speakers—and even prescriptive grammarians—differ on what they consider standard. All of our U.S. presidents speak Standard English (most if not all of the time), but one can easily discern that they speak different kinds. All varieties of Standard American English have a group of grammatical features, most notably pronunciation, that distinguish them from one another. However, none have the features that traditional, prescriptive grammarians have typically classified as nonstandard, features like *ain't*. More specifically, none have the features *most speakers know* are classified as nonstandard. *Vernacular* is the term that is now used in place of *nonstandard*, which is often felt to be too judgmental. *Vernacular* is also used in other senses. In one other sense, it refers to a person's most relaxed style of speech, one in which there is practically no self-monitoring. The term AAVE, which refers in reality to a cluster of regional and social varieties (as does AASE), includes nonstandard forms of AAE. The other term, AASE, refers to standard varieties, which have none of the grammatical features that most people would label nonstandard. (See below for more discussion on standards and vernaculars, and see also the chapter on vernacular dialects of English.)

History

There have been several hypotheses on the origin and historical evolution of AAE. Keep in mind that *evolution* does not imply change for the better or the worse in the social sciences. It refers merely to changes in form over time. Practically all scholars recognize that AAE (especially AAVE) is more different from other, non–African American dialects of English (henceforth OAD, for "other American dialects") as a group than OAD are from one another. The issue is why. There are currently two main groups of hypotheses: the Anglicist and the creole substrate hypotheses.

The first group of hypotheses suggests that the distinctiveness of AAE is due overwhelmingly to the retention in AAE of grammatical features that have receded or disappeared in OAD; some of these features are still present in the British Isles. These hypotheses also assign a significant role to divergence in accounting for AAE's distinctiveness: over the last century and a half or so, AAE has diverged from OAD, developing new features not found in OAD or making central to its overall grammar features that in OAD have remained less robust or nonexistent. Habitual *be* is offered as an example of the latter possibility (e.g., *He be doing his homework every night after dinner* 'He does his homework every night after dinner').

Creole substrate hypotheses view an important influence on AAE as historically stemming from creole languages once spoken more widely in the U.S. by slaves imported from other areas, notably the Caribbean. According to these hypotheses, AAE is the result of language shift in the U.S.'s African-descent population, whose early members mostly spoke West African and creole languages. Their descendants shifted to English, but it was their own special form of English: AAE.

These two groups of hypotheses are unlike the *creolist* hypotheses that were advanced formerly. Those hypotheses claimed that AAE evolved out of a creole language, once widely spoken in U.S., particularly the plantation South. They claimed in addition that today's AAE is the outgrowth of the decreolization of that former creole: due to increasing education and contact with English, African Americans linguistically accommodated, making their language more and more like English, until it actually became a dialect of English.

The creole substrate hypotheses propose that the influence of creole languages spoken here and there in various areas left traces in AAE, and that in creating the new language that AAE was, speakers incorporated creole features. In other words, in shifting from creole languages to a new one (AAE), speakers retained a few features from their creole first languages. Also, there were speakers of various West African languages who, in contact with English, created in the emerging AAE some elements similar to those created in creole language genesis. They also retained a few West African language features in their new English variety (AAE).

The West African languages believed to have been spoken by Africans in the U.S. during the formative period of AAE belong to the Niger-Congo language family, including the languages Kikongo, Twi, Ibo, Mende, Yoruba, Hausa, Bambara, and Ewe-Fon (the last is a cluster of highly similar language varieties). Among the words in AAE that are considered to have originated in African languages are *yam*, *tote*, *banjo*, *gumbo* ('okra', 'a seafood stew with okra'), *cooter* ('turtle'), *goober* ('peanut'), and many personal names, such as *Cuffy* or *Coffy*, *Cudjo* or *Cudjoe*, *Zola*, and *Phoebe* (homophonous with the Greek name). There are also a number of expressions that are translations of ones in West African languages, for example, *sweet-mouth* ('to flatter') and *bad-mouth* ('to malign').

Social Context

African Americans and Their Language Varieties

Most but not all African Americans speak AAE. Probably around 95% speak some kind of AAE (we have no reliable figures), even though they may use only a few of the grammatical features that linguists associate with AAE. They may also use a variety of AAE only sometimes, employing another variety of English, for

---

NON–AFRICAN AMERICANS WHO SPEAK AAE

There are some non–African Americans who speak AAE, normally those who have grown up in close proximity to African American communities. For example, some Puerto Ricans in New York City, whose neighborhoods abut and overlap with African American ones, have AAE in their linguistic repertoire. Some use it as their only truly native variety. Some non–African Americans are not native speakers but attempt to speak AAE because they may be attracted to facets of African American popular culture (e.g., hip-hop, the "gangsta" lifestyle portrayed in rap music videos, the lifestyle of television shows, "urban fashion," etc.). Or they may be involved in close personal relationships with African Americans, as a result, for example, of having married an African American, living in an African American community, or socializing mostly with African Americans in the military. With the personal relationship groups especially, they may subconsciously acquire features of AAE grammar.

example, in some social situations. That other variety may be a local white vernacular English, which they use in majority-white social situations.

Some African Americans speak language varieties other than AAE. Some speak local white vernaculars and standards. Some speak non-English varieties such as Gullah, the English-related creole language spoken in the Sea Islands off South Carolina and Georgia and in the coastal area from South Carolina south to Florida. A few in Louisiana speak Cajun French (a variety of French) or Louisiana French Creole, which is related to French through its vocabulary primarily but has a distinct status as a creole language. (For more on this, see the chapter on language varieties of Louisiana.) Still others speak Cape Verdean Creole and some American Indian languages, the latter as a result of the commingling of African-descent and Native American populations throughout U.S. history (Spears and Hinton 2010).

The Ebonics Controversy

Ebonics is probably the term for AAE that most people recognize, due to the Ebonics controversy that broke out in 1996. The Oakland School Board had passed a resolution that many people misinterpreted as calling for the teaching of Ebonics in public schools. In reality, the basic intention of the resolution was to have teachers who teach pupils speaking AAVE, the nonstandard variety of AAE, acquire a basic knowledge of the grammar and use of nonstandard AAE in order that they might be better equipped to teach their students some variety of Standard English.

In its wake, there was a stunning outpouring of disparagement and ridicule of this variety, frequently characterizing it as speech reflecting sloth, ignorance, and degradation stemming from slavery. Many African Americans—and other black commentators (not all blacks in the U.S. are African American)—joined in heaping abuse on Ebonics. Some of the widely disseminated, negative, and false ideas about African American language and culture are accepted by blacks too. They, as members of other groups, sometimes fall victim to believing negative stereotypes circulated about them, their language, and their culture generally. (Language is part of culture.) Anthropologists call this phenomenon "internalized oppression." A related example of internalized oppression is that many female students I have taught believe a woman would not make a good president.

Linguists were horrified by the reaction, since we believed that enough correct information on Ebonics—indeed, on all language varieties—had been disseminated to make most people aware that all language varieties are legitimate, systematic, governed by grammatical rules, expressively adequate, and fully worthy of our respect. Much of the invective hurled at Ebonics was actually antiblack sentiment couched in terms of language. In other words, attitudes about African Americans and blacks in general were being expressed via remarks about language. Language attitudes in the typical case are attitudes about their speakers. (See Smitherman

2004 for a useful review of the Ebonics controversy and an earlier 1979 court case, *King et al. v. Ann Arbor School District Board*, concerning the role of AAVE in the schooling of African American K–12 students speaking it.)

Other Varieties

In addition to those varieties that are classified with respect to standardness, AAVE and AASE, there are also regional varieties of AAE. The regional varieties have been little discussed (see, however, Butters 1989; Wolfram and Thomas 2002). In addition, there are African American diaspora varieties in Liberia, Nova Scotia, and the Samaná Peninsula of the Dominican Republic (see Spears 2008 and the references therein). The diaspora varieties have been studied, primarily over the last 20 years, in order to gain insight into the history of AAE. Since African American populations left the U.S. for other countries in the nineteenth century, there is a possibility that they have preserved grammatical features no longer present in AAE. This is so because diaspora varieties are usually more conservative, preserving features that are lost in the parent variety through language change. Diaspora-variety research has been done principally with the goal of finding evidence for or against the claim that AAE was once a creole language, quite similar to the creole languages of the Caribbean such as Jamaican Creole (Patwa) and Trinidadian Creole English.

Some Linguistic Features

As noted above, standard varieties of English can be said to be characterized negatively, that is, by a list of grammatical traits that they do not have. This is a useful but ultimately oversimplified way of talking about standards; it suits the purposes of this discussion, however. These vernacular (i.e., nonstandard) traits include, for example,

- the use of *ain't* and the use of multiple negation, as in *They ain't got none* and *He don't never go nowhere*;
- the use of nonstandard (vernacular) past participles, as in *They haven't went yet* and *The milk is froze*; and
- the use of certain verb forms such as habitual, invariant *be*, as in *She be studyin all the time*.

Standard varieties are those that do not have any of the grammatical traits figuring in lists of nonstandard grammatical traits appearing in prescriptive grammars. (Prescriptive grammars and dictionaries are not always in full agreement.)

Consequently, AASE does not have any *salient* grammatical features figuring in the lists of nonstandard grammatical features, that is, those features that most speakers, especially more educated ones, are aware of and that we find in prescriptive grammars. Observe that I will refer to AASE as one variety although actually it also includes many regional and social varieties. This variety does have features that are distinctive to African American varieties, but none from the non-standard feature list. This statement surprises many people because they assume that any grammatical feature that occurs only in AAE varieties must be nonstandard. But this is not so.

There are some distinctive AAE grammatical features that have escaped traditional, prescriptive grammarians' attention and the attention of the general public and thus have never appeared on any such lists. It is not farfetched to reason that if these grammarians knew about such features, they would put them on the nonstandard list, owing to the stigma that U.S. society has historically attached to most things black. This stigmatizing, however, is nowadays changing noticeably. Features of African American language and African American culture generally are now more often accepted without stigma. Examples of this come from areas of AAE itself, for example, rap vocabulary, music (jazz, rhythm and blues; and rap); and fashion (such as cornrow hairstyles) and "urban fashion" (such as the once popular baggy jeans and greatly oversized T-shirts associated with hip-hop culture).

(For lists of many more grammatical features of AAVE, see Green 2002; Mufwene et al. 1998; Rickford 1999; Rickford and Rickford 2000; and Wolfram and Thomas 2002.)

Grammatical Camouflage

The distinctive AAE grammatical traits that appear in AASE are camouflaged (Spears 1982). It is practically impossible for anyone not a specialist in AAE grammar to detect them. Since most AASE speakers are often sensitive to the stigma still attached to things black, they would probably try to rid their speech of these features if they knew what they were. AAE specialists, for our part, are sometimes reluctant to discuss camouflaged, distinctively black grammatical features for fear that speakers' knowledge of them might inadvertently promote the attrition and perhaps eventual disappearance of these features—and possibly of AASE itself. Linguists often act to preserve language varieties, trying not to do anything that might hasten their demise. Every language variety is precious in that it carries the history and culture of a people.

One example of an already rather well-known camouflaged grammatical feature occurring in both AASE and AAVE is what linguists call "stressed *been*," usually written *BIN*. *BIN* is pronounced with more emphasis (stress), and in most varieties always with high pitch. Consider the following sentences, which most hearers would assume to be the same sentence:

(1) She's BIN married. (AASE)

   'She's been married a long time and still is married.'

(2) She's been married. (OAD)

> 'She's been married before (but isn't now).'
> 'She's been married (and still is—no length of time implied).' (Compare *She's been married since last Saturday.*)

The two sentences are grammatically different, however. *BIN* is a type of auxiliary that occurs only in AAE. It is distinct from the past participle of *be*, which occurs in all English dialects and has a different meaning, as indicated by the glosses. This, like other AAE features, has spread outside black communities and outside of AAE into other communities and language varieties, for example, Puerto Rican and Dominican English in many parts of New York City. This feature has never been classified as nonstandard by prescriptivist grammarians, as noted above, most likely because they did not know of its existence.

Note the following AAVE sentence:

(3) She BIN married. (AAVE; same meaning as example 1)

You probably noticed that this sentence has a nonstandard grammatical feature: the absence of any form, contracted ('s) or not, of the auxiliary verb *have*. These examples are useful because they offer a good example of how AAVE, AASE, and OAD differ.

Some nonstandard grammatical features that occur in AAVE also occur in vernacular OAD (for example, Appalachian English and Ozark English) and indeed in varieties spoken by the great majority of the English-speaking American population. (Many Americans erroneously believe that most English speakers by far speak standard varieties.) For example,

(4) She done ate all of it. (VERNACULAR [NONSTANDARD])

> 'She has eaten all of it.'/'She's eaten all of it.' (STANDARD)

This example has the nonstandard auxiliary verb *done* and a nonstandard past participle of *eat*. The standard past participle is *eaten*.

Defining AAE

As already noted, *BIN* is an example of a distinctively black grammatical feature. There is an entire list of such features, and linguists expect to discover more. Some are well known, such as habitual, invariant *be* and *BIN*. Others are known only to AAE specialists. They are somewhat difficult to discover because most are deeply camouflaged. Other things being equal, linguists who are native speakers of AAE are in a better position to ferret out camouflaged grammatical features. Distinctively black grammatical features (hereafter DBGF), that is, ones found in AAE varieties only (except in cases where they have spread to other varieties), permit a definition of **AAE**: any variety of American English having a core group of DBGFs. Some DBGFs are found in virtually all AAE varieties, others in only a few. An example of the former is *BIN*. An example of the latter is the conjunction (or complementizer) *say* (sometimes occurring more camouflaged as *said*):

(5) Joe told me **say** they left = Joe told me **said** they left. (AAVE)

'Joe told me **that** they left.' = 'Joe told me they left.' (standard—AASE and OAD)

The conjunction *say* is particularly interesting because it is a **creolism**: a grammatical trait found in at least some creole languages in addition to AAE (see the chapter on language contact as well as Spears 2008). As such, it provides a clue concerning the origin and history of AAE. Another creolism is associative and plural *them*. It occurs in sentences such as (6). The full form is *and them*, usually pronounced *an' 'em*, while in creoles it is *dem*. The associative sense is illustrated in the following example:

(6) John an' 'em left this morning. (AAVE)

'John and his friends/family/gang/colleagues left this morning.'

Further Reading

An in-depth discussion of race, ethnicity, class, and racism, along with other ills afflicting societies, can be found in Desmond and Emirbayer's *Racial Domination, Racial Progress: The Sociology of Race in America* (2010). AAE has been studied empirically more than any other social variety of English. The literature on it is quite extensive. The following works, however, serve well as a distillation of much that has been published. A classic that is still important is William Labov's *Language in the Inner City* (1972). (Labov's work ushered in the era of modern, empirically sophisticated AAE studies.) A systemic treatment of AAE grammar is presented in Green's *African American English* (2002). Unlike many writers, she presents the grammatical features of AAE as a system. The best introductory discussion of AAE for an audience with no linguistics background is Rickford and Rickford's *Spoken Soul: The Story of Black English* (2000). Like Green's book, it discusses topics related to use: literature, preaching, and verbal styles. John Baugh's *Out of the Mouths of Slaves: African American Language and Educational Malpractice* (1999) focuses on educational issues. Geneva Smitherman's classic, *Talkin and Testifyin: The Language of Black America* (1977), was written before the bulk of grammatical research on AAE but remains an excellent reference for communicative practices. *African-American English: Structure, History and Use*, edited by Mufwene et al. (1998), as well as Rickford's *African American Vernacular English* (1999) and Wolfram and Thomas's *The*

Development of African American English (2002), are indispensable for information on grammar and history. *The Social Contexts of African American English* (Lanehart 2001) is a valuable source for discussion of grammar, history, and communicative practices. For the most recent extended discussion of AAE history, especially as related to creoles, see Spears (2008).

Writing has recently begun to appear on a gender-based variety, African American Women's Language (Troutman 2001; Lanehart 2002). Actually, we might say that most of the earliest studies on AAE were also gender based, but not self-consciously so, since they repeatedly focused on speakers in all-male groups.

Problem Sets

Semantics and Pragmatics

Some grammatical features of AAE have been much discussed. In these problems I focus on less known aspects of AAE grammar that readers have probably not read about. (See Wolfram's chapter for more AAE problems.) The first group of problems in this section deal with the semantics and pragmatics of *be done*, which is found solely in AAVE. This double-auxiliary form may express tense, aspect, and/or disapproval. Like the entire set of disapproval markers in AAE, it expresses disapproval of what the clause containing it expresses or of what an adjacent clause expresses. All of the disapproval markers are camouflaged: they seem to be words that are familiar to speakers of OAD, but they are not.

The system of disapproval markers in AAE grammar constitutes a reflection in grammar of what is sometimes called a *principle* of AAE speech, that is, a common, culture-linked style of speaking that is manifest in much AAE speech. The term for this communicative principle is *directness* (Spears 2001), which refers to saying exactly what one thinks, eschewing euphemisms or "telling it like it is." Directness may characterize the message communicated or the expressions used to communicate a message, which those not familiar with the culture often consider to be overly blunt or obscene. (Bluntness and obscenity are culturally relative. For example, the word *bloody*, considered obscene in most Commonwealth countries, is unremarkable in the U.S.)

Instead of saying, *That suit doesn't really flatter you*, one might say, for example, *You look like a fool in that suit.* Since African Americans (who are culturally African American) hear much direct speech, they are used to it and often find it humorous. Different versions of directness occur in the speech practices of other communities. An example is *dugri*, the direct speech of Israeli Sabras, native-born Israeli Jews, primarily of European descent (Katriel 1986).

Be done: In this problem, we will examine only some aspects of the grammar of this form. *Be done*, as noted, actually has several meanings in AAVE, one of which is the disapproval meaning. To figure out two meanings of *be done*, including the disapproval one, examine the sentences in Table 7.1 and then answer the questions below.

TABLE 7.1 Example sentences with *be done*

	African American Vernacular English	Standard
(7)	If he lay a hand on my kid again, I be done knock him upside the head.	'If he lays a hand on my kid again, I'm going to knock him upside the head so quick!'
(8)	If I get home after five, he be done left.	'If I get home after five, he'll have left.'
(9)	If they go in there and see a bunch of ghosts and things, they be done jump out the window.	'If they go in there and see a bunch of ghosts and things, they're going to jump out of the window so fast!'
(10)	Before you finish your homework, the baby be done already fell asleep.	'Before you finish your homework, the baby will have already fallen asleep.'
(11)	If they put sugar in my gas tank again, I be done had a fit.	'If they put sugar in my gas tank again, you'd better believe I'll really have a fit!'
(12)	By the time you get to the mall, they be done gone back home.	'By the time you get to the mall, they'll have gone back home.'

1. The meanings in the main clauses of the even-numbered sentences all express the same tense. What tense is it: past, future, present perfect, future perfect, or past perfect? (In these sentences the main clauses all follow the commas, while the first clauses, the ones before the commas, are all subordinate clauses.) If you are not sure what the tense terms mean, discuss them with your instructor.

2. Notice that the first clauses in the even-numbered sentences describe ordinary types of events that would not cause much of an emotional reaction for the average person. However, the first clauses in the odd-numbered sentences are emotionally charged. Are the events described in the first clauses of the odd-numbered sentences likely to have the approval or disapproval of the average person?

3. Now consider the time (or tense) relationship between the clauses of the AAVE sentences. Think about the event expressed by each clause. Which clause's event occurs first in real time? For example, in sentence (7), does "laying a hand on my kid again" occur before or after "my knocking him upside the head"? Put "1st" or "2nd" in each cell of Table 7.2 depending on whether the clause occurs first or second in real time. The first sentence is done for you.

TABLE 7.2 Clause sequence in *be done* sentences

Sentence number	Occurrence in real time	
	First clause	Second clause
(7)	1st	2nd
(8)		
(9)		
(10)		
(11)		
(12)		

4. Keeping in mind examples (7)–(12) and what you discovered in the previous questions, respond to the following:
    a. What meaning does *be done* express when the first clause occurs first in real time and the second clause occurs second in real time?
    b. What tense does *be done* express when the first clause occurs second in real time and the second clause occurs first in real time?

5. Considering what you have learned about AAVE so far, how would the following sentences be translated from Standard English into AAVE? (Just concentrate on using *be done* in a grammatically correct way. Do not worry about other details of AAVE grammar.) After your translation, state in parentheses whether the *be done* in your AAVE translation expresses disapproval or not. Do this by writing "disapproval" or "not disapproval" in parentheses after your translation. Sentence (13) is translated as an example:

    (13) If he leaves junk all around his room again, I'm going to throw it in the trash!

    If he leave junk all around his room again, I be done threw it in the trash! (Disapproval)

    (14) By the time I graduate from college, my daughter will have graduated from middle school.
    (15) If the police beat up anybody in this neighborhood again, we'll have the biggest demonstration you've ever seen!
    (16) If I catch you looking at that website again, I'm going to put Net-Nanny on that computer!
    (17) If we get to church after 11 o'clock, they'll already have started the service.

6. Now consider the two following AAVE sentences in both of which one of the clauses expresses disapproval (the first repeated from above):

(18) If they put sugar in my gas tank again, I be done had a fit!
(19) If you let that puppy in here again, he be done peed on the floor!

    a. How does the real-time sequence of the clauses in sentence (18) compare with that of the clauses in (19)? That is, what is the clause sequence in each example sentence?

    b. Does the time sequence correspond to that in the disapproval sentences in Table 7.1?

7. Does either (18) or (19) have a future perfect clause?

Now, consider the event expressed by each clause of (18) and (19).

8. In (18), does the *if* clause or the second clause express the event disapproved of?
9. In (19), does the *if* clause or the second clause express the event disapproved of?
10. Based on your answers to (8) and (9), which of the following is the best generalization about conditional sentences (those with an *if* clause) with the *be done* of disapproval:

    a. The disapproved-of event can be expressed by the *if* clause only.

    b. The disapproved-of event can be expressed by the consequent (main) clause only.

    c. The disapproved-of event can be expressed by either the *if* clause or the consequent clause.

11. What is the tense of the *be done* clauses in disapproval sentences?

Phonology

Postvocalic word-final /l/ deletion: As in other varieties of English, postvocalic final /l/ may be phonetically realized with velarization [ɫ], it may be weakened to an off-glide, or it may undergo deletion. Spears's Midwestern variety of AAE provides examples of these phonetic realizations in the pronunciations of /l/, for example, *seal* ([si:ɫ] and [siw]) and *pool* ([pu:ɫ], [pu:], and [pu]). Often, the vowel preceding the deleted /l/ is long, but it can be short in certain cases. Table 7.3 shows possible pronunciations for words with postvocalic word-final /l/. (Note: As in many varieties of English, pre-consonantal vowels preceding voiced consonants are lengthened in monosyllabic words, hence the lengthened vowels in the third column.)

12. Based on the data in Table 7.3, which vowels permit postvocalic word-final /l/ deletion? (Use natural classes in your answer, e.g., front vowels, high front vowels, etc. Provide a "minimal" answer; for example, if "mid vowels" accounts for the data, do not answer "mid lax vowels," even if it accounts for the data too.)

13. Now consider the data in Tables 7.3 and 7.4 together and refine your analysis.

TABLE 7.3 Word set #1: Postvocalic word-final /l/ in a Midwestern variety of AAE

Orthography	Phonemic representation	With velar /l/	With /l/ deletion
seal	/sil/	[siːɫ]	★[siː]
sill	/sɪl/	[sɪːɫ]	★[sɪː]
sale	/seɪl/	[seɪːɫ]	★[seɪː]
sell	/sɛl/	[sɛːɫ]	★[sɛː]
pool	/pul/	[puːɫ]	[puː]
pull	/pʊl/	[pʊːɫ]	[pʊː]
poll	/powl/	[powːɫ]	[powː]
tall	/tɔl/	[tɔːɫ]	[tɔː]

TABLE 7.4 Word set #2: Postvocalic word-final /l/ in a Midwestern variety of AAE

Orthography	Phonemic representation	With velar /l/	With /l/ deletion
Cal	/kæl/	[kæːɫ]	★[kæː]
dull	/dʌl/	[dʌːɫ]	★[dʌː]
doll	/dɑl/	[dɑːɫ]	★[dɑː]

TABLE 7.5 Word set #3: Postvocalic word-final /l/ in a Midwestern variety of AAE

Phonemic representation	With velar /l/	With /l/ deletion
/pul/	[puːɫ]	[puː]
/pʊl/	[pʊːɫ]	[pʊː]
/powl/	[powːɫ]	[powː]
/tɔl/	[tɔːɫ]	[tɔː]

Now answer the question taking the new data into consideration: what vowels permit postvocalic word-final /l/ deletion? (As before, use natural classes in your answer.)

14. As you have read above, two phonological rules may apply to the phonemic representations in Table 7.4: (1) postvocalic word-final /l/ deletion and (2) vowel lengthening preceding voiced consonants. To produce the pronunciations in the third column in Table 7.5, do these two rules have to apply in a certain order? If so, how must the two rules be ordered?

References

Baugh, John. 1999. *Out of the mouths of slaves: African American language and educational malpractice.* Austin: University of Texas Press.

Butters, Ronald R. 1989. *The death of Black English: Divergence and convergence in Black and White vernaculars.* Frankfurt: Peter Lang.

Desmond, Matthew, and Mustafa Emirbayer. 2010. *Racial domination, racial progress: The sociology of race in America.* New York: McGraw-Hill.

Green, Lisa J. 2002. *African American English: A linguistic introduction.* Cambridge: Cambridge University Press.

Katriel, Tamar. 1986. *Talking straight:* Dugri *speech in Israeli Sabra culture.* New York: Cambridge University Press.

Labov, William. 1972. *Language in the inner city.* Philadelphia: University of Pennsylvania Press.

Lanehart, Sonja L., ed. 2001. *The sociocultural and historical contexts of African American English.* Philadelphia: John Benjamins.

Lanehart, Sonja L. 2002. *Sista, speak! Black women kinfolk talk about language and literacy.* Austin: University of Texas Press.

Mufwene, Salikoko S., John R. Rickford, Guy Bailey, and John Baugh, eds. 1998. *African-American English: Structure, history and use.* New York: Routledge.

Rickford, John R. 1999. *African American Vernacular English.* Waltham, MA: Blackwell.

Rickford, John Russell, and Russell John Rickford. 2000. *Spoken soul: The story of Black English.* New York: John Wiley & Sons.

Smitherman, Geneva. 1977. *Talking and testifyin: The language of black America.* Detroit: Wayne State University Press.

Smitherman, Geneva. 2004. Language and African Americans: Movin on up a lil higher. *Journal of English Linguistics* 32.3: 186–196.

Spears, Arthur K. 1982. The Black English semi-auxiliary *come. Language* 58: 850–872.

Spears, Arthur K. 2001. Directness in the use of African-American English. In Sonja L. Lanehart, ed., *Sociocultural and historical contexts of African-American English,* 239–259. Amsterdam: John Benjamins.

Spears, Arthur K. 2008. Pidgins/Creoles and African American English. In Silvia Kouwenberg and John Victor Singler, eds., *The handbook of pidgins and creoles,* 512–542. Waltham, MA: Blackwell.

Spears, Arthur K., and Leanne Hinton. 2010. Language and speakers: An introduction to African American English and Native American languages. In Arthur K. Spears, ed., Language, inequality, and endangerment: African Americans and Native Americans, special issue, *Transforming Anthropology* 18.1: 3–14.

Troutman, Denise. 2001. African American women: Talking that talk. In Sonja L. Lanehart, ed., *Sociocultural and historical contexts of African-American English,* 211–238. Amsterdam: John Benjamins.

Wolfram, Walt, and Erik Thomas. 2002. *The development of African American English.* Waltham, MA: Blackwell.

8

CHICANO ENGLISH

Carmen Fought

Introduction

The data presented in this chapter are from my fieldwork with Latinos and Latinas in Los Angeles, California, in the mid-1990s (Fought 2003). My original plan was to study only Spanish in the community, but once I arrived and started talking to people, I realized that the variation and changes going on in the English dialects of the community were very interesting as well. Bilingual Latino communities in the U.S. are what linguists refer to as language contact areas. Like other bilingual or multilingual areas of the world, they provide a chance to study unique and interesting language patterns, because when two languages coexist in one community for a long time, they often come to influence each other. (See also the chapter "Language Contact.") Many people (not linguists) think this is bad somehow, that two languages influencing each other will lead to the deterioration of both languages. But change and deterioration are not the same thing. One of the first things that new students of linguistics learn is that all living languages change and that this process is both natural and inevitable. Language change is also one of the phenomena that linguists are most interested in.

In Mexican American communities in Los Angeles, both the Spanish and the English spoken are different from varieties of those languages used in other regions or countries. In Chicano Spanish, for example, speakers say *Te llamo pa' trás*, a literal translation of the English phrase *I'll call you back*, which is not used by speakers in monolingual Spanish-speaking countries such as Mexico. The more typical monolingual expression would simply be *Te llamo*. (For more examples, see the chapter on Southwest Spanish.)

The English spoken by Latinos in Los Angeles covers a large range of variation. A particular speaker, for example, someone with a white-collar job, might use a very standard-sounding dialect, with only occasional phonetic features to mark the ethnicity of that person as Latino or Latina. Other speakers (or even the same one on a different occasion) might use a variety called Chicano English, the variety that I focused on in my fieldwork and that I will discuss in more detail below. Even between older-generation and younger-generation speakers in the same community, there are some slight differences in the characteristics of Chicano English.

History

One of the reasons I chose to study this dialect is that it reflects the ways in which the social and historical context can affect language variation. When recent groups of Mexican immigrants arrived in Los Angeles, they learned English as a second language. Like other adult second-language learners, they spoke an "accented" variety of English that included phonological and other patterns from their first language, Spanish. The children of these immigrants, however, generally grew up using both Spanish and English. And they used the "learner English" of the community as a basis for developing a new native dialect of English, which linguists have labeled Chicano English. Note that linguists generally prefer to classify the varieties of learners as *interlanguages* since the interlanguage varieties, taken as a group, show much more variation than established dialects. Established language varieties, like Chicano English (which also happens to be a relatively new variety), show less variation (especially across speakers) than interlanguages. Linguists express this by stating that established languages' grammars have crystallized. Chicano English now has special rules of its own that set it apart both from Spanish and from other dialects of English (see below), and like all dialects, this one continues to change and evolve.

Social Context

Myths about Chicano English and Issues of Language Prejudice

One important fact to remember: you can't tell from hearing a person speak Chicano English whether he or she *also* speaks Spanish. If you grew up in a bilingual Latino community, you probably already knew this. People outside the community, however, may think they are hearing a "Spanish accent" when they hear Chicano English, because of Spanish's influence on its historical development. In fact, many of the people who now speak Chicano English grew up monolingual in English. They don't speak any Spanish at all, especially if they are third generation or later. They can't even order a meal at Taco Bell in Spanish!

People who don't know much about this dialect often get confused about this point, though. A coworker of mine asked me recently, "Why do so many Mexican American students seem to have such a hard time learning English, even if they were born here in the U.S.?" She then gave me the specific example of a Mexican American student who worked in her office. I happened to know that the student she was talking about was a native speaker of English, specifically of

Chicano English. This example illustrates a myth that the general public has about Chicano English: that it is a broken version of English spoken by people whose first language is Spanish. On the contrary, Chicano English speakers have in reality learned English perfectly, like children of all ethnic backgrounds who grow up in the U.S., but the variety of English they've learned is a nonstandard one, and one that happens to reflect the historical contact with Spanish. And it cannot possibly be just a nonnative variety spoken by second-language learners of English if it is spoken by people who know *only* English!

This misperception of Chicano English speakers (i.e., guessing that they have a Spanish accent when in fact they don't know any Spanish) has unfortunate repercussions in the educational system. Some monolingual English-speaking kids have had to take special tests for "limited-English" speakers (tests that were supposed to be for bilinguals!), because they spoke Chicano English. In the Los Angeles School District, a test is administered to any student whose parents report, in a survey sent home by the school, that Spanish is spoken at home (even if only the parents speak it). Often, students who are completely fluent in English and fairly poor in Spanish are classified as LEP (Limited English Proficient) because of the nonstandard forms they use in responding to the questions. Mexican American students whose parents don't speak Spanish at home might show equally low scores due to being Chicano English speakers, but these students are not tested.

Someone who did not understand all of this, such as an educational administrator, might conclude (mistakenly) from the test results that bilingual Mexican American children are likely to be hindered in learning English properly because of their Spanish. But, in fact, that is not true at all. All the evidence we linguists have suggests that being bilingual is a good thing. It's being ignorant about dialects that's hazardous to your intellectual growth.

These types of linguistic misperceptions are part of the reason why sociolinguists' field of study is important to our society. Often, children who speak nonstandard dialects may be inaccurately classified as "not knowing much English" or even "having a speech defect," with terrible consequences for the child. We hope that we can get more information into the educational system about how dialects work. In addition, by describing language patterns in more detail, we can dispel some myths in our culture that lead to language prejudice (e.g., that someone who **codeswitches**, moving back and forth between two languages, doesn't speak either language well). (For more on codeswitching see the discussion in the chapter "Language Contact.") Finally, as discussed earlier, studying languages in contact helps us to learn more about how social organization affects variation and about how languages change over time.

Because research by linguists on the English spoken in Mexican American communities is fairly new, there are many things we still do not know. For example, what is the relationship between *Chicano English*, a term usually reserved for varieties spoken by speakers of Mexican American ethnicity in the southwestern regions of the U.S., and *Puerto Rican English*, a variety found among speakers of Puerto Rican ethnicity on the East Coast? Because both varieties grew out of contact with Spanish, we might expect some similarities but also some differences. An interesting study to compare with those on Chicano English is Zentella (1997). Although the focus is on Puerto Rican English, many issues such as bilingualism, language shift, and language attitudes are similar to those in Mexican American communities. We also know very little about regional differences within Chicano English. Is the dialect used by speakers in Tucson, Arizona, different from the one I studied in Los Angeles? There are likely to be at least some differences, but at this point we do not have enough research to be able to discuss these issues.

It is also difficult to estimate the number of speakers of Chicano English. To begin with, there has been some debate in the literature about what this term encompasses. Most researchers in the area agree with Santa Ana (1993) that nonnative speaker varieties should be treated separately. I also agree with this conclusion, but at times it can be difficult to know where to draw the line on the continuum between native and nonnative. As mentioned earlier, regional differences may also be a factor, and many regions have not been studied at all. Do Mexican Americans in Ohio, for example, speak Chicano English? However, if we keep in mind that Latinos are now the largest minority ethnic group in the U.S., that a majority of them still live in the Southwest, and that a large percentage of them are now people who were born here, we can guess that the number of speakers of Chicano English in the country is quite large. It is a variety that is vibrant and growing.

Some Linguistic Features

As I mentioned above, there is variation in how different speakers use Chicano English, just as there is variation among speakers in all dialects of English. Whatever dialect you use, you probably don't speak exactly like other friends or relatives from the same hometown. You probably try to sound as little like your parents as possible. And if they try to sound like you . . . well, let's not go there. So I will describe here some of the features that tend to show up in Chicano English, but keep in mind that a particular speaker may not use all or even most of them.

Phonology

The phonology of Chicano English is what makes it most distinct. It retains many sounds that show the influence of sounds from Spanish, although the vowels and consonants are still very different from Spanish. This is, after all, a dialect of English. I won't provide the details about which sounds contrast or vary in Chicano English, because you are expected to do that for yourself in the exercise below. Besides the vowels and consonants, Chicano English has distinct prosodic patterns, patterns in the stressing of syllables or the rising and falling of pitch (called *intonation*), that also set it apart from other dialects of English. If you have a chance to hear someone speak Chicano English, listen for rhythmic patterns that sound distinctive to you.

PROSODY

Prosody refers to speech elements such as length, intonation, tone, or stress that occur "on top of" the sound segments; these are also called *suprasegmentals*.

Syntax

The syntax of Chicano English includes certain nonstandard features, most of which can also be found in other dialects, spoken by people of other ethnicities. A good example is multiple negation (e.g., *He didn't do nothing about it*), which is used by working-class speakers who are African American or European American as well. Chicano English speakers also may use a pattern that linguists call "inversion in embedded questions." In many dialects, when you take a question like *What was he talking about?* and insert it into another sentence, the subject and verb are switched, as though it were a statement instead of a question: *I asked him what he was talking about.* Often, in Chicano English, these forms look more like the original question, so that you instead get *I asked him what was he talking about.*

Verb forms are often regularized in Chicano English. Linguists use the term **regularized** to describe a process whereby speakers of a particular dialect "clean up" irregularities in a language pattern to make it more consistent. For example, the third person singular form of the verb in English is different from all the other forms: the verb is identical in *I do, you do, we do, they do,* but then out of the blue you get *he/she does,* with the extra *-s* morpheme and a vowel quality change. Chicano English speakers may regularize the third person, as in the example *He don't want me to end up like my sister.*

Something similar happens with reflexive pronouns, like *myself.* Most of the forms consist of the possessive pronoun (*my, our, your, her*) plus *self* or *selves.* But in Standard English in the third person we suddenly get a different type of pronoun as the base (*him* + *self, them* + *selves*) rather than the third person possessive pronouns *his, their.* Chicano English speakers (as well as speakers of some other dialects) sometimes preserve the basic pattern by regularizing these forms to be *hisself* and *theirselves.*

There are other syntactic patterns that show up in Chicano English, but these are a few of the main ones. While the phonology of Chicano English is very distinctive, the morphological and syntactic patterns tend to overlap with a number of other dialects.

Semantics

Anyone who has had a debate with someone from another region about the question of *soda* versus *pop* knows that the meanings or uses of particular words can also be a feature of specific dialects. There are some semantic patterns found in Chicano English that distinguish it from other dialects. A number of these patterns are found in the area of modal auxiliary verbs such as *can*, *should*, *must*, and *might*. One example is the modal *could*. In many dialects of English this modal is used to refer to something that might happen now or in the future, as in *She could write it now if she wanted to* or *She could get an A if she studies hard next year*. But in Chicano English, it can also be used to refer to a present ability without implying some contingency. Standard dialects of English would use the modal *can* for this when no contingency is implied. A possible Chicano English example is as follows, clarified with a short dialogue between two speakers:

> A: Class, who can speak Spanish? [asks the teacher]
> B: David could speak Spanish, teacher.

By saying that *David could speak Spanish* the student means 'David is able to speak the Spanish language right now', not in the future. In other dialects, if you said *David could speak Spanish*, some contingency would be implied, as in *David could speak Spanish right now—if he wanted to*.

Several additional words have a meaning in Chicano English that is distinct from their meaning in other dialects of English. I will not list all of them here, but I will give a couple of representative examples. The first is the use of the word *barely* to mean 'just recently', as in *I barely broke my leg*. In my dialect, this would mean something like 'It was just a small break, a hairline fracture, and it almost doesn't count as a break.' In Chicano English, however, this means 'I just broke my leg a short while ago'. Another example is the use of the word *tell* to mean 'ask'. As an example, I asked one of the people I was interviewing, who had told me he wasn't very fluent in Spanish, if he thought he would be able to answer a few simple questions in Spanish. He replied, "It depends on what you tell me." Some of these semantic differences seem as though they can be traced to the historical contact with Spanish, but others cannot.

Further Reading

Chicano English and the other varieties of English spoken in Latino communities have only recently begun to be the focus of sociolinguistic research (as compared with studies of other dialects of English, such as African American varieties). There were a few studies in the 1980s, and then very little follow-up for several decades. (See, for example, Ornstein-Galicia and Metcalf's 1984 collection of papers.) Early researchers in Latino communities focused primarily on the type of Spanish spoken instead. Some later works have begun to address this gap. Santa Ana (1993) provides an overview of Chicano English, addressing among other things the issue of whether nonnative speaker varieties should be counted as Chicano English. He concludes that the two types of dialects (native and nonnative) should be treated separately. Zentella (1997), mentioned earlier, gives a comprehensive picture of patterns of bilingualism among Puerto Rican American speakers in New York City, including a detailed study of codeswitching.

Schecter and Bayley (2002) offer a detailed study of two different Latino communities in the U.S., looking at the politics of ethnicity and the role of language in the construction of cultural identities. Fought (2003) is the first modern, comprehensive study of Chicano English. It provides sketches of the phonology, syntax, and semantics of this dialect, as well as some more detailed sociolinguistic studies of language change in the community. It also covers issues of bilingualism, language attitudes, and portrayals of language in the media.

Problem Sets

Notes about Real Language Data

If you've already done some phonology problems in your workbook, you're probably used to seeing small data sets that focus on just a few sounds. The data come from some exotic language like Kikuyu or Igbo that you've never heard of before. If you're able to solve the problem (and all of us have times when we just get stuck), it usually has a neat solution, maybe some clear minimal pairs that show you that two sounds are in contrast or something like that.

If you ever decide to go out into the world to study a new dialect or language (and I hope some of you might go on to do that), you will quickly find out that real language data are not much like phonology problems in your book. First of all, the people in the community are not going to speak in problem sets. Nobody has put the data into neat columns focusing on just a few sounds. You will have to figure out for yourself from the data what is interesting and what isn't. Second, some patterns may be neat, but others may be a little ambiguous or messy. And to make matters worse, you might not have very much data for a particular sound or pattern, so that you end up having to take your best guess as to whether a word represents a new pattern or just a fluke.

If you decide to research a little-studied language from the Brazilian rain forest, figuring out the sound patterns can be very, very difficult. But sometimes studying a different dialect of a language you know well (such as English) can be just as hard, though in other ways. You need to set aside your ideas of what you think the patterns should be, based on your own dialect. If there is no difference between the voiced sound [w] and the voiceless sound [w̥] in your dialect, then it's obvious to you that these are the same. But in some dialects of English, *weather* and *whether* begin with completely different sounds, and people living in that area can tell these words apart just by hearing them. This means that [w] and [w̥] contrast in that dialect and count as different sounds.

In assembling the data for the phonology problems below, I have transcribed a number of words from three different speakers, all of whom are of Latino ethnicity and live in the Los Angeles area. The first speaker, Rosanna (a pseudonym, as are all the names), immigrated from Mexico as a young adult. She is a nonnative speaker who speaks English fairly well but whose first language is Spanish. The second speaker, Joaquín, was born in the U.S. and grew up speaking Chicano English. He is bilingual and speaks both English and Spanish with native fluency.

He is from the slightly older Chicano generation (he's 45). Chuck is a younger-generation Chicano English speaker, age 17. He is monolingual and does not know much Spanish at all. Each of these three people has a slightly different dialect. For this exercise, you will assume that they are representative of a larger group of speakers like them.

Since I know from studying these dialects which types of sounds are interesting, I've selected words that highlight those sounds and have put them in the lists. However, I have not attempted to divide the list into groups focusing on particular sound pairs. I've tried to make it a little bit more like real data collection. You have to figure out for yourself what's interesting. Sometimes you'll have a neat pattern, like a minimal pair, but other times you won't. You'll have to use the skills you've learned for analyzing phonological data and try to determine which sounds count as "the same" and which are completely different. Sometimes you will feel that you need more data. If this happens, take your best guess as to what is going on, and explain what other types of words you would want to collect. Remember that in the lists below, since these are dialects of English after all, some words may be pronounced the same as they are in your own dialect. Also, some words may occur more than once on the list, with different pronunciations.

Phonology

Part A: Look at the data in Table 8.1 from Rosanna, age 56, a nonnative speaker of English, and answer the following questions.

TABLE 8.1 Data from Rosanna (a nonnative speaker of English whose first language is Spanish; age 56)

dad [dɛd]	she [ʧi]	his [his]
ideas [aɪdijas]	because [bikas]	calmed [kʌm]
the [də]	aunt [ɛnt]	her [xʌr]
he [xi]	chairs [ʃɛrs]	Al Anon [ɛlanan]
hitchhike [hɪʃhaɪk]	spent [əspɛnt]	herself [xərsɛlf]
school [skʊl]	together [tugɛðər]	that [dɛt]
cashiers [kæʃɪrs]	credits [krɛdɪs]	through [tru]
if [if]	shorthand [ʧɔrhɛnd]	habit [hɛbɪt]
these [dɪz]	handle [hɛndəl]	support [supɔrt]
all [al]	was [was]	children [ʧɪldrɛn]
years [yɪrs]	lucky [laki]	something [sʌmtiŋ]
husband [hasbɛnd]	would [wu]	immature [iməʧur]
up [ap]	run [ran]	home [xom]
but [bat]	chairs [ʧɛrs]	stuff [staf]
the [da]	punishing [panɪʃɪn]	understood [ənərstud]
shows [ʧos]	them [dɛm]	enthusiasm [ɛntusiyæsəm]

Note: [x] is a voiceless velar fricative.

1. Transcribe each word from Rosanna's data as you would pronounce it your-self. (If you are not a native speaker of English, ask a native speaker to pro-nounce the words for you and transcribe that person's pronunciation. Don't look the words up in a dictionary. The dictionary pronunciations may not be suitable for this exercise.) As you compare your transcriptions and the tran-scriptions of Rosanna's data, respond to the remaining questions.

2. There is one sound that appears in Rosanna's dialect that does not occur at all in native varieties of English. What is it?

3. There is also a sound that occurs in native varieties of English that seems to be completely missing in Rosanna's dialect. What is it? What does she substitute for the native English sound?

4. a. The following pairs of sounds belong to different phonemes in native dialects of American English. But some of these pairs are merged into one phoneme in Rosanna's wordlist. Find three sets of vowels and two sets of consonants in this list that seem to be merged in Rosanna's dialect com-pared to the native dialect of English that you have transcribed. Explain your answer using data from Rosanna's wordlist.

i.	/i/–/ɪ/	vii.	/ʧ/–/ʃ/
ii.	/ɛ/–/æ/	viii.	/d/–/ð/
iii.	/u/–/ʊ/	ix.	/t/–/θ/
iv.	/a/–/ʌ, ə/	x.	/s/–/z/
v.	/m/–/n/	xi.	/n/–/ŋ/
vi.	/l/–/r/		

    b. Are there any patterns you can identify in the distribution of the variants for each pair of sounds, or do they seem random?

5. In general, Spanish has phonotactic constraints that do not allow as many consonants in a syllable as English allows. In particular, Spanish does not allow initial consonant clusters consisting of /s/ + obstruent. What process(es) does Rosanna seem to be using to deal with this difference in phonotactic con-straints between English and Spanish? Do these processes occur regularly every time, or are they variable?

6. Most dialects of English have a phonetic process where vowels in unstressed syllables tend to be reduced to [ə], as in the first syllable of *define* [də.ˈfaɪn] versus *definition* [ˈdɛ.fə.nɪ.ʃən]. Does Rosanna have this process? If so, is it con-sistent or variable?

7. What guesses could you make about Spanish based on these data? Many of you probably know some Spanish, but even if you don't, you should be able to guess, for instance, what sounds do and don't count as separate phonemes in this language, based on Rosanna's speech.

Part B: Now look at the other two data sets, from Joaquín, an older native speaker of Chicano English, and Chuck, a younger native speaker (Tables 8.2 and 8.3).

TABLE 8.2 Joaquín (older-generation native CHE speaker; age 45)

kids [kɪdz]	decided [disaɪdɛd]	she's [ʃiz]
together [tugɛðər]	she's [ʧiz]	that [dæt]
child [ʧaɪl]	school [skul]	all [al]
speak [spik]	they [de]	institution [ɪnstɪtuʃən]
everything [ɛvriθiŋ]	dentist [dɛnɪs]	years [yɪrz]
L.A. [ɛle]	teaching [tiʧin]	losing [luzin]
culture [kʌlʧər]	times [taɪms]	she [ʃi]
was [wʌz]	draft [dræf]	put [pʊt]
health [hɛlθ]	Chico [ʧiko]	stuff [stʌf]
neighborhood [nebərhʊd]	these [ðiz]	reading [ridin]
social [soʃəl]	dances [dænsɛz]	Spanish [spænɪʃ]
least [lis]	worries [wəriz]	to know [tu no]
their [dɛr]	her [hʌr]	get [gyɛ]
wouldn't [wʊn]	financial [faɪnænʃəl]	teacher [tiʧər]

TABLE 8.3 Chuck (younger-generation native CHE speaker; age 17)

she's [ʃiz]	that's [ðæs]	change [ʧenʤ]
truck [trʌk]	back [bæk]	father [faðər]
there's [dɛrz]	minutes [mɪnəts]	then [dɛn]
that [dæt]	was [wʌz]	show [ʃo]
eighteen [etin]	hot [ha]	last [læs]
cabs [kæbs]	looking [lʊkin]	because [bikʌs]
husky [hʌski]	depressed [diprɛst]	specially [spɛʃəli]
neighborhood [nebərhʊ]	dazed [dez]	thinks [θɪŋks]
to go [tu go]	Chicano [ʧikano]	ducked [dʌkt]
left [lɛf]	clock [klak]	shake [ʃek]
shot [ʃat]	something [sʌmθin]	home [hom]
mature [məʧʊr]	freeze [friz]	besides [bisaɪds]
up [ʌp]	this [dɪs]	difference [dɪfrɛns]

8. Read all of the phonetic transcriptions for Joaquín's and Chuck's data out loud. If the pronunciation for a word in their data differs from yours, transcribe your own pronunciation (or that of a native speaker of English, if you are not a native speaker).

9. Is the extra sound from Rosanna's dialect (see [2]) still evident in each of these two dialects? What about the sound that is missing in her speech? Does it show up?

10. Now look at your answer to (4) above. Does Joaquín or Chuck have any phonemic contrasts that Rosanna didn't have? Which sounds are now clearly distinguished? Which sounds still seem to be merged or in variation in each of the two native speaker dialects?

11. What about the phonetic processes you analyzed in (5)–(6) above (vowel reduction, etc.)? What processes in the dialects of Joaquín and Chuck are similar to those used by Rosanna? What processes seem to work differently?

12. Are there any differences between the older variety of Chicano English (Joaquín) and the newer variety (Chuck)? If so, what are these?

References

Fought, Carmen. 2003. *Chicano English in context*. New York: Palgrave/MacMillan.

Ornstein-Galicia, Jacob, and Allan Metcalf, eds. 1984. *Form and function in Chicano English*. Rowley, MA: Newbury House.

Santa Ana, Otto. 1993. Chicano English and the nature of the Chicano language setting. *Hispanic Journal of the Behavioral Sciences* 15.1: 3-35.

Schecter, Sandra R., and Robert Bayley. 2002. *Language as cultural practice: Mexicanos en el norte*. Mahwah, NJ: Lawrence Erlbaum.

Zentella, Ana Celia. 1997. *Growing up bilingual*. Oxford: Basil Blackwell.

9

JAMAICAN CREOLE

Peter L. Patrick

Introduction

Jamaican Creole (JC) is a Caribbean English-lexified creole language, spoken primarily on the island of Jamaica (pop. 2.7 million people) but also in North America and Britain. When creolists say **English-lexified creole**, we mean that it is a language closely related to English in terms of vocabulary but nevertheless grammatically distinct from English. A creole language is one that was created as a result of intense language contact between a **superstrate** language (that is, a dominant colonial language—English in this case) and less powerful **substrate** languages (several West African ones). (On creole languages see also the chapter on language contact.) JC is a language that is separate from English and is in no way inferior to English, although many people, including some Jamaicans, think of it as a low-status language, due in part, no doubt, to the status of Jamaica in the world political economy.

It is a language of ethnic identification: practically all Jamaicans speak *di Patwa*, as it is popularly called, and practically nobody speaks it except those of Jamaican heritage. (The word *Patwa*, stressed on the first syllable, derives from French *patois*, but the Jamaican language itself has no French lineage and is not related to well-known French-lexified Creoles like those spoken in Haiti or Louisiana. Indeed, its vocabulary is almost wholly English.)

History

JC is the product of British colonialism, slavery, and the plantation economy, leading to language contact and creolization between Africans and English speakers. It began developing into a language after 1655, when English soldiers captured Jamaica from Spain, and was largely formed by about 1750. This was after a century that saw a massive increase in the African population. However, some important grammatical features are not attested for a century after 1750.

West and Central African sources included languages of the Kwa and Bantu families. Jamaican Maroons, rebel slaves who defeated the English army and established autonomous settlements by treaty in 1739, maintained knowledge of Twi, an ancestral Akan language (spoken in Ghana). This group also developed a special Maroon Spirit Language, which resembles Suriname creoles (Bilby 1983). English-language input into the formation of JC included nonstandard regional English dialects from London, Bristol, the West Midlands, and Liverpool, as well as Scots and Irish English.

Today over 90% of Jamaicans are of African descent, often with European heritage as well. Later arrivals (after 1845) claim Indian, Chinese, and Syrian heritage, but they did not influence the birth of the language.

Since the early 1900s many Jamaicans have migrated abroad, about 10% of the population in each decade since 1950. Over half a million Jamaican-born people live in the U.S. today. They and their descendants live in significant numbers in Toronto, Canada, and such U.S. urban areas as greater Miami (over 100,000) and New York City (nearly 250,000). In certain smaller cities (Baltimore and Philadelphia), they make up over 5% of the foreign-born residents.

Like other Caribbean peoples, these transnational families remain in close contact with family members back home in Jamaica. In Britain, Jamaicans have been present since the seventeenth century but migrated in significant numbers after World War II, making up the largest group of the 500,000 or more Caribbean migrants arriving in the 1960s and 1970s. While JC speakers in the U.S. have tended to assimilate to African Americans socially and linguistically, in the United Kingdom (including Britain and Northern Ireland), they form the majority of African-descent people from the Western Hemisphere. New speech varieties have emerged that linguists discuss under names such as London Jamaican (Sebba 1993), British Black English (Sutcliffe 1982; Edwards 1986), British Afro-Caribbean English, and British Creole (Patrick 2004).

The Social Context

The Sociolinguistic Situation

JC was long subordinated to Standard English by an elite minority who monopolized power and controlled the official culture. Limited access to Standard English for most people resulted in the **creole continuum**, a chain of minimally distinct speech varieties stretching from the **acrolect** (varieties closest to Standard Jamaican English [SJE]) to the most **basilectal varieties** (those furthest from the standard, showing the greatest continuity with their African roots). Even the end of the continuum closest to SJE merges subtly into SJE. This continuum model was developed by DeCamp (1971) because discrete, categorical approaches (community bilingualism, standard plus dialect, and diglossia) proved inadequate to describe the Jamaican language situation, as these approaches assume that there are clearly distinguishable speech varieties and that one can always tell when someone is speaking one as opposed to the others. (*Diglossia*, also discussed in the language contact chapter in this volume, refers to a society where there is at least some bilingualism and where the two [or more] languages have distinct functions in society.)

In addition to the acrolectal and basilectal varieties, there are mesolectal varieties, comprising the broad middle range of speech varieties on the continuum, used by most Jamaicans and used in many situations (Patrick 1999). The mesolect, then, lies between SJE (a variety of English, not a creole) and the creole varieties that are furthest from English. It incorporates some elements of English structure into the systematic but variable JC grammar. JC grammar shows systematic variation. **Variation** refers to the fact that in many cases, there are two or more ways (pronunciations, words, phrases, etc.) to say the same thing. For example, in English *walking* and *walkin'* are two ways of pronouncing one and the same word. In this respect, JC is like all languages: it shows variation. Creole-language mesolects, however, tend to have somewhat more systematic variation than other language varieties that do not exist in a creole continuum. Variation—the different ways of saying the same thing and the evaluations of each way of saying it—is patterned in a strong and stable way. Variation of the type I am discussing is inherent in languages. Indeed, linguists call it **inherent variation** (see the language contact chapter). This variation is not produced synchronically (during one period of time) through language mixing (of creole varieties with each other or with English). Variation has been present in JC (and in all languages) since they first began. Nevertheless, Jamaicans do codeswitch, for example, from a variety of JC to English or vice versa. They also styleshift, for example, from a more formal style of a certain variety of creole, or from SJE, to a less formal variety (Patrick 1997). (The majority of the world's speakers codeswitch, and virtually all of them styleshift. See the chapter on language contact.)

SJE is a recognized national variety of English, genetically descended (in the linguistic sense) by normal transmission, originally from British dialects and then from one generation on to the next over the centuries. However, basilectal JC grammar differs radically from English grammar and emerged from profound language contact and structural mixing during the period when it was formed. It is not genetically descended from English nor from African languages, though elements from each merged to different extents in the creation of JC. *Genetically descended* in linguistics means that a language (English, for example) has only one language "parent" (the English of the preceding generation), which in turn had only one, and so on. This is unlike creoles, which usually have several parent languages—a superstrate language and several substrate languages (or, in some cases, one superstrate and one substrate).

The Use of JC

SJE is largely the medium for education and literacy, despite JC's increasing penetration into broadcast and print media since Jamaica's independence in 1962.

The government has recently begun pilot bilingual education programs using JC and SJE. Only in the twenty-first century has the Jamaican government seriously begun exploring language planning and recognition of JC as a national language. Yet JC remains a rich and vibrant cultural force, the language of home and family, everyday life, and mass politics and culture. It has achieved worldwide popularity through Jamaican vocal music (most famously reggae, especially the songs of Bob Marley) and an internationally honored literature, with distinguished poets and writers including Edward Baugh, Louise Bennett, James Berry, Jean Binta Breeze, Erna Brodber, Michelle Cliff, Linton Kwesi Johnson, Claude McKay, Pamela Mordecai, Mervyn Morris, Mutabaruka, Velma Pollard (also a creolist), Dennis Scott, and Olive Senior. JC is also known throughout the world by the spread of Rastafarian culture, including Rastafarians' distinctive variety of JC, Dread Talk (Pollard 1994).

Some Linguistic Features

Orthography

There is no popularly recognized spelling system for JC. Linguists have long used or adapted the phonemic orthography (Jamaican Language Unit 2001) first devised by Frederic Cassidy (1961) and used in the *Dictionary of Jamaican English* (Cassidy and Le Page 1967). Recently, efforts have been made to popularize it as well (e.g., author Carolyn Cooper [n.d.] publishes a regular newspaper column using it).

In everyday practice, Jamaicans have long used their own idiosyncratic, often inconsistent English-based systems (Cooper calls this "chaka-chaka spelling"). For some aspects of JC they are quite useful and make pronunciation transparent.

Palatalization

Historically, velar stops before low vowels in English words could sometimes be palatalized to [c] and [ɟ] and followed by palatal glides, giving [cj] and [ɟj] (in the International Phonetic Alphabet [IPA]), so that a word such as *garden* could be pronounced [ɟjaːrdən]. This palatalization plus glide before low vowels occurred traditionally in northern Ireland; eastern Virginia; Charleston, South Carolina; and the Midlands and Southwest of England. It was even considered essential to polite speech in London in the 1700s. It was never phonemic in English and has gradually disappeared from many English dialects since 1800. (See Cassidy and Le Page 1967; Patrick 1999.)

The transfer of English words to JC at the time when palatalization before low vowels was common in English led to JC having the palatalized velar phonemes /kj/ and /gj/ (using IPA symbols) alongside the plain velar phonemes /k/ and /g/. Jamaicans often spell the palatalized velar consonants using *ky* (or *cy*; e.g., *cyat, kyat* 'cat') and *gy* (e.g., *gyaadn* 'garden'), a practice adopted here. Palatalization also occurs before high front vowels, as in many languages, but under different conditions—this is not considered here. The problem sets will allow you to explore JC palatalization further.

Tense and Aspect

An important feature distinguishing Caribbean creoles from their European lexifier languages is the structure of their tense, mood, and aspect (TMA) systems. **Tense** has to do with the way verbs locate **situations** (i.e., events, actions, and states of affairs) in time, for example, present, past, and future. (In this discussion, I use terms that are more readily understandable than some of those used by linguists in talking about tense and aspect.) **Aspect** treats events, actions, and states, that is, situations, in another way. Aspect has to do with their duration, distribution through time (repeated, frequent, or habitual), or delimitation (beginning or end) or the speaker's point of view (e.g., looking at a situation from the inside, as it is unfolding). The expression of **mood** is intimately related to that of tense and aspect. Mood—for example, indicative and subjunctive—expresses a speaker's attitude toward or evaluation of the meaning a clause conveys and is expressed by auxiliary verbs and the absence of third person singular, present tense, indicative -*s* in English: *he take* versus *he takes*, for example. (Mood will not be discussed further.)

English typically marks tense and aspect through auxiliary verbs and inflectional suffixes, both of which are limited in JC compared to English. JC instead usually marks tense and aspect (and mood) by putting a tense-aspect free morpheme in front of the verb—or by leaving the verb in its **stem form**, that is, with neither markers in front nor affixes. The morphemes in front of the verb are called **TMA particles**, since they are used to mark mood too.

In what follows, you will find a basic description of some ways to express tense and aspect in JC. Not all grammatical subtleties are included.

One way of marking **progressive aspect** in JC is by putting /a/ before the verb stem. (An example of progressive aspect in English is the sentence *She is selling mangoes.*) Progressive aspect indicates that a situation is ongoing at the time the sentence refers to (present, past, etc.). Progressive aspect in JC is not influenced by tense: it is the same for present and past actions, and /a/ itself does not convey tense. (In English, where the verb suffix /-ɪŋ/ or /-ɪn/ serves the same function as /a/ in JC, tense is marked on the obligatory preceding auxiliary verb *be*.) The following JC examples illustrate this:

(1) a. Mi a ron   'I am running'
     b. Mi a ron   'I was running'

(2) a. Dem a chat   'They are talking'
     b. Dem a chat   'They were talking'

The tense (past, present, future) of the preceding JC examples is usually figured out by using the social context of the speaker's remark or conversation.

Habitual aspect is like progressive aspect because it refers to an ongoing situation. Habitual aspect expresses that an action, event, or state of affairs has been in effect for a significantly long period of time, whereas progressive aspect focuses just on the time when the sentence is being uttered. Whether a length of time is significantly long or not depends on the conversational context and expectations. The English sentence *She sells mangoes* signals habitual aspect. Note that this sentence implies that it is her job. *She is selling mangoes* indicates only that she is doing it now, or perhaps these days, but not for a significantly long period of time.

Habitual aspect and also progressive aspect can be used to express uninterrupted situations or ones that are interrupted—in other words, ones that occur over and over again. An example of an interrupted situation occurs in the sentence *He's hitting the nail with the hammer.* The hitting is interrupted, occurring over and over again. But every time he hits the nail, it's considered part of the same ongoing situation.

Historically, habitual aspect used to be usually marked identically to progressive aspect, and it is still possible—though rare—to use /a/ + *verb* (stem) to convey the habitual meaning. In contemporary JC, habitual aspect is usually expressed with just the plain verb stem, with no preceding TMA particle. Example (3) may (in some speech contexts) express habitual meaning, as indicated by the gloss. It does so with the optional /a/ or without it. (The parentheses indicate that /a/ is optional):

(3)   Mi (a) ron   'I run (habitually)'

(Remember that, with /a/, this sentence may also express progressive aspect, as in the examples above.) More details about tense and aspect in JC will be provided in the problem sets.

Further Reading

Jamaican was the first Caribbean English creole to be extensively described using modern linguistic methods. The first generative grammar of a creole was Bailey's (1966), and the first comprehensive etymological dictionary was Cassidy and LePage's (1967). JC remains among the best-researched creoles, having been the subject of language studies of many kinds, unlike most creoles. The references section provides an idea of the range of scholarship on JC.

Problem Sets

For the problems in this chapter, when precision is required, as in Table 9.1 and in the problem sets on palatalization, IPA is used within phonetic brackets []. Where phonetic detail is irrelevant, and/or phonemic representation is required, the Cassidy orthography is used, enclosed in phonemic slashes / /. Occasionally, English or JC words are marked, as in dictionary fashion, to indicate their stress patterns. They may be given either in English spelling or in phonemic slashes with stress marking.

Palatalization

Table 9.1 illustrates English words belonging to different historical word classes. (**Word classes** are simply groups of words whose pronunciations have often changed together throughout the history of a language, in this case English.) The third column lists the pronunciations in the prestigious southern British "Received Pronunciation" (RP) accent (used by the royal family and other high-status groups). Though RP was not the historical input to JC, it conveniently preserves vowel distinctions made in many former and present-day British English varieties. In regard to vowels, it is also important to note that JC has a phonemic length distinction with low vowels: /a/ and /a:/ (for example, in JC orthography, /kat/ 'cot' contrasts with /kaat/ 'caught').

The table also gives the vowels for the equivalent words in JC, phonemically transcribed, indicating whether these JC words may variably occur with the

TABLE 9.1 English vowels and word classes with Jamaican Creole equivalents

Word class	English example words	Corresponding RP vowel	JC vowel	JC example word	Palatal glide
Short *a*	cat, gas, *can'dle, Ca'nada*	[æ] short low front unrounded V	/a/	/kyat/	y
Short *o*	cot, *cot'tage, com'mon*	[ɒ] short low back rounded V	/a/	/kat/	–
Broad *a*	can't, cast, calf	[a:] long low back unrounded V	/aa/	/kyaan/	y
Long open *o*	caught, call, cawed	[ɔ:] long mid backrounded lax V	/aa/	/kaat/	–
a before *r*	card, *gar'den, gar'gle*	[a:] long low back unrounded V	/aa/	/kyaad/	y
o before *r*	cord, *cor'ner, Gor'don*	[ɔ:] long mid back rounded lax V	/aa/	/kaad/	–

Note: The Jamaican Creole material uses Jamaican Creole orthography graphemes, not the International Phonetic Alphabet.

palatalized phoneme. Not every word that is eligible always has a palatalized velar, but words that are not eligible never receive one.

Note: In JC words of two or more syllables, I will mark primary stress before the stressed syllable (e.g., *'after*). Notice that stress in JC does not always fall where American English speakers might expect.

Examine the data in Table 9.1 carefully and answer the following questions:

1. To arrive at a statement of where the palatalized velar phonemes /ky/ and /gy/ in JC show up, use one phonetic feature to fill in the blank in the following statement:

   JC words that have the palatalized velar phonemes /ky/ and /gy/ correspond to words in RP that have /k/ and /g/ in front of _____ vowels.

2. Now, along with the data in the table, take into account the JC pronunciations of the additional words in (4), which also show a palatal glide (in JC orthography):

   (4) *English word*   *JC word*
        'garage   /'gyaridj/
        me'chanic   /me'kyanik/
        New'castle   /nyu'kyasl/

   Note that these are all short-*a* words because the syllables beginning with the palatalized velars belong to the short-*a* word class. Note also that *garage* is stressed on the first syllable in British English, rhyming with *carriage*. *Newcastle* occurs in British English with two different stress patterns: one on the first syllable, and one – as here in JC– on the second.

   Assuming that these words conform to the statement provided in the first question, what must the corresponding RP vowel be in these three words? Explain your answer.

3. Now consider the following word in (5) with a variant (different) pronunciation of the JC word for *mechanic*:

   (5) *English word*   *JC word*
        'mechanic   /'makanik/

   If one assumes that this variant pronunciation existed in English and that it had a low unrounded vowel in the second syllable, then what has been presented thus far about palatalization would predict that the corresponding JC word would have /ky/. But this English model was *not* incorporated into JC with /ky/. Comparing the words in (4) with the others in Table 9.1, what about the phonology of the word in (5) could account for /k/ instead of /ky/? (Hint: Think about where stress falls in the words.)

4. Now consider the following example word, assuming that the English model had /k/ preceding a low unrounded vowel:

(6)   rein'carnate /riiyenkaa'niet/ but not (ungrammatical)
      */riiyen'kyaaniet/

Taking into consideration how many syllables precede the palatalized consonants in the rest of the data, explain why /ky/ does not occur in this JC word.

Tense and Aspect

Take into account what has been presented about JC tense and aspect in this chapter and respond to the following:

5. Translate this English sentence into JC: *The woman is selling mangoes.* (These are the words you will need: *di* = the; *uman* = woman; *sel* = sell; *manggo* = mango.)
6. a.   What are the two ways to translate into JC *The woman* (habitually) *sells mangoes?*
    b.   Which translation would one hear most of the time nowadays?

Stativity takes account of whether a verb's meaning describes a state (**stative** verbs) or an action/event (**nonstative** or **dynamic** verbs; I will use the term *dynamic*). Thus, a verb itself may be stative or dynamic. These aspects inhere in the meaning of the verb itself. Stative verbs themselves convey the meaning that a situation is ongoing; the situation may be short, long, or even of permanent duration. For example, *have* is a stative verb. If you say *She has brown hair*, you're talking about a usually permanent situation. If you say *He has a pimple*, you're usually talking about a situation of short duration: normally, the pimple will soon go away. Typical stative verbs, in both English and JC, have meanings such as 'have', 'know', 'belong', 'need', 'contain', 'trust', 'want', 'cost', 'depend', and so on.

Just as in English, stative verbs in JC are not normally marked as having progressive aspect by a word or suffix (the TMA particle /a/ in JC or the morpheme *-ing* in English). So, in English, for example, one can say *I belong to a club* but not *★I am belonging to a club* (starred because it is ungrammatical). So, in JC, stative verbs do not appear with progressive (or habitual) /a/: their inherent meaning already refers to an ongoing situation, as do the progressive and habitual aspects. (There are actually some exceptions, but they won't concern us.)

7. Is the English verb *sell* stative or dynamic? (Hint: Is it ungrammatical in the progressive, for example, *He's selling mangoes?*)

Only dynamic verbs can be marked as progressive. So the JC TMA marker cannot occur with stative verbs to express progressive aspect. Remember that stative verbs, by virtue of their meaning, refer to ongoing situations.

8. Translate the English sentence *I (habitually) want mangoes* into JC, in the way it would normally be said nowadays. (English *want* is *waan* in JC.)

Nouns and Determiners

In this section we will look at JC nouns and articles; the latter are called *determiners* by linguists. Rather than getting into a rather complicated discussion of grammatical details, we will simply think about how sentences can be translated between JC and English. (For more information, see Patrick 1999 and 2004.) Keep in mind that in this discussion, you will learn more about nouns than you were told in the discussion above. Consider the following examples:

(7) a. *Di uman waan di manggo.*   'The woman wants the mango.'
     b. *Di uman waan manggo.*   'The woman wants mangoes.'
     c. *Di uman waan di manggo-dem.*   'The woman wants the mangoes.'
     d. *Di uman waan wan manggo.*   'The woman wants a mango.'
     e. *Di uman waan manggos.*   'The woman wants mangoes.'

Note that there are two ways to translate *The woman wants mangoes* into JC, one provided in (7b) and the other in (7e).

9. Morphologically, how is the JC noun *manggos* in (7e) more like the English sentence's noun than the JC noun in (7b)?
10. Which sentence, (7b) or (7e), is more basilectal (more different grammatically from English)?
11. Translate the following into English in the present tense.
    a. *Di uman waan di chrii-dem.* (*chrii* = tree)
    b. *Di uman waan di manggo chrii.*
    c. *Di uman waan wan mekyanik.* (mekyanik = mechanic)
    d. *Wan mekyanik waan manggo.*
    e. *Di uman sel manggo.*

References

Bailey, Beryl Loftman. 1966. *Jamaican Creole syntax*. Cambridge: Cambridge University Press.

Bilby, Kenneth. 1983. How the "older heads" talk: A Jamaican Maroon spirit possession language. *Nieuwe West-Indische Gids* 57.1–2: 37–88.

Cassidy, Frederic G. 1961. *Jamaica talk: Three hundred years of the English language in Jamaica*. London: MacMillan.

Cassidy, Frederic G., and Robert B. Le Page, eds. 1967 (1980, 2nd ed.). *Dictionary of Jamaican English*. New York: Cambridge University Press.

Cooper, Carolyn. n.d. *Jamaica Woman Tongue* [blog using Jamaican Creole]. http://carolynjoy cooper.wordpress.com/

DeCamp, David. 1971. Towards a generative analysis of a post-creole speech continuum. In Dell Hymes, ed., *Pidginization and creolization of languages*, 349–370. Cambridge: Cambridge University Press.

Edwards, Viv. 1986. *Language in a black community*. Clevedon: Multilingual Matters.

Jamaican Language Unit. 2001. Spelling Jamaican the Jamaican way. *Teaching materials on Jamaican Creole orthography*. Kingston, JA: University of the West Indies at Mona. http://www.mona.uwi.edu/dllp/jlu/documents/spelling-jamaican-the-jamaican-way-Handout.pdf

Patrick, Peter L. 1997. Style and register in Jamaican Patwa. In Edgar W. Schneider, ed., *Englishes around the world: Studies in honour of Manfred Görlach*. Vol. 2, *Caribbean, Africa, Asia, Australasia*, 41–56. Amsterdam: John Benjamins.

Patrick, Peter L. 1999. *Urban Jamaican Creole: Variation in the mesolect*. Varieties of English Around the World G17. Amsterdam: John Benjamins.

Patrick, Peter L. 2004. Jamaican Creole: Morphology and syntax. In Bernd Kortmann, Edgar W. Schneider, Clive Upton, Rajend Mesthrie, and Kate Burridge, eds., *A handbook of varieties of English*. Vol. 2, *Morphology and syntax*, 407–438. Topics in English Linguistics. Berlin: Mouton de Gruyter.

Pollard, Velma. 1994. *Dread talk: The language of Rastafari*. Kingston, JA: Canoe Press.

Sebba, Mark. 1993. *London Jamaican: Language systems in interaction*. London: Longman.

Sutcliffe, David. 1982. *British Black English*. Oxford: Blackwell.

10

SOUTHWEST SPANISH

MaryEllen Garcia

Introduction

"Andale pues. Ay te miro." If you can understand this way of leave-taking, then you are familiar with the dialect of Spanish that will be examined in this chapter. For those of you who do not, it translates roughly as "Alright, then. See you around." Not every Mexican American or Chicano would use these very words, but it is within the bounds of the wide-ranging dialect that linguists call Southwest Spanish. Of course, no translation can give the full flavor and effect of an utterance in this dialect, spoken as it is by a group of people who share a common culture, ancestry, and history, as well as a common ethnic language.

The term **Southwest Spanish** (SWS) refers to the Spanish spoken by speakers of Mexican heritage. It is a cover term for many local dialects and encompasses a wide range of linguistic phenomena. The majority of the estimated 20.5 million Mexican-heritage speakers live in the southwestern U.S., which includes Texas, California, New Mexico, Arizona, and Colorado. All of these states share a very long Hispanic tradition due to their exploration and settlement history, first by Spain and subsequently by Mexico. However, this group has extended its presence beyond this region in recent times, which will be addressed in the next section.

History

The Spanish explorations from the sixteenth through the eighteenth centuries accounted for early settlements in New Mexico (1598) and in Texas (El Paso del Norte, 1659, and San Antonio, 1718). With religious conversion as their goal, Spanish priests established missions along California's Pacific coast (San Diego, 1769). Spanish descendants from New Mexico founded a colony in the San Luis Valley in Colorado in 1851.

Mexico's political independence from Spain in 1810 meant that by the nineteenth century, immigration northward was by Mexican nationals rather than Spanish colonizers. The Treaty of Guadalupe Hidalgo, signed in Texas in 1848 after the U.S. war against Mexico, gave much land formerly belonging to Mexico to the U.S., making the Rio Grande the geographic and political boundary between the two countries. The cession of lands by Mexico in the mid-1800s paved the way for Anglo-Americans to expand westward in greater numbers, soon becoming the dominant group in the Southwest culturally, socially, politically, and linguistically. More Mexican immigration occurred due to the expansion of the U.S. railway system to the West in the late 1800s, coupled with the growth of agricultural enterprise in California and Texas.

The twentieth century saw the greatest immigration northward, from 1910 to 1930, largely due to the Mexican Revolution and its aftermath. Thousands of Mexican nationals emigrated to the U.S. primarily for economic reasons. The bracero program, lasting from 1942 to 1964, allowed temporary workers to hold jobs legally in agriculture, the railroads, and food processing. In the 1980s, amnesty for Mexicans who had crossed the border without legal documentation created the opportunity for members of this group to legalize their status in the U.S. Between 1990 and 2000, Nevada's Hispanic population more than tripled, and the number of Mexican-origin immigrants dramatically increased in the Midwest, South, and Northeast.

In brief, the Hispanic tradition in the Southwest begins much earlier than the Anglo tradition in this region. Further, while the Rio Grande, the political border between the U.S. and Mexico, has been an important symbol of the official cultural and linguistic separation of the two countries, it has been only somewhat effective as a physical barrier between them. Entry into the U.S. from Mexico via the border states is a contentious issue even today. Whatever the entry point, continued immigration from Mexico as well as from Central and South America has contributed to the linguistic mix of the Spanish spoken in the Southwest. Although the term SWS has a regional focus, it also encompasses the Spanish of Mexican-heritage speakers who now reside in different parts of the U.S., particularly the Midwest and the South.

Social Context

The primary reasons for Mexican immigration to the U.S. in the twentieth century were political and social change in Mexico and greater economic opportunity to the north. Many of those who crossed the Rio Grande were from the working classes in Mexico who were willing to work at hard labor, in agriculture, or in the service sector—in brief, trading their sweat equity for a chance that their children might have a good public education and better lives than they themselves had left. However, the dominant English-speaking society was wary of this generally darker-skinned, racially mestizo (i.e., mixed) group who did not speak English well, if at all. The immigrants were seen as unskilled and uneducated, taking lower-paying jobs and living in the poor parts of town. Social and cultural marginalization was the norm for this group in many cities in the Southwest. It was in this social context that Mexican Americans born to immigrant parents struggled to learn English and to integrate themselves into the more advantaged group in their communities.

Their class-based alienation from the mainstream was reinforced by their use of Spanish; a society that spoke only English viewed them with suspicion. The sons and daughters of the immigrants born in the U.S. were made to speak only English and were punished for speaking Spanish in school, even though it was usually their primary home language. While this practically ensured that they would learn English, it damaged their self-esteem and fostered a reluctance to pass along their mother tongue to their own children, that is, to the third generation. This not only jeopardized the maintenance of Spanish in the community but also on a very personal level presented a barrier to communicating with elders in the family, who were likely to be monolingual in the ethnic language. The failure of many schools to teach bilingually also put up a barrier to the transmission of Spanish, particularly of the more formal, academic variety. While language shift to English may be ongoing in older communities, it is the influx of new immigrants that bolsters the present-day vitality of the language in the Southwest and elsewhere. For the near future, the projected increase in the Hispanic population in the U.S. may provide the impetus for the revitalization of Spanish in both older and newer Mexican-heritage communities.

The Spanish spoken by Mexican Americans is from an oral tradition, considered vernacular Spanish by linguists, that has been handed down across centuries. As is typical of oral traditions, the spoken language reflects a variety not found in textbooks, with features such as archaic forms, regional vocabulary, and folksy pronunciations. *Vernacular* indicates an informal speech style that all speakers may use on occasion, and the term is also used in a second sense to mean a nonstandard variety, as it is elsewhere in this book. (For more on *vernacular* and *dialect*, see the introductory chapters and the chapters on vernacular dialects of English and African American English.) Spoken by a community in a locale where English is prevalent and has more prestige, this vernacular Spanish from Mexico has incorporated some features from the language and society it is in contact with.

Many folk terms exist to refer to this variety, such as *Spanglish*, which refers to a mix of Spanish and English. The mixing of these languages is also captured by the term *Tex-Mex*, which adds a regional focus. The term *Pocho Spanish* refers to the Mexican-heritage transplant to the U.S. who can no longer speak Spanish "correctly" because of the "contamination" from English. All of these terms can be used to denigrate this contact dialect and its speakers by implying that it is not a true linguistic variety. In contrast, although linguists recognize that some people judge bilingual vernaculars as "incorrect" or even "bad Spanish"—terms that exhibit biased, subjective linguistic prejudice—they do not make value judgments in studying language and recognize all dialects as rule-governed and worthy of respect. The term SWS is a way to refer to the Mexican American dialect objectively, without the emotional and judgmental baggage that other terms might carry with them.

Some Linguistic Features

This bilingual speech variety, a combination of Mexican Spanish and informal English, is similar to other Spanish-English varieties in the U.S. Only some of the more notable features of SWS will be presented here, including characteristic **pronunciation** (phonetics, phonology), **vocabulary** (lexicon), **codeswitching** (alternation between languages), and **Caló** (street slang). (For more on *codeswitching*, please see the "Language Contact" chapter.)

Some Pronunciations in the SWS Vernacular

SWS is a dialect of Latin American Spanish and so has the same inventory of phonemes and the same phonology as other Latin American dialects do. It also exhibits many of the same variable pronunciations that are typical of vernacular Spanish around the world. Not surprisingly, some of these variable pronunciations are also used by speakers of standard dialects when speaking informally. Vernacular pronunciations often result in more regular patterns (**paradigms**), differing from those in the standard because they are not constrained by rules of correctness (**codification**) as standards are. Some variations in pronunciation in the vernacular are due to the extension of phonological tendencies (**rules**) to a broader range of phonetic environments, as in the following examples.

Diphthongization

In the standard variety, two adjacent vowels are pronounced in one syllable if one is high /i, u/, with the high vowel phoneme becoming a glide, as in *miedo* /miedo/ → [mje.ðo] 'fear' and *bueno* /bueno/ → [bwe.no] 'good'. In the vernacular, this rule can extend to mid vowels /e, o/, as in *peor* 'worse', pronounced [pjor], and *poema* 'poem', pronounced [pwe.ma].

DIPTHONGIZATION, CONTRACTION, MONOPHTHONGIZATION, AND HIATUS

Dipthongization is an unconscious phonological process that converts two vowels into one syllable. Languages also employ the process of **monophthongization**, in which a diphthong becomes a single vowel. **Contraction**, a process very similar to monophthongization, is the elimination of a vowel, resulting in one syllable instead of two. On the other hand, in careful pronunciation vowels may be pronounced separately even if one immediately follows the other. This separation is called a **hiatus**.

Contraction or Omission of Vowels

In the standard variety, two adjacent vowels are pronounced as if lengthened, as in *creer* [kré:r] 'to believe' or *leer* [lé:r] 'to read', or with a slight pause (hiatus) between them, as in *ahora* [a.ó.ra] 'now' or *maestra* [ma.és.tra] 'teacher'. In the vernacular, two like vowels may contract into one, resulting in [krér] and [lér], and a sequence of different vowels may have one omitted, resulting in [ó.ra] and [més.tra]. Both processes eliminate the hiatus in the word, changing a pronunciation disfavored in most languages to a favored one.

Deletion of Fricative Consonants

In the standard varieties of Spanish, the stop (**occlusive**) consonants /b, d, g/ can weaken to the fricative (or **spirant**) [β, ð, ɣ], respectively, between vowels, as well as in other environments. A further process of weakening may delete the intervocalic fricatives in this and other vernacular Spanish varieties. In SWS phonemic /b/, for example, may be barely perceptible or absent altogether (deleted) following a stressed syllable, resulting in *necesitaba* 'I/he needed' [ne.se.si.tá:] or *estaba* 'I/he was' [es.tá:], with the stressed vowel lengthened. Another example is the loss of phonemic /d/ between vowels, as in *nada* [ná.a] 'nothing' and *todo* [tó.o] 'everything'. The deletion of intervocalic -d- is also well known in Andalusian, a dialect of southern Spain that is closely related to the vernacular dialects of the Americas.

The Lexicon of SWS

The Importance of Word Borrowing

Evidence of contact with English in SWS is found in the areas of the vocabulary (lexicon/*léxico*) and semantics via loan translations (calques/*calcos*), phrases based on English translated into Spanish. As the chapter "Language Contact" explains, words are often borrowed when people live with two languages and two cultures in the same geographic space.

LOAN TRANSLATIONS AND CALQUES

Loan translations, also called *calques*, are word-for-word translations of words or phrases from one language to another.

What about Borrowings in SWS?

Words tend to be borrowed into another language when the item or concept is lacking in that culture or society. In various parts of the Spanish-speaking world, words are often borrowed from English to fill lexical voids, for example, *jersey* 'sweater', *esmoquin* 'smoking jacket, dinner jacket', *esquiar* 'to ski', *estándar* 'standard', and *esnobismo* 'snobbery'. Notice that the borrowed words (*préstamos*) are incorporated phonologically into the pronunciation patterns of the language doing the borrowing, as is normal when one language borrows from another. SWS has many more *préstamos* than do the monolingual varieties, as it is spoken in an English-speaking environment. Here are a few contextualized examples of borrowings used in SWS that are not also used in Standard Spanish. The standard (monolingual) form of the *préstamo* is given in parentheses.

(1) La familia Gómez fue a un <u>piquenique</u> en el parque.
'The Gómez family went on a <u>picnic</u> in the park.'
('picnic' = *día de campo*)

(2) Ellos tienen que pagar sus <u>biles</u> el primer día del mes.
'They have to pay their <u>bills</u> on the first day of the month.'
('bills' = *cuentas*)

(3) Las <u>brecas</u> de la <u>troca</u> no trabajan.
'The <u>brakes</u> of the <u>truck</u> don't work.'
('brakes' = *frenos*, 'truck' = *camión*)

Note that the monolingual Spanish versions in some cases might not have the same cultural connotations or in other cases might not be part of the bilingual speaker's lexicon.

Another lexical result of Spanish-English language contact is the false cognate (*cognado falso*), a word that exists in both languages and has a common origin but whose meanings are no longer interchangeable. Not only are the words similar in form, but they also legitimately belong to both languages. It is how they are used *semantically* that accounts for the differences between the SWS vernacular and a monolingual variety of Spanish. For example, in (3) above, monolingual Spanish would use *funcionar* to refer to 'work' in regard to machines and *trabajar* only when referring to people. But in SWS *trabajar* is extended to machines as well as people. In the bilingual community, Spanish words that are similar phonologically and semantically to English may be appropriated to achieve cognitive efficiency for the speaker.

FALSE COGNATES

False cognates are words that seem to be identical in two languages but have different meanings or are not totally interchangeable.

Other examples of false cognates are found in the examples below. The monolingual Spanish lexical choices are given in parentheses.

(4) El hijo de María <u>atiende</u> el <u>colegio</u> en Austin.
'Maria's son <u>attends</u> <u>college</u> in Austin.'
('attends' = *asiste a*, 'college' = *la universidad*)

(5) Estudiamos mucho en la <u>librería</u> para mejorar nuestros <u>grados</u>.
'We study in the <u>library</u> a lot to improve our <u>grades</u>.'
('library' = *biblioteca*, 'grades' = *notas, calificaciones*)

(6) Ella <u>realizó</u> que tenía que <u>registrarse</u> para ese curso.
'She <u>realized</u> that she had to <u>register</u> for that course.'
('realized' = *se dió cuenta (de)*, 'register for' = *inscribirse en*)

Loan Translations

Another influence from English appears to be the result of translating literally from one language to another, creating a loan translation. However, when a community is accustomed to using certain expressions for certain concepts, it is no longer a conscious, active translation process by the speaker but is now simply the normal way of expressing these concepts and meanings. For example, *dar pa' tras* 'to give back', *mandar pa' tras* 'to send back', and *ir pa' tras* 'to go back, return' are a few of many expressions with *pa' tras* 'back'. (Compare to monolingual *devolver* 'to give/to send back' and *volver* 'to go back, return'.) Roundly disparaged by many monolingual speakers who would prefer that dialects not be influenced at all by contact languages, *pa' tras* is very productive; that is, it can be used to create many words and expressions. Therefore, it is an important building block for the SWS vernacular. Other examples of loan translations built on English meanings but using Spanish words are the following:

(7) Voy a poner la ropa en mi <u>máquina</u> <u>de lavar</u>.
'I'm going to put the clothes in the <u>washing machine</u>.'
('washing machine' = *lavadora*)

(8) El dentista decidió <u>correr por mayor</u> de la ciudad.
'The dentist decided to <u>run for mayor</u> of the city.'
('to run for mayor' = *hacerse candidato para alcalde*)

(9) Ella <u>tuvo un buen tiempo</u> en la fiesta.
'She <u>had a good time</u> at the party.'
('to have a good time' = *divertirse, pasarlo bien*)

Codeswitching

The languages used in any bilingual community are considered distinct codes, and switching between them is called **codeswitching**. This chapter does not discuss the syntactic rules involved in codeswitching but rather what may motivate speakers to switch between languages in the same utterance or conversation.

In a typical conversation, some switches may be employed to fill a **semantic gap**; for example, switches of a single noun, verb, or phrase may be used because that word or phrase is associated with the other language, such as *brother-in-law* or *Luby's Cafeteria*. Some switches may have to do with cohesion, such as the use of **discourse markers** to underscore transitions in the discourse, such as *okay*, *but*, *pues* 'well', and *entonces* 'then', or to acknowledge listeners, such as with *you know*. Some may be related to a speaker's **stylistic resources**, such as emphasizing a point by using a word or phrase in the other language, or emphasizing a phrase or sentence by repeating it in a second language after it was already expressed in the other language. In the same vein, speakers may unconsciously remember an utterance from another conversation and **quote** it in the language used by the original speaker. Others may use switches for interactional reasons, for example, following the lead of a previous speaker by **accommodating** to her language choice. Further, the speaker's own **identity** may come into play with emblematic tags, such as *¿verdad?* or *¿qué no?* to signal ethnicity, or fillers, such as *este* instead of *uh*, used to hold the floor. Also, a switch can occur for **formulaic routines**, for example, to close a dialogue: *Andale, pues* or *Have a nice day*. (Valdés 1982 suggests most of these categories.)

SEMANTIC GAP

Semantic gap refers to areas of meaning that the other language does not express precisely or at all.

DISCOURSE MARKERS

Discourse markers are words or phrases, such as *pues*, *well*, or *OK*, that are usually not very meaningful in themselves and are used repeatedly in speech for a variety of important purposes, providing the listener with cues about the structure of the discourse and the speaker's meaning.

FORMULAIC ROUTINES

Formulaic routines are common phrases often used as a way of performing socially expected courtesies, such as greetings, thanks, leave-takings, and such.

Even though the reasons for many switches may be apparent, it may not be possible to account for all of them. In the case of SWS, codeswitching can be one strategy used by less fluent speakers of Spanish to maintain some ethnic language ability. However, for other communities, linguists recognize that the mixing of two codes can lead to the creation of a new bilingual mixed language.

(See the chapter "Language Contact" and Thomason 2001 for an introduction to this topic.)

Pachuco Caló

Many bilingual speakers in the southwestern U.S. know the word *Caló*, referring to a speech style that was popular with Mexican American youth during the 1940s and 1950s, called *Pachucos*. Pachuco Caló was used by these young people as a way of displaying their unique identity that was bilingual and bicultural, defiant of the social and linguistic norms of their parents. This insider speech style also served as a way of displaying the speaker's cleverness and creativity by wordplay and novel expressions.

CALÓ

Caló is a special, in-group way of speaking in the Mexican American community, considered a secret slang.

PACHUCOS

Pachucos, originally meaning 'youths from El Paso', later was applied to young men who dressed, acted, and spoke like the earlier El Paso youths.

Caló began as a criminal argot, used as a secret code to hide meanings from authorities by another marginalized population, the Spanish Gypsies, officially called the Rom. From the Pachuco youth, Caló gradually spread to general SWS. Once-secret meanings can now be found in specialized Caló dictionaries and in dictionaries of Mexican American Spanish.

ARGOT

An *argot* is a secret way of speaking associated with criminals universally.

ROM

Rom is the preferred name for the group of people previously known as Gypsies. Their traditional language is Romani, an Indo-Aryan language more closely related to Sanskrit than it is to Spanish.

Caló includes many elements of general SWS, such as word borrowing, phrasal calquing, and codeswitching, as well as Mexican idioms (**modismos**), slang, and taboo words, that is, words that are avoided in polite society but can be deliberately used to display strong emotion and defiance of conventional norms. Traditional Pachuco Caló includes words that can be traced back to Sanskrit via Rom,

TABLE 10.1 Categories of traditional Pachuco Caló

From Gypsy Caló	Gloss	Examples	Gloss
bato, vato	'young man, guy'	¡Quiúbole, ese bato!	'What's up, guy?'
bute, buti /-ri	'many, much, a lot'	Estoy buti cansado.	'I'm really tired.'
calcos	'shoes'	calcos chaineados	'shined shoes'

Neologisms	Gloss	Example	Gloss
rucaila	'girl, young woman'	Y me dijo la rucaila …	'And the girl said to me …'
capirucha	'capital'	Él es de la capirucha.	'He is from the capital (city).'
cáfiro	'coffee'	¿Ya está el cáfiro?	'Is the coffee ready?'

Wordplay	Gloss	Example	Gloss
la birria,la bironga	'the beer'	¿Tomaste la birria? ¿Tomaste la bironga?	'Did you drink the beer?'
Simón	'yes, sure'	Simón, claro que sí.	'Sure, of course.'
Nelson	'no, no way'	Nelson, no voy.	'No way. I'm not going.'

Pachuco phrases	Gloss	Example	Gloss
al alba	'aware, sharp'	Ponte al alba.	'Watch out.'
de aquellas	'extremely good'	¡Es de aquellas!	'It's really cool!'
águilas	'keep an eye out'	Águilas, la chota.	'Hey, look, the cops.'

neologisms (invented words, or **neologismos**), plays on words, metaphors, and other strategies. Some examples of traditional Pachuco and contemporary SWS Caló are listed in Table 10.1.

Summary

In sum, this chapter has shown that the Spanish of Mexican Americans, known as SWS, is a vernacular that shares phonological processes with the vernaculars of Latin America and Spain. Linguists consider all language varieties to be legitimate, having their own social spheres of appropriateness and their own grammatical norms or rules. The primary difference between vernacular Spanish dialects in monolingual communities outside of the U.S. and SWS (as well as other varieties of Spanish spoken in English-speaking areas) is the influence of English. That influence shows up primarily in the lexicon and in codeswitching.

Further Reading

Scholarship on SWS has been done in the tradition of structural dialectology (e.g., Espinosa 1909) and in a variety of other structural and descriptive approaches (e.g., Hernández-Chávez, Beltramo, and Cohen 1975). Dictionaries of this dialect (for example, Cobos 1983; Fuentes and López 1974; Galván and Teschner 1994) have provided definitions of single-word borrowings and other notable lexical usages. There have been syntheses of research on the Mexican American linguistic repertoire (e.g., Peñalosa 1980) or theoretically oriented discussions of it (Sánchez 1994).

The field has changed significantly since 1975 when one bibliographer lamented "the lack of research on syntax, semantics, sociolinguistics, theoretical issues, and so forth" (Teschner, Bills, and Craddock 1975: xxii). Recent studies have included work in codeswitching, word borrowing, discourse analysis, the ethnography of communication, pragmatics, language choice, and language maintenance and shift, as well as theoretical and pedagogical questions. Some of these perspectives are reflected in various chapters of anthologies (for example, Duran 1981; Amastae and Elías-Olivares 1982; Elías-Olivares 1983; Elías-Olivares et al. 1985). These early volumes have inspired others, which readers are invited to discover on their own.

Problem Sets

Phonology

Reducing Hiatus: Beginning Level

1. After examining the data in Table 10.2, list the vowels that become glides in standard dialects and then describe the phonological context in which vowels become glides. (For the purposes of this exercise you may assume that the spelling of the Spanish words in the leftmost column represents the underlying form of the vowels. The periods in the transcriptions indicate syllable structure.)

TABLE 10.2 Beginning-level reducing hiatus data

Orthography	Standard	Vernacular SWS	Gloss
peine	[péj.ne]	[péj.ne]	'comb'
teatro	[te.á.tro]	[tjá.tro]	'theater'
peor	[pe.ór]	[pjór]	'worse'
trueno	[trwé.no]	[trwé.no]	'thunderclap'
golpear	[gol.pe.ár]	[gol.pjár]	'to hit'
lealtad	[le.al.tád]	[ljal.tád]	'loyalty'
león	[le.ón]	[ljón]	'lion'
pelear	[pe.le.ár]	[pe.ljár]	'to fight'
toalla	[to.á.ya]	[twá.ya]	'towel'
almohada	[al.mo.á.da]	[al.mwá.da]	'pillow'

TABLE 10.3 Intermediate-level reducing hiatus data

Orthography	Standard	Vernacular	Gloss
regatear	[re.ga.te.ár]	_____	'to haggle'
peón	[pe.ón]	_____	'peasant'
me habló	[me.a.bló]	_____	'he/she spoke to me'
teórico	[te.ó.ri.ko]	_____	'theoretic'
crear	[kre.ár]	_____	'to create'
te odia	[te.ó.dja]	_____	'he/she hates you'
se alarmó	[se.a.lar.mó]	_____	'he/she became alarmed'
te amo	[te.á.mo]	_____	'I love you'
lo hace	[lo.áse]	_____	'he/she does it'
cohete	[ko.é.te]	_____	'rocket'

2. What additional vowels may also become glides in vernacular SWS?
3. Using the features [+high] or [-high] and [+low] or [-low], restate the type of vowels that may become glides in (a) Standard Spanish dialects versus (b) vernacular Spanish dialects.

Reducing Hiatus: Intermediate Level

4. Now use your answer to (3) to fill in the blanks in Table 10.3 for the vernacular forms that may occur in varieties such as SWS. (Make sure to show syllable structure.)

Lexicon

Match the categories in (a)–(h) to the definitions below by writing the letter in the appropriate space.

a. Loan translation   d. Borrowed word   g. False cognate/lexical calque
b. Neologism   e. Gypsy Caló   h. Pachuco phrase
c. Semantic extension   f. Taboo word

5. _____ Lexical item originally from another language, such as *troca*, *bil*, and *dólar*.
6. _____ A string of words that has Spanish words but depends on English for its meaning, like *mandar pa' tras* 'to send back'.
7. _____ A word that has a similar form in the other language but that has a different meaning in formal Spanish, such as *aplicación* for 'application' or *atender* for 'to attend (school)'.
8. _____ An implicit comparison between one thing and another with which it shares a semantic feature, such as *bolillo*, 'a white roll', for 'Anglo person'. (This is also a type of metaphor.)

9. _____ A new nonsense word, such as *tú sábanas* 'you sheets' for *tú sabes* 'you know', which displays the combining of a real word and added syllables.

10. _____ An expression used by Mexican American teens in the 1940s and 1950s to sound cool, like *ponte trucha* for 'watch out'.

11. _____ Refers to topics that shouldn't be talked about in polite society; may be used frequently to rebel against authority, like *no tiene huevos* 'he doesn't have testicles' to represent 'courage'.

12. _____ Words introduced into Spanish by the Gypsies in Spain in the nineteenth century. Some of the words can be traced back to Sanskrit, like *bato* for 'guy'.

Codeswitching Exercise

Match these terms with their descriptions or examples below. The codeswitch into English is indicated by the use of capital letters. Provide a label from the following list for the part that is <u>underlined in the items</u>.

a. Single word/semantic gap
b. Triggered switch
c. Accommodation
d. Quotation

e. Formulaic routine
f. Discourse markers
g. Stylistic resources/emphasis
h. Identity markers (tags, fillers, etc.)

(These categories and some examples below are from Valdés 1982.)

13. _____ Susie recalls what her doctor told her:
"Me dijo <u>THAT IF I DON'T FEEL WELL, YOU KNOW, I NEED TO GET THE MEDICINE.</u>"
'He said to me' <u>THAT IF I DON'T FEEL WELL, YOU KNOW, I NEED TO GET THE MEDICINE</u>.

14. _____ Margie explains to her friend:
"Cada vez que iba, sabes, yo pagaba <u>TWENTY DOLLARS.</u>"
'Every time I went, you know, I paid' <u>TWENTY DOLLARS</u>.

15. _____ Porque allí hay <u>WALNUTS</u>. YOU DON'T LIKE THEM?
'Because it has' <u>WALNUTS</u>. YOU DON'T LIKE THEM?'

16. _____ 'Todo el tiempo vamos a comer <u>STEAKS</u>, tú sabes.'
'All the time we go to eat <u>STEAKS</u>, you know'

17. _____ <u>WELL</u>, a veces, <u>YOU KNOW</u>, me lo quiero pintar.
<u>WELL</u>, 'sometimes', <u>YOU KNOW</u>, 'I want to color it.'

18. _____ Mis hijos no saben nada de matemáticas. Nada. <u>NOT A THING</u>.
'My kids don't know anything about math. Nothing.' <u>NOT A THING</u>.

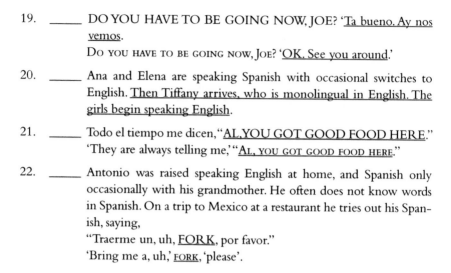

19. _____ DO YOU HAVE TO BE GOING NOW, JOE? 'Ta bueno. Ay nos vemos.

Do you have to be going now, Joe? 'OK. See you around.'

20. _____ Ana and Elena are speaking Spanish with occasional switches to English. Then Tiffany arrives, who is monolingual in English. The girls begin speaking English.

21. _____ Todo el tiempo me dicen, "AL, YOU GOT GOOD FOOD HERE."

'They are always telling me,' "AL, YOU GOT GOOD FOOD HERE."

22. _____ Antonio was raised speaking English at home, and Spanish only occasionally with his grandmother. He often does not know words in Spanish. On a trip to Mexico at a restaurant he tries out his Spanish, saying,

"Traerme un, uh, FORK, por favor."

'Bring me a, uh,' FORK, 'please'.

References

Amastae, Jon, and Lucía Elías-Olivares, eds. 1982. *Spanish in the United States: Sociolinguistic aspects.* Cambridge: Cambridge University Press.

Cobos, Ruben. 1983. *A dictionary of New Mexico and southern Colorado Spanish.* Santa Fe: Museum of New Mexico Press.

Duran, Richard P., ed. 1981. *Latino language and communicative behavior.* Norwood, NJ: Ablex.

Elías-Olivares, Lucía, ed. 1983. *Spanish in the U.S. setting: Beyond the Southwest.* Rossylyn, VA: National Clearinghouse for Bilingual Education.

Elías-Olivares, Lucía, Elizabeth A. Leone, René Cisneros, and John Gutierrez. 1985. *Spanish language use and public life in the USA.* The Hague: Mouton.

Espinosa, Aurelio M. 1909. *Studies in New Mexican Spanish, part I: Phonology.* Biblioteca de Dialectología Hispanoamericana 1, ed. Amado Alonso and Angel Rosenblat (1930). Buenos Aires: Instituto de Filología.

Fuentes, Dagoberto, and José A. López. 1974. *Barrio language dictionary: First dictionary of Caló.* La Puente, CA: El Barrio Publications.

Galván, Roberto A., and Richard V. Teschner. 1994. *El diccionario del español chicano / The dictionary of Chicano Spanish.* Lincolnwood, IL: National Textbook Co.

Hernández-Chávez, Eduardo, Anthony F. Beltramo, and Andrew D. Cohen. 1975. *El lenguaje de los chicanos.* Arlington, VA: Center for Applied Linguistics.

Peñalosa, Fernando. 1980. *Chicano sociolinguistics.* Rowley, MA: Newbury House.

Sánchez, Rosaura. 1994. *Chicano discourse: Socio-historic perspectives.* Houston, TX: Arte Público [Rowley, MA: Newbury House].

Teschner, Richard V., Garland D. Bills, and Jerry R. Craddock. 1975. *Spanish and English of United States Hispanos: A critical, annotated, linguistic bibliography.* Arlington, VA: Center for Applied Linguistics.

Thomason, Sarah G. 2001. *Language contact: An introduction.* Washington, DC: Georgetown University Press.

Valdés, Guadalupe. 1982 [1976]. Social interaction and code-switching patterns: A case study of Spanish/English alternation. In Jon Amastae and Lucía Elías-Olivares, eds., *Spanish in the United States: Sociolinguistic aspects*, 209–229. Cambridge: Cambridge University Press.

11

DOMINICAN SPANISH

Barbara E. Bullock and Almeida Jacqueline Toribio

Introduction

The diversity of the Spanish dialects spoken in the Caribbean has stimulated significant popular and scholarly attention. What emerges from the linguistic literature is that the Spanish of the Dominican Republic, while sharing many lexical and structural properties with other Caribbean varieties, also presents significant linguistic innovation, manifesting specific phonological, morphological, and syntactic features that differentiate this Spanish dialect from all others (cf. Henríquez-Ureña 1940; Jiménez Sabater 1975; Bullock and Toribio 2009).

The geography of the Dominican Republic alone entails that it is and has been linguistically much less insular than either Puerto Rico or Cuba since it occupies the eastern two-thirds of Hispaniola, an island shared with Haiti, a country of Creole and, to a much lesser extent, French speakers. (See the chapter on Haitian Creole for more information.) The relatively porous border between the two nations has created a situation of Spanish-Creole language contact that endures to this day. However, the extent to which there may be Creole-Spanish convergence remains to be investigated, as there are no apparent linguistic features of Dominican Spanish that can be unquestionably attributed to Haitian origins. Creole influence is imputed to be confined to the Spanish spoken by the *fronterizos*, those who live along the border (Lipski 1994), but it is possible that Dominicans' perception of "Haitianized" Spanish is founded more on racial and cultural stereotypes than on linguistic reality (cf. Bullock and Toribio forthcoming). Today, it is arguably the case that Dominican Spanish experiences more incursions from American English than from any other language.

History

In order to properly situate the unique linguistic development of contemporary Dominican Spanish, it is necessary to survey the historical context in which the dialect developed and thereby to understand the various contact situations that have arisen. Before the advent of the Spanish presence on Hispaniola in the fifteenth century, the island had served as a home to the Taíno. Taíno indigenous words are plentiful in Dominican Spanish, as they are elsewhere in varieties of Caribbean Spanish. Lexical items such as *jaiba* 'freshwater crab', *guano* 'a type of palm', *maní* 'peanuts', *macuto* 'a woven basket', *tusa* 'corncob', *bohío* 'hut', and the everyday expression *un chin* 'a small amount' speak to contact between the Spanish and the indigenous peoples. Other traces of Taíno forms particular to the Dominican Republic are found in toponyms (e.g., Cibao, Higüey, Maguana, Bahoruco, Dajabón) and, occasionally, in given names (e.g., Annacaona, Caonabo). Some Taíno words have even been borrowed into English from Spanish, for example, *maíz* 'corn', *canoas* 'canoes', *hamacas* 'hammocks', and *huracanes* 'hurricanes'. (We would like to thank MaryEllen Garcia for pointing these out.)

The Taíno population suffered greatly under the colonization of Santo Domingo (the original name for the Spanish part of Hispaniola), succumbing in large numbers to disease, to forced labor (the *encomienda* system), and to warfare against the Spanish colonizers. The dwindling numbers of Taíno laborers and the persistent refusal of the survivors to tolerate the harsh working conditions meant that the Spanish soon turned to the importation of African slaves, a move that set the stage for a new source of language contact that is reflected in the Africanisms found in the Dominican lexicon: for example, *guineo* 'banana', *mondongo* 'tripe stew', *cachimbo* 'tobacco pipe', and *fucú* 'evil spirit'.

When rich deposits of gold were discovered in Peru and Mexico, Spain's enthusiasm for its Caribbean colony waned and Santo Domingo was virtually abandoned for more than a century to the colonists, Indians, African slaves, maroons, and renegades who remained. The French, however, began to invest in Saint-Domingue (Haiti), importing massive numbers of slaves to work the prosperous sugar plantations until the slaves came to vastly outnumber the Europeans. The slave revolts of the late eighteenth century that led to Haitian independence also ultimately resulted in the Haitian occupation of Santo Domingo. The barriers—of language, religion, and skin color—that existed between the Haitians and the Dominicans made for uneasy alliances. And although the Haitians eventually helped the Dominicans gain their independence from Spain, there is a history of animosity between these two peoples that, at times, has been punctuated by horrific violence. This is reflected in a profound sentiment of *anti-haitianismo*, a polarizing brand of nationalism deliberately cultivated by the twentieth-century dictator Rafael Leonidas Trujillo Molina that remains widespread throughout the Dominican Republic (cf. Paulino 2005).

Given a great deal of political unrest and a depressed socioeconomic climate in the Dominican Republic, Dominicans began entering the U.S. in the early 1960s as transient immigrants and stayed to find employment, raise their families, and form enclave communities. The Dominican presence is especially strong in the South Bronx and in Upper Manhattan's Washington Heights, variously known as Quisqueya Heights (from the original Taíno name for the Cibao region, meaning 'mother of all lands'), *el pequeño Cibao* 'the little Cibao', and *el platanal* 'the plantain grove'. Migration to New York is so common that in the Dominican Republic the term *Dominican York* is often used to refer to a Dominican who lives anywhere in the U.S. However, while Dominicans have traditionally migrated to New York, and to the gateway communities of Bergen-Passaic (New Jersey), Providence (Rhode Island), Lawrence (Massachusetts), and Miami (Florida), over the last decade they have begun to establish new communities in smaller cities such as Raleigh and Charlotte (North Carolina), Grand Rapids (Michigan), and Reading and Harrisburg (Pennsylvania) (cf. Jensen et al. 2006). According to the U.S. Census Bureau's American Community Survey, approximately 1.4 million persons of Dominican origin resided in the U.S. in 2010, making them the fifth-largest immigrant group from Latin America and the Spanish-speaking Caribbean (following Mexicans, Puerto Ricans, Salvadorans, and Cubans).

Social Context

In the U.S., Dominicans are intensely loyal to their linguistic norms, maintaining and advancing the Dominican Spanish dialect even in the context of other, more conservative Latin American dialects. The continued use of the Dominican vernacular is a strong indicator that the immigrant community considers its language to be an important feature of its identity. Nevertheless, the difference between the community vernacular and the prescribed norm significantly impacts Dominicans' language behavior. In New York City and the surrounding area, Dominican Spanish is identified and evaluated as being of marginal status. Indeed, Zentella (1997) found that Dominicans themselves expressed highly negative opinions about Dominican Spanish, and 80% stated that Dominican Spanish should not be taught in schools. Especially vulnerable to the consequences of linguistic prejudice are children and adolescents, who are exposed to the variety at home and acquire forms that often become the basis for teachers' negative impressions and attendant efforts at remediation. To be sure, educators often fail to appreciate the ways in which dialects differ and the practical difficulties and familial alienation that imposing a normative standard may present. As observed by Hudson (1980: 200), "a child who gives up the forms of his local group and adopts those that are widely accepted in the nation would in fact be adopting forms that are the identifying symbols of another group."

But even in the Dominican Republic, where speakers are not confronted with direct criticism from (or comparison to) speakers of other Spanish dialects, Dominicans experience a great deal of linguistic insecurity. Dominican Spanish is stigmatized and undervalued for lacking certain features of an idealized standard—the

Castilian or European variety. Further contributing to their negative evaluations of their own speech is the widespread belief that Dominican Spanish has been "contaminated" by Haitian Creole, that is, that it is no longer "pure" Spanish. This accounts for Dominicans' dim view of the variety spoken in the northwest, where the contact with the neighboring nation is most pronounced. The popular view is that the best Spanish variety approximates the European norm and that the worst variety is spoken by those who are believed to be influenced by the language of the Haitians. Dominicans' predilection for the European Spanish variety, and repudiation of the influence of the Haitian language, speaks to a national "other-ing" and racialization of Haitians (cf. Toribio 2006).

These ideologies are upended for Dominicans who migrate to the U.S. These Dominican immigrants quickly realize that in the black/white racial dichotomy of their new country, it doesn't matter what they believe they are: in the U.S., they, like Haitians, are considered African descendants. Ill prepared to interpret and accept discrimination on these grounds, Dominican immigrants often seek out strategies for making themselves distinct from African Americans, and their use of the Spanish language affords one simple means of doing so. It is unquestionable that the social and racial context in which Dominicans find themselves—both on the island and in the U.S.—has contributed in large measure to their language loyalty as an expression of their heritage.

Some Linguistic Features

As noted, Dominican Spanish demonstrates phonological, morphological, and syntactic properties that distinguish it from other varieties of Spanish. Perhaps most salient is the regional variation in pronunciation. Persons with origins in the capital city of Santo Domingo are said to *hablar con la -l* 'speak with the -l', whereas those from the southern coastal region *hablan con la -r*, and those from the northwestern agricultural countryside of the Cibao Valley *hablan con la -i* (usu-ally pronounced with the glide [j]). Sample pronunciations are illustrated by the proper names in (1). (Note that periods indicate syllable breaks and that the apos-trophe precedes the stressed syllable.)

(1) | *Normative Spanish* | *Santo Domingo* | *Southern Coast* | *Cibao Valley* |
|---|---|---|---|
| Elsa [ˈel.sa] | [ˈel.sa] | [ˈeɾ.sa] | [ˈei.sa] |
| Arturo [aɾ.ˈtu.ɾo] | [al.ˈtu.ɾo] | [aɾ.ˈtu.ɾo] | [aj.ˈtu.ɾo] |

NORMATIVE SPANISH

We will use the term **normative Spanish** to label an idealized standard variety. This sort of variety is referred to as Standard Spanish in the chapter on Southwest Spanish. As in the case of English, there is more than one standard variety of Spanish.

More notably, the Dominican Spanish dialect has witnessed a decrease in morphological distinctions that may be due to other phonological processes. A feature attested across regional and social dialects is the weakening and deletion of syllable-final /s/. This segment can signal morphological information, such as plurality on articles, adjectives, and nouns, as in (2), in which the plural noun phrase 'the pretty houses' is rendered homophonous with the singular.

(2)		*Normative*	*Dominican*
la casa bonita (sg.)		[la.ˈka.sa.βo.ˈni.ta]	[la.ˈka.sa.βo.ˈni.ta]
las casas bonitas (pl.)		[las.ˈka.sas.βo.ˈni.tas]	[la.ˈka.sa.βo.ˈni.ta]

Another phonological segment that is subject to alteration is /n/, which can be velarized or deleted in syllable-final position, though in the latter case the nasal quality may remain on the preceding vowel. In various verbal conjugations, the phonological reduction of /s/ and /n/ can result in the neutralization of person/number markings, as with the examples of the imperfect tense of the verb *comer* 'to eat' in (3).

(3)		*Normative*	*Dominican*
comía 'I ate'		[ko.ˈmi.a]	[ko.ˈmi.a]
comías 'You (familiar) ate'		[ko.ˈmi.as]	[ko.ˈmi.a]
comía 'You (formal) ate'		[ko.ˈmi.a]	[ko.ˈmi.a]
comían 'They ate'		[ko.ˈmi.ãn]	[ko.ˈmi.aŋ]/[ko.ˈmi.ã]/
			[ko.ˈmi.a]

In normative Spanish, person and number in verbal paradigms are distinguished by inflectional endings, such as -*s* (second person singular) and -*n* (third person plural). Because of this richness of verbal morphology, subject pronouns in Spanish do not have to be expressed. In fact, in normative Spanish *Hablas español* 'You speak Spanish' without the expressed subject *tú* is more common than *Tú hablas español*. This would lead one to hypothesize that the loss of morphology should necessitate the presence of subject pronouns in Dominican Spanish.

While there is little evidence for a causal connection between morphological reductions and overt syntactic subjects, it is unmistakable that Dominican Spanish presents an increased incidence of subject pronouns when compared to other Spanish varieties (cf. Otheguy, Zentella, and Livert 2007). As shown in the examples in (4), drawn from our corpus of spoken language, Dominican Spanish allows for personal subject pronouns (*ellas* 'they:fem.', *yo* 'I', *uno* 'one') to be freely employed, without the usual discursive restrictions expected in normative Spanish.

(4)   a.   Hay unas muchachitas que están juntas conmigo que *ellas* viven pa' fuera, entonces *ellas* vinieron a estudiar en la escuela del Pino, entonces *ellas* saben mucho inglés. *Yo* no me acuerdo en el país que *ellas* vivían.

'There are some girls who are with me that *they (fem.)* live abroad, so
they came to study at school in El Pino, so *they* know a lot of English.
I don't remember what country *they* lived in.'
b. Cuando *uno* mezcla un idioma con el de *uno* se le hace difícil real-
mente para *uno* pronunciar las cosas.
'When *you* mix a language with *your* own it becomes difficult for
you to pronounce things.'

This tendency has proliferated throughout the pronominal system and is
observed even for inanimate subjects, as in (5), where in normative Spanish no
pronoun can be used.

(5) a. Pero yo no sé qué le pasó [a la camioneta] porque *ella* tiene gasolina
y *ella* estaba caminando bien.
'I don't know what happened to it [to the pickup truck] because *it*
has gas and *it* was running fine.'
b. *Ella* [la escuela] es bien, dan muchas clases, los profesores son buenos.
'*It* [the school] is fine, they give lots of classes, the teachers are good.'

Another prominent distinguishing feature of Dominican Spanish is the pattern
of word order attested in questions. Whereas normative Spanish requires that the
verb appear before the subject, as in (6a) and (7a), Dominican Spanish allows for
preverbal subjects, as in (6b) and (7b).

(6) a. Papi, ¿qué dice ese letrero? (normative Spanish)
Daddy, what says that sign
b. Papi, ¿qué *ese* *letrero* dice? (Dominican Spanish)
Daddy, what that sign says
'Daddy, what does that sign say?'

(7) a. ¿Cuánto gana un médico? (normative Spanish)
how much earns a doctor
b. ¿Cuánto *un* *médico* gana? (Dominican Spanish)
how much a doctor earns
'How much does a doctor earn?'

It should be pointed out that many of these features are individually manifested
across varieties of Spanish. What is noteworthy is that they coexist in Dominican
Spanish and that this constellation of properties has come to characterize this
language variety.

Summary

The linguistic features outlined above are typical of Dominican Spanish; however, Dominicans, both on the island and in the U.S., demonstrate a great deal

of variation with respect to these features, mixing structures representative of the distinctive Dominican dialect with those that are modeled on normative Spanish. In addition, in the context of widespread bilingualism among Dominicans in the U.S., some variation may be contact induced (e.g., the use of *una suera* [u.na.ˈswe. ɾa] borrowed from English, 'a sweater', which incorporates the *r*-dropping of the New York City and Long Island pronunciation of *sweater* [ˈswɛ.ɾa] into Spanish phonology and morphology).

Further Reading

An insightful perspective on the twin, divergent histories of the Dominican Republic and Haiti is presented in Wucker's *Why the Cocks Fight* (1999). A survey of contemporary Dominican immigration and integration into the U.S. is found in Torres-Saillant and Hernández's *The Dominican Americans* (1998), and a popular ethnography of a Dominican ethnic enclave is presented in Levitt's *The Transnational Villagers* (2001). A particularly enthralling portrayal of Dominican history and culture (with ample examples of colloquial Dominican Spanish) is found in Diaz's Pulitzer Prize–winning novel *Brief Wondrous Life of Oscar Wao*. The sociolinguistic situation of Dominicans and Dominican Americans is profiled by Toribio (2003, 2006) and by Bailey (2002), and their educational challenges are foregrounded in the work of Pita and Utakis (2002) and in Bartlett and García's *Additive Schooling in Subtractive Times* (2011). The linguistic properties of the Dominican Spanish variety are sketched in Lipski's *Latin American Spanish* (1994) and are more fully documented in Jiménez Sabater's *Más datos sobre el español de la República Dominicana* (1975) and Henríquez-Ureña's *El español en Santo Domingo* (1940). A more recent treatment of rural Dominican Spanish is offered by Bullock and Toribio (2009), and a linguistic overview of the contact between Spanish and Haitian Creole in the border regions is offered by Ortiz López (2011).

Problem Sets

Sociolinguistics

1. In their studies of Dominican Americans in the northeastern U.S., Bailey (2002) and Toribio (2003) have observed that black Dominican Americans often employ Spanish in distinguishing themselves from African Americans. For these speakers, language is central to the performance of ethnic identity, a fact that may contribute to language loyalty and may be implicated in Spanish-language maintenance. Now, consider the case of white Dominican Americans, whose assimilation into the dominant social structure may be easier. What predictions would you make with regard to their Spanish-language loyalty? What individual and societal forces would promote maintenance or loss of the Spanish language among these speakers?

2. Scholars in history and sociology have documented the enduring legacy of a nationalistic anti-Haitian doctrine in the Dominican Republic. One consequence examined by Bullock and Toribio (forthcoming) is Dominicans' reluctance to learn Haitian Creole. Can you think of similar examples in which attitudes toward particular languages in the U.S. have been shaped by social ideologies and/or historical events?

Phonology

3. The regional dialects of Dominican Spanish in Table 11.1 are distinguished by their pronunciations. Carefully examine the data presented and respond to the questions that follow.

TABLE 11.1 Data from regional dialects of Dominican Spanish

Normative Spanish	Regional dialects in the Dominican Republic			Gloss
	Santo Domingo	Southern Coast	Cibao Valley	
[ˈfweɾ.te]	[ˈfwel.te]	[ˈfweɾ.te]	[ˈfwej.te]	'strong'
[al.ˈfõn.so]	[al.ˈfõn.so]	[aɾ.ˈfõn.so]	[aj.ˈfõn.so]	(name)
[ˈpor.ke]	[pol.ˈke]	[poɾ.ˈke]	[poj.ˈke]	'why'
[suɾ]	[sul]	[suɾ]	[suj]	'south'
[ak.ˈsjõn]	[ak.ˈsjõŋ]	[ak.ˈsjõŋ]	[ak.ˈsjõŋ]	'action'
[pa.ˈpel]	[pa.ˈpel]	[pa.ˈpeɾ]	[pa.ˈpej]	'paper'
[al.ˈkal.de]	[al.ˈkal.de]	[aɾ.ˈkaɾ.ðe]	[aj.ˈkaj.ðe]	'mayor'

a. List the sounds that alternate between normative Spanish and the regional dialects.
b. Make a general statement using natural classes about the class of sounds that is affected in these alternations.
c. Determine the phonological environment in which the allophones alternate in the regional dialect pronunciations.

4. Dominican Spanish speakers are often insecure about their pronunciation and employ hypercorrect forms (cf. Bullock and Toribio 2010). *Hypercorrection* refers to errors that speakers make when they are trying to pronounce a word more accurately. Compare the normative and hypercorrect Dominican pronunciations in Table 11.2. Then, using what you discovered in (3), match each of the four Dominican forms with the regional dialect that it is most likely to come from and justify your decision.

TABLE 11.2 Dominican hypercorrection data

Orthography	Normative Spanish	Dominican hypercorrection	Gloss
haitiano	[aj.ˈtja.no]	[al.ˈtja.no]	'Haitian'
voy	[boj]	[boɾ]	'(I) am going'
buey	[bwej]	[bwel]	'ox'
muy	[muj]	[muɾ]	'very'

5. Examine the pronunciations given in Table 11.3 and answer the questions that follow.

TABLE 11.3 /s/–deletion data from Dominican Spanish

Orthography	Normative Spanish	Dominican Spanish	Gloss
busco	[ˈbus.ko]	[ˈbu.ko]	'I look for'
pasta	[ˈpas.ta]	[ˈpa.ta]	'paste'
español	[es.pa.ˈɲol]	[e.pa.ˈɲoj]	'Spanish'
dos hijos	[do.ˈsi.hos]	[do.ˈsi.ho]	'two children'
dispone	[dis.ˈpo.ne]	[di.ˈpo.ne]	'disposes'
disco	[ˈdis.ko]	[ˈdi.ko]	'record'
después	[des.ˈpwes]	[de.ˈpwe]	'then'
hospitales	[os.pi.ˈta.les]	[o.pi.ˈta.le]	'hospitals'
bates	[ˈba.tes]	[ˈba.te]	'baseball bats'
este	[ˈes.te]	[ˈe.te]	'this'
inglés	[iŋ.ˈgles]	[iŋ.ˈgle]	'English'
ajíes	[a.ˈhi.es]	[a.ˈhi.e]	'peppers'
comiste	[ko.ˈmis.te]	[ko.ˈmi.te]	'you ate'

a. Determine the phonological environment in which /s/ is deleted in Dominican Spanish.
b. Compare the pronunciations above to the hypercorrect forms in Table 11.4 and explain the rule of hypercorrection that Dominican Spanish employs.

TABLE 11.4 Hypercorrect forms in Dominican Spanish

Orthography	Normative Spanish	Dominican hypercorrection	Gloss
Bárbara	[ˈbaɾ.βa.ɾa]	[ˈbaɾ.βa.ɾas]	(name)
hola	[ˈo.la]	[ˈo.las]	'hello'
preparado	[pɾe.pa.ˈɾa.ðo]	[pɾes.pa.ˈɾa.ðo]	'prepared'
otra	[ˈo.tɾa]	[ˈos.tɾa]	'another'

Morphology

6. Dominican Spanish displays a morphological phenomenon known as double plural marking (see Núñez-Cedeño 2003, 2008). Examine the data in Table 11.5 in light of the previous phonology exercise.

TABLE 11.5 Double plural marking data

Singular	Gloss	Normative plural	Dominican double plural
['la.ta]	'can'	['la.tas]	['la.ta.se]
['es.to]	'these'	[és.tos]	['e.to.se]
[mu.'heɾ]	'woman'	[mu.'he.ɾes]	[mu.'he.ɾe.se]
[pa.'pel]	'paper'	[pa.'pe.les]	[pa.'pe.le.se]
[a.'hi]	'pepper'	[a.'hi.es]	[a.'hi.se]

a. Describe the formation of the normative Spanish plural from the singular by first listing the allomorphs and then explaining their distribution.
b. Identify the Dominican double plural allomorphs and describe their distribution.
c. Stems such as *ágil* ['a.hil] 'agile' cannot take either of the double plural allomorphs: **ágilse/*ágilese*. Suggest possible phonological explanations for this gap.

Syntax

7. An intriguing characteristic of Dominican Spanish is the availability of the pronoun *ello*, which has no equivalent expression in other varieties of the language. Consider the distribution of *ello* in the following examples and respond to the questions that follow. The normative Spanish equivalent constructions would not allow the *ello*.

(8) Ello   llueve   con   frecuencia.
    ello   rains   with   frequency
    'It rains frequently.'

(9) Ello   había   mucha   comida   en   esa   fiesta.
    ello   was   much   food   at   that   party
    'There was lots of food at that party.'

(10) Ello   parece   haber   huelgas.
     ello   seem   to-be   strikes
     'There seem to be strikes.'

a. The Dominican *ello* corresponds to two different subjects in English. Please list them and then explain how they are similar to one another by considering what, if anything, they refer to.

b. What types of verbs allow for the subject pronoun *ello*?

c. Does the unacceptability of *ello* in the following construction confirm your previous responses? Explain your answer.

(11) *Ello   compró   Cheo   una   vaca.
      ello   bought-3sg.   Cheo   a   cow
      'Cheo bought a cow.'

References

Bailey, Benjamin. 2002. *Language, race, and negotiation of identity: A study of Dominican Americans*. New York: LFP Scholarly Publications.

Bartlett, Lesley, and Ofelia García. 2011. *Additive schooling in subtractive times: Bilingual education and Dominican immigrant youth in the Heights*. Nashville, TN: Vanderbilt University Press.

Bullock, Barbara E., and Almeida Jacqueline Toribio. 2009. Reconsidering Dominican Spanish: Data from the rural Cibao. *Revista Internacional de Lingüística Iberoamericana* 14: 49–73.

Bullock, Barbara E., and Almeida Jacqueline Toribio. 2010. Correcting the record on Dominican [s]-hypercorrection. In S. Colina, A. Olarrea, and A. Carvalho, eds., *Romance linguistics 2009*, 15–24. New York: John Benjamins.

Bullock, Barbara E., and Almeida Jacqueline Toribio. Forthcoming. From Trujillo to the terremoto: The effects of language ideologies on the language attitudes of the rural poor of the northern Dominican border. *International Journal of the Sociology of Language*.

Diaz, Junot. 2007. *The brief wondrous life of Oscar Wao*. New York: Riverhead Books.

Henríquez-Ureña, Pedro. 1940. *El español en Santo Domingo*. Buenos Aires: Biblioteca de Dialectología Hispanomericana V.

Hudson, R.A. 1980. *Sociolinguistics*. Cambridge: Cambridge University Press.

Jensen, Leif, Jeffrey H. Cohen, Almeida Jacqueline Toribio, Gordon DeJong, and Leila Rodríguez. 2006. Ethnic identities, language and economic outcomes among Dominicans in a new destination. *Social Science Quarterly* 87: 1088–1099.

Jiménez Sabater, Max A. 1975. *Más datos sobre el español de la República Dominicana*. Santo Domingo: Ediciones Intec.

Levitt, Peggy. 2001. *The transnational villagers*. Berkeley: University of California Press.

Lipski, John. 1994. *Latin American Spanish*. New York: Longman Linguistics Library.

Núñez Cedeño, Rafael. 2003. Double plurals in Dominican: A morpho-pragmatic account. In P. Kempchinsky and C. Piñeros, eds., *Theory, practice, and acquisition: Papers from the 6th Hispanic Linguistic Symposium and the 5th Conference on the Acquisition of Spanish*, 68–82. Somerville, MA: Cascadilla Press.

Núñez Cedeño, Rafael. 2008. The /-e/ in popular Dominican Spanish: An expressive marker not a double plural. *Spanish in Context* 5: 196–223.

Ortiz López, Luis. 2011. Spanish in contact with Haitian Creole. In M. Diaz Campos, ed., *The handbook of Hispanic sociolinguistics*, 855–904. Hoboken, NJ: Wiley-Blackwell.

Otheguy, Ricardo, Ana Celia Zentella, and David Livert. 2007. Language and dialect contact in Spanish in New York: Toward the formation of a speech community. *Language* 83: 770–802.

Paulino, Edward. 2005. Erasing the Kreyol from the margins of the Dominican Republic: The pre- and post-nationalization project of the border, 1930–1945. *Wadabagei: A Journal of the Caribbean and Its Diaspora* 8: 39–75.

Pita, Marianne D., and Sharon Utakis. 2002. Educational policy for the transnational Dominican community. *Journal of Language, Identity and Education* 1.4: 317–328.

Toribio, Almeida Jacqueline. 2003. The social significance of language loyalty among black and white Dominicans in New York. *The Bilingual Review/La Revista Bilingüe* 27: 3–11.

Toribio, Almeida Jacqueline. 2006. Linguistic displays of identity among Dominicans in national and diasporic settlements. In C. Davies and J. Brutt-Griffler, eds., *English and ethnicity*, 131–155. New York: Palgrave.

Torres-Saillant, Silvio, and Ramona Hernández. 1998. *The Dominican Americans*. Westwood, CT: Greenwood.

Wucker, Michelle. 1999. *Why the cocks fight: Dominicans, Haitians, and the struggle for Hispaniola*. New York: Hill and Wang.

Zentella, Ana Celia. 1997. Spanish in New York. In O. García and J. Fishman, eds., *The multilingual apple: Languages in New York City*, 167–201. Berlin: Mouton de Gruyter.

12

CHINESE

Lauren Hall-Lew and Amy Wing-mei Wong

Introduction

The Chinese language comprises a large variety of languages and dialects, some-times mutually unintelligible, belonging to the Sino-Tibetan language family. Varieties of Chinese are spoken in China and throughout Asia as well as in many communities throughout Europe, Australia, Africa, and the Americas. According to the 2010 American Community Survey (U. S. Census Bureau n.d.), *Chinese*—an umbrella term covering all Chinese varieties—was estimated to be the third most frequently spoken language at home in the U.S., after English and Spanish.

Speakers of Chinese varieties in the U.S. are characterized by a high degree of heterogeneity. Most importantly, they vary greatly in terms of their national and geographic origins. While a large number are immigrants and descendants from across mainland China, throughout early American history the Chinese-speaking population also consisted of immigrants from Hong Kong and Tai-wan, as well as from other overseas communities of the Chinese diaspora in Southeast Asia and in Central and Latin America. Varieties of Chinese spoken in the U.S. are linguistically heterogeneous as well, given that the label *Chinese* encompasses at least seven major mutually unintelligible regional varieties (or *fāngyán*, a term used in Chinese dialectology meaning 'regional speech'), each with its own more or less mutually intelligible subvarieties. As a result, someone from mainland China's Fujian province, for instance, may not be able to speak to someone from China's Guangdong province, if both speakers are using their native varieties. Nevertheless, the mutually unintelligible varieties of Chinese are united linguistically by a shared writing system, which has a long history dating back to approximately the second millennium BC. (See the section below on writing systems.)

The seven major regional varieties of spoken Chinese are as follows:

1. Mandarin: a variety spoken natively by about 70% of the Han Chinese. It can be further classified into several subgroups: Northern (which includes standard varieties like Mainland *Pǔtōnghuà*, Taiwan *Guóyǔ*, or Singapore *Huáyǔ*), Eastern, and Southern.
2. *Yuè*: a prominent variety spoken in the Guangdong and Guangxi provinces in southern China. It has historically been the dominant variety in communities of the Chinese diaspora spanning Southeast Asia to the Americas and the Caribbean. It includes subvarieties such as Cantonese, often considered the prestige variety within the *Yuè* group, and Toisanese (also commonly know as Taishanese, from the Mandarin term), which is a *Sìyì* dialect that was the most prominent variety in American Chinatowns prior to the 1970s.
3. *Mǐn*: spoken in all of Fujian province and the northeastern part of Guangdong province in China, as well as in Taiwan and other overseas Chinese communities. It can be further divided into Southern *Mǐn* (which includes Hokkien and Teochew) and Northern *Mǐn* (which includes Fuzhounese).
4. *Wú*: spoken in the Yangtze (Changjiang) delta and the coastal region around Shanghai. It is usually further divided into Northern *Wú* (which includes Shanghainese) and Southern *Wú*.
5. *Kèjiā* (or *Hakka*): spoken by the people of Hakka (a word of Cantonese origin meaning 'guest' or 'stranger') in isolated communities scattered throughout southern China and in diaspora settlements.
6. *Xiāng*: spoken predominantly in the central and southwestern parts of Hunan province in China.
7. *Gàn*: a less known and studied Chinese variety spoken chiefly in the eastern part of Hunan province and in Jiangxi province in China.

A 2008 survey showed that all of the seven *fāngyán* groups were spoken in the U.S. to varying degrees by Chinese immigrants and international students (Wiley et al. 2008). Given the vast linguistic diversity that characterizes spoken Chinese, estimates of the numbers of Chinese speakers in and out of the U.S. are necessarily rough and approximate. Globally, it is estimated that over 1.2 billion people (about one-fifth of the world's population) speak some variety of Chinese as their native language (Lewis 2009). In the U.S. alone, data from the 2010 U.S. American Community Survey estimated that 2,723,737 people (or almost 1% of the population over the age of five) spoke Chinese as their primary language at home (U.S. Census Bureau n.d.).

History

The 1830 U.S. Census recorded three Chinese residents, possibly the earliest U.S. immigrants of Asian descent; significant Chinese immigration to the U.S. began a bit later, in the 1840s. Most of these early immigrants came from Guangdong province in southern China. Immigration was motivated by the California Gold Rush of 1848–55, which coincided with social and political turmoil in China, including the Opium Wars in 1842 and the Tai Ping Rebellion of 1850–64. Many Chinese migrants sought to escape from the violence and hardship that these events caused and sought a new life in California, which became known in Cantonese varieties as Gum Shan ('Golden Mountain'). During the 1860s and 1870s, Chinese immigration was further encouraged by the major railroad companies operating in California, which promised work building the western portion of the Transcontinental Railroad. These early Chinese immigrants were low-wage laborers who spoke dialects of *Yuè* such as Toisanese and Cantonese. In the U.S., the vast majority of migrants lived in Chinatowns, both in major Western cities as well as in small rural towns (Lee 1949). Chinatowns segregated the Chinese from the rest of the community through both internal and external pressures, including social and economic convenience as well as social and economic discrimination (Yung and the Chinese Historical Society of America 2006; Wang 2007).

Strong anti-Chinese movements in California during the last quarter of the nineteenth century forced some Chinese Americans to move away from the West Coast. Chinatowns began to emerge in major eastern cities such as New York, Boston, and Baltimore, although the Chinese American population on the East Coast would not compare to that of the West Coast until the 1950s. Anti-Chinese movements led to the U.S. Congress passing the Chinese Exclusion Act in 1882, prohibiting further immigration and barring those already in the U.S. from naturalization. This act became the first legislation in U.S. history to ban the immigration of a specific ethnic group.

As a consequence of the Chinese Exclusion Act, Chinese immigration dropped drastically for about 60 years, except for a brief surge of Chinese immigration after San Francisco's major earthquake in 1906. The earthquake destroyed most birth certificates and immigration records in city hall, opening up opportunities for all Chinese San Franciscans to claim U.S. citizenship and subsequently send for relatives living in China. This era of "paper son" migration included many people who entered the country via San Francisco through falsified birth certificates claiming family relations with Chinese Americans. Because their immigration was tied to those Chinese already in the U.S., these new migrants tended to speak *Yuè* varieties as well, adding to the development of distinctly U.S. Chinatown varieties of *Yuè* (Dong and Hom 1980). "Paper son" and subsequent Chinese immigration was cut short by the Immigration Act of 1924. This included the Asian Exclusion Act, which banned U.S. immigration from any Asian country, thereby resulting in a decades-long gap in Chinese immigration to the U.S.

Up until World War II, Chinese Americans lived primarily in segregated Chinatowns and were limited to working menial jobs and living in overcrowded, substandard housing (Yung and the Chinese Historical Society of America 2006). English was used only in areas visited by tourists, and Chinese was not used outside of the borders of Chinatowns. This state of social and linguistic segregation began to break down during World War II, when the U.S. alliance with China led to the repeal of the Chinese Exclusion Act in 1943, paving the way for more and more anti-Chinese laws to be repealed in the following years (Chow 1977). The most important and lasting change to U.S. immigration legislation was the Immigration and Nationality Act of 1965, which eliminated "national origins" as a basis for distributing immigration quotas and set an annual immigration quota of 20,000 from any given country, giving preference to skilled workers and those seeking family reunification. This act led to a major demographic shift across major urban centers in the U.S. in general, and particularly in various U.S. Chinatowns (Wang 2007). The passage of the act as law in 1968 was followed by a surge in immigration from Taiwan and Hong Kong. Many of these immigrants were anticommunist elites originally from different parts of China who had fled to Taiwan or Hong Kong after the 1949 Chinese Communist Revolution. Since the end of the twentieth century more Chinese-speaking immigrants from across China and South Asia have been able to enter the U.S., in part through the establishment of formal diplomatic relations between the U.S. and the People's Republic of China (PRC) in 1979 and the increasingly liberal emigration policies on the part of the PRC.

Today, Chinese immigrants from mainland China and their descendants constitute the majority of the Chinese American population (59.5%), followed by immigrants and their descendants from Taiwan (15.9%), Hong Kong (9.4%), and areas of the non-U.S. Chinese diaspora (15.3%) (Shinagawa and Kim 2008). The most recent group of immigrants from mainland China is the most diverse in terms of their geographic, linguistic, and socioeconomic backgrounds. While the majority of the first immigrants were Yuè-speaking peasants or rural laborers, the new arrivals came from both rural and urban China, and many of today's urban immigrants are highly educated and professionally skilled. Many primarily speak varieties of Mandarin (sometimes along with other home dialects, such as Fuzhounese). The growing presence of Mandarin speakers challenges the long-held dominance of Toisanese and Cantonese in U.S. Chinatowns.

Another major demographic shift since the 1960s is that Chinese immigrants now often settle in states other than California (and Hawai'i, with its own long history of Asian immigration), specifically in New York, New Jersey, Texas, Illinois, Maryland, and Virginia. That said, more than half of all Chinese Americans in 2006 lived in the two states of California and New York (53%), with the highest concentration in metropolitan areas such as New York and New Jersey on the East Coast; San Francisco, San Jose, and Oakland in Northern California; and Los Angeles and Long Beach in Southern California (Shinagawa and Kim 2008). However, Chinese Americans today increasingly live outside of urban centers, in more middle-class or upper-middle-class suburban communities. Historically, changes in immigration law coincided with a relaxation in laws prohibiting home ownership for people of color, starting with a 1948 U.S. Supreme

Court ruling against housing discrimination based on race. By the 1960s Chinese Americans were no longer confined to crowded Chinatowns and obtained the freedom to find better jobs and own land and property. Many recent arrivals are now able to bypass living in Chinatowns and instead are moving directly into the newer residential suburbs where the former Chinatown residents had also settled, leading to the phenomenon of "New Chinatowns" (Laguerre 2006; Fong 2008) and "ethnoburbs" (Li 2009) in areas like San Francisco, Los Angeles, and New York City.

The Social Context

In the U.S. the steady increase of Chinese immigrants from diverse geographic and linguistic backgrounds, together with their American-born children, grand-children, and great-grandchildren, has resulted in a high degree of multilin-gualism and multidialectalism within American Chinese communities. With the exception of native Mandarin- and Cantonese-speaking immigrants, who tend to speak only either Mandarin or Cantonese, most Chinese immigrants are multi-dialectal and speak more than two varieties of Chinese. The various varieties of Chinese alongside English create a complex pattern of *diglossia* or *polyglossia*. (On diglossia see also the chapter "Language Contact.") English is the *beyond-community* high variety that enjoys socioeconomic and academic status and is used in wider public contexts. It is the preferred, if not default, language of choice to address people outside of the Chinese communities, including Asians and Asian Americans whose ethnicity is unknown to the speaker (and who could be Chinese, Vietnamese, Korean, Japanese, etc.). Cantonese and, increas-ingly, Mandarin, are the *within-community* high varieties used in public and more formal contexts among groups of people of Chinese descent. Other Chinese varieties, and possibly some nonstandard varieties of English, may be said to con-stitute the low varieties spoken at home and in other local and private contexts. A similar diglossic or polyglossic situation characterizes Chinese communities in other English-dominant countries, such as Canada and the United Kingdom (Li Wei 2007).

POLYGLOSSIA

Polyglossia is a sociolinguistic term that refers to the use of multiple (*poly-*) language varieties (*glossia*) by members of a speech community. In a poly-glossic speech community, each of the coexisting language varieties serves a specific range of social functions and varies in terms of prestige and for-mality. High varieties tend to have greater social prestige and are used in more formal contexts such as the classroom and religious settings. Low varieties tend to be used in relatively informal setting such as the home.

The post-1965 influx of Chinese immigrants created a market for Chinese media in the U.S. Numerous radio and television programs targeted for Chinese audiences are produced and broadcast in various U.S. cities. Programs produced in mainland China, Hong Kong, and Taiwan are also available through different Chinese satellite and cable television providers as well as the Internet. The two high varieties of Chinese, Standard Mandarin and Standard Cantonese, are used in these programs.

Chinese publications are also widely available in Chinatowns across the country. The fact that the Chinese writing system is not alphabetic but consists instead of a set of more or less logographic characters permits different varieties of Chinese to share the same written language—*báihuà*, 'plain speech' or 'Vernacular Chinese', a register of written Chinese that was popularized after the New Cultural Movement of the 1910s in China and is used today for Chinese publications worldwide. Today, over 15 Chinese-language newspapers are printed and sold in the U.S.; some, such as *Singtao Daily*, the *World Journal*, and the *China Press* (*Qiaobao*), have nationwide circulation. Others, such as *Chicago Chinese News*, the *Austin Chinese Times*, and the *St. Louis Chinese Journal*, serve more local Chinese communities.

Motivated by the desire to preserve their heritage language and to promote a sense of ethnic identity among their U.S.-born and raised children, Chinese Americans began to set up Chinese-heritage language schools as early as 1848. By 1997 there were at least 634 nonprofit and for-profit Chinese language schools across the country (Chao 1997), with, for example, about 20 located throughout New York City (Pan 1997). Nonprofit Chinese language schools are usually affiliated with nonprofit organizations such as Chinese benevolent associations or religious institutions. They generally offer programs tailored to students of Chinese descent during the weekend, after school, or in the summer. Earlier Chinese language schools usually offered classes in Cantonese. Recently, the number of Mandarin classes has caught up to—if not surpassed—the number of Cantonese classes (Semple 2009), reflecting not only the major shift in immigration patterns over the last couple of decades but also the PRC's growing influence and integration into the world economy. Since students in Chinese language schools have traditionally been Chinese-heritage students with at least basic listening and speaking abilities, classes have typically emphasized reading and writing skills.

In addition to community language schools, public bilingual programs in Chinese and English are also available. This is in part a consequence of the 1974 civil rights case *Lau v. Nichols*, in which eight-year-old Kenny Lau, on behalf of his school's 1,800 (majority) Chinese American students, sued the San Francisco School District over English-only instruction. The U.S. Supreme Court ruled in favor of the mandatory adoption of bilingual-bicultural education for non–English-speaking students, leading to the formal adoption of bilingual education programs. Many traditional bilingual education programs in the U.S. aim to help students who have limited English proficiency transition to mainstream,

English-only classrooms as quickly as possible, and their linguistic goal for the students is the acquisition of English. Recently, there has been a rise in the number of two-way or dual-language-immersion bilingual education programs in Mandarin and English open to all children regardless of their language or ethnic background. The goal of these programs is to enable students to become bilingual and biliterate in English and Chinese (see Starr 2011).

Despite the availability of Chinese media, Chinese-heritage language schools, and other institutional support for the maintenance of the Chinese language, language shift to English is taking place rather rapidly within Chinese communities in the U.S., particularly among the American-born generations. Shinagawa and Kim (2008), citing data from the 2006 American Community Survey (ACS), report that while only 34.1% of first-generation (i.e., foreign-born) Chinese Americans reported speaking English "very well," the percentages rise dramatically for those who are U.S.-born (i.e., second generation and beyond) or who were born overseas but arrived in the U.S. before the age of 16 (i.e., the 1.5 generation). Of the 1.5 generation, 70.4% reported speaking English "very well," while 93.8% of the U.S.-born Chinese Americans did. Additionally, only about 27.6% of the U.S.-born Chinese Americans are estimated to speak their heritage language at home. Taken together, these estimates suggest that the rate of shift from Chinese to English is accelerating. Jia (2008) found that even for first-generation Chinese Americans, their Chinese language skills continue to decline with increasing English immersion, with reading and writing more susceptible to attrition than listening and speaking skills.

Some Linguistic Features

Research specifically on varieties of Chinese in the U.S. has been rather sparse in comparison to the vast wealth of literature on varieties spoken across Asia (but see Dong and Hom 1980; Starr 2011). What follows is a very brief list of some linguistic features that are common across Chinese languages, focusing on those varieties important to Chinese-speaking communities in the U.S. and pointing out some features that have been of interest to linguistic researchers. Sources for this section include Norman (1988), Li and Thompson (1989), Matthews and Yip (1994), Bauer and Benedict (1997), and our own research.

Phonetics and Phonology

Most varieties of Chinese have a typologically simple syllable structure. A typical syllable in Chinese consists maximally of an onset consonant, a vowel nucleus, a coda consonant, and a tone, such as the word *máng* 'busy' in Standard Mandarin, where [m] is the onset, [a] the vowel, and [ŋ] (spelled *ng*) the coda consonant, and the rising tone is indicated by a diacritic, ´. Syllables often do not have a coda consonant. For example, *má* 'hemp' comprises only an onset, a vowel nucleus, and a tone. Generally speaking, all varieties of Chinese tend to have a rather restricted set of coda consonants, but different Chinese varieties vary in what consonants are allowed as codas. Standard Cantonese allows a larger coda consonant inventory than Standard Mandarin. For instance, Standard Cantonese allows /p/, /t/, and /k/ as syllable codas, while Standard Mandarin does not. Chinese varieties, in general, do not have consonant clusters in either the onset or coda position.

Chinese languages are *tonal*, meaning that the pitch of a morpheme is phonemic, distinguishing otherwise phonologically identical syllables from one another and correlating those different syllables with different meanings. (On tones, see also the chapter on Navajo.) For example, the Standard Mandarin syllable *ma* that we mentioned earlier can be associated with any one of four different tones (represented by the diacritics above the vowel), resulting in four words with different meanings: *mā*, in high tone, means 'mother'; *mǎ*, in low tone, means 'horse'; *má*, in rising tone, means 'hemp'; and *mà*, in falling tone, means 'scold'. Shanghainese, on the other hand, has only two contrastive tones. Standard Cantonese has six or seven basic tones, depending on the region. Many varieties of Chinese also have an additional neutral tone, which varies in its realization depending on the tones of the surrounding syllables.

As in any language family, there is a wide range of phonetic and phonological variation within and across regional varieties of Chinese. The sound systems of Chinese varieties in the U.S. correspond to the varieties found in Asia, but analyses within the U.S. focus specifically on Cantonese and Toisanese, since those varieties dominated the earliest American Chinatowns and are still widely used today. Although Toisanese and Cantonese both belong to the *Yuè* group, phonological differences exist between these two varieties. For example, syllable–initial [tʰ] in Cantonese in words like 田 'farm' [tʰɪŋ] and 頭 'head' [tʰɐw] is realized as [h] in Toisanese, such that 'farm' and 'head' are pronounced as [hiŋ] and [hɐw], respectively.

Morphology, Syntax, and Word Order

There is some debate in linguistic typology over whether or not to classify Chinese languages as monosyllabic or *isolating* languages. In an isolating language (as opposed to a *synthetic* language), every word consists of just one syllable. While this was true for Classical Chinese, most modern Chinese languages concatenate syllables to form new words, and many nouns, verbs, and adjectives consist of two or more syllables. At the same time, every syllable of every word carries its own meaning; that is, every syllable is a separate morpheme, unlike words in a language like English. For example, the Standard Mandarin word *túshūguǎn* means 'library', and each of its syllables has its own meaning that combines to form the one word: *tú* means 'picture', *shū* means 'book', and *guǎn* means 'hall'. In contrast, the syllables [laɪ], [brɛ], and [ri] in the English word do not have their own meanings and are not separate morphemes.

The basic word order of Chinese languages is Subject-Verb-Object (SVO), but they also have some features more typical of Subject-Object-Verb (SOV) languages such as prepositional phrases that precede the verbs they modify, as in (1):

(1) Zhāngsān   chángcháng   zài   túshūguǎn   wēnxí   gōngkè
    Zhangsan   always   in   library   review   homework
    (subject)   (adverb)   (prepositional phrase) (verb)   (object)
    'Zhangsan always reviews his homework in the library.'

Chinese languages are also ***topic-comment*** or *topic-prominent* languages, in that they all make use of sentence structures such as (2):

(2) zhè běn shū   wó   yǐjīng   kàn guò le
    This book   I   already   read
    (Topic)   (Comment)
    'I have already read this book.'

In topic-comment sentences, the topic of the sentence—what the sentence is about—simply comes before the rest of the sentence. These sentences translate into English as something like "As for X [topic], Y [comment]." So, in the above example, the topic *zhè běn shū* 'this book', is introduced first in the sentence, followed by the comment *wó yǐjīng kàn guò le* 'I already read'.

The Chinese languages are *noninflectional* and *analytic*, so unlike varieties of English and the other languages and linguistic varieties discussed in this book, the Chinese languages have few overt grammatical inflections, such as for tense, case, or number. For example, the Standard Mandarin noun *shū* can mean either 'book' (in [3a]) or 'books' (in [3b]). Similarly, the verb *mǎi* is used to mean 'bought' (3a, 3b), 'buys' (4), or 'to buy' (5), without undergoing any structural modification.

(3) a. Wó   gāngcái   *mǎi*   le   zhè   běn   *shū*
       I   just now   buy   ASPECT   this   CLASSIFIER   book
       'I bought this book just now.'
    b. Wó   gāngcái   *mǎi*   le   sān   běn   *shū*
       I   just now   buy   ASPECT   three   CLASSIFIER   book
       'I bought three books just now.'

(4) Zhāngsān   jīngcháng   *mǎi*   cǎipiào
    Zhangsan   often   buy   lottery tickets
    'Zhangsan often buys lottery tickets.'

(5) Wó   xiànzài   chū   *mǎi*   cǎipiào
    I   now   go   buy   lottery tickets
    'I am going out to buy lottery tickets.'

Although in (3a) and (3b) the aspect marker *le* comes after the verb and—together with the adverb *gāngcái* 'just now'—contributes to the interpretation of a past meaning, *le* is not a past tense inflectional suffix. It is a verbal particle that indicates perfective aspect; that is, it indicates that an event is completed and should be viewed as a whole. (See the chapter on Jamaican Creole for the definition of linguistic aspect and mood.) Chinese uses a variety of particles to indicate aspect or mood.

Another notable fact about the syntax of Chinese languages is the use of ***serial verb constructions***, which are phrases consisting of two (or more) adjacent verbs without any overt morphological marking indicating the relationship between the verbs. All the verbs in a serial verb construction share the same subject and occur within the same clause. For example, in the following Mandarin sentence from Li and Thompson (1989: 595), *mǎi piào jìn qu* is a serial verb construction.

(6) wó   mǎi   piào   jìn qu
    I   buy   ticket   enter go
    'I bought a ticket and went in.'

As is illustrated in (6), the adjacency of the verb phrases *mǎi piào* 'bought a ticket' and *jìn qu* 'went in' indicates that each verb phrase is related to the other in the joint formation of one single, combined meaning (e.g., one event or state) predicated of the same subject. For example, it could be that one event occurs after the other, as in (6), or that one event is done to achieve the other, or that the subject of the sentence is alternating back and forth between the two. It could also be that the first verb describes the circumstances in which the second verb takes place.

Chinese languages are also known for their use of *classifiers* and *measure words*, which occur between quantifiers and nouns or between demonstratives and nouns (Schachter 1985: 39; Senft, 2000). For example, to say 'a book' (*yī běn shū*), 'three books' (*sān běn shū*), or 'this book' (*zhè běn shū*) in Standard Mandarin, one must use the classifier *běn* between the numeral or demonstrative and the noun. Without the classifier *běn*, the phrases are not grammatical.

CLASSIFIERS

Classifiers, sometimes called ***measure words***, are a class of words or morphemes in some languages that are used to "classify" nouns according to their characteristics such as shape, animacy, and size when the nouns are being counted. (See also the Navajo chapter for the related concept of classificatory verbs.)

Classifiers are often matched with the nouns they classify according to some characteristic of the noun (e.g., physical properties). For example, the classifier *tiáo* is often used with nouns that denote objects that tend to be long and thin like ropes, ribbons, rivers, and so on. You can find more examples in the problem sets below.

Writing System

As discussed in previous sections, the only domain of language that unites all varieties of Chinese is the writing system, which is comprised of characters (logographic) rather than an alphabet (alphabetic). Regardless of the way a word is pronounced across the various Chinese languages or dialects, the way the character is written is relatively uniform. The major division in terms of Chinese writing systems is between traditional and simplified forms; the former are used more in communities such as Taiwan and Hong Kong, and the latter are used throughout mainland China and elsewhere (e.g., Singapore). For instance, the character for 'book' in traditional form is 書, whereas the simplified form is 书. Both forms can be found in communities in the U.S. There are a few dialectal variations in characters used in written Chinese, but the range of variation tends to be more restricted in writing than in speech.

Chinese characters may be quite simple or quite complex, being comprised of anywhere from 1 to 33 strokes (but on average around 15). Each character has its own form, pronunciation, and meaning. Historically, many characters were formed by phonetic compounding, where the resulting character has two elements: a phonetic element encoding the pronunciation of the character and a semantic element encoding some aspects of the meaning. For example, the Chinese character for 'comment' or 'evaluate' is "評". It consists of two parts: the part on the left, 言 , is derived from the character for 'words'. This part suggests that the meaning of the character has something to do with speech. The right part of the character, 平, pronounced as *píng*, provides some clues to the likely pronunciation of the word 評 (which is also *píng* in this example). Not all characters, however, were formed this way, and many do not include a phonetic element; others, such as some of those used for loanwords, may be used purely for their pronunciation and contribute none of the semantics. (For more about the Chinese writing system, see Norman 1988 and Yan and Liu 1997.)

Pinyin, or more formally Hanyu Pinyin, is the most common transcription system used to romanize Standard Mandarin (and is the one used in this chapter). Yale romanization is most commonly used for transcribing Cantonese, especially for varieties in the U.S. Jyutping is another romanization system for Cantonese that is gaining popularity since its development in 1993. For more about the Pinyin and Yale systems, see Li and Thompson (1989) and Matthews and Yip (1994), respectively.

Further Reading

Linguistic research on the use of Chinese languages in communities in the U.S. has focused on education, applied linguistics, and sociolinguistics. For example, several studies have been conducted in communities across the U.S. on the maintenance of varieties of Chinese among the American-born descendants of immigrants, that is, on bilingual proficiency among the children, grandchildren, and great-grandchildren of immigrants (e.g., Chen 1992; Mouw and Xie 1999; Luo and Wiseman 2000; Zhou and Xiong 2005; Cheng 2006; Williams 2006; Jia 2008; Starr 2011). Luo and Wiseman (2000) found that the language use of a Chinese American child's peer group most strongly influences that child's use and retention of his or her heritage language, whereas Williams (2006) found that the strongest predictor for Chinese language use was whether or not the individual had been born in the U.S. or not, with influences such as family expectations and personal expressions of identity also being important factors.

Research in sociolinguistics and linguistic anthropology has considered economic shifts within Chinese American communities, such as movements out of Old Chinatowns and into middle-class suburbs, with respect to their effects on language attitudes and language use (e.g., Cheng 2006). For example, Wang (2007) gave a historical argument for the ways in which Chinese monolingualism in Old Chinatowns became ideologically associated with economic struggle and oppression, motivating the next generation to move away from bilingual competency and toward English monolingualism. Wong (2007, 2010) found that in New York City Chinese Americans' use of regional dialect features of English was correlated with their social networks and lifestyle orientations, particularly with respect to Chinese cultural practices. Hall-Lew (2009, 2013) showed how English-dominant Chinese Americans living in middle-class "New Chinatowns" are advancing local patterns of English phonological variation and change.

Sociolinguistic research on varieties of Chinese in China has also been increasing in recent years. One recent volume edited by Li Yuming and Li Wei (2013) covers topics ranging from the role of language in the media, education, and social policy to analyses of how language is used in everyday life, both on the mainland as well as in Hong Kong, Macau, and Taiwan.

Problem Sets

Phonology

A loanword (or *borrowing*) is a word borrowed from one language into another language, a common language contact phenomenon. (See also the chapter "Language Contact.") This problem set examines loanwords borrowed from English into Cantonese. English loanwords are common in all varieties of Cantonese that are in close contact with English, such as Hong Kong Cantonese as well as those varieties spoken in the U.S. By examining data on how loanwords are adapted into Cantonese, you will learn more about the phonology of this variety of Chinese.

(Please note: Pronunciations in the following data sets are presented in phonetic transcription. Periods are used to mark syllables in the words. The superscript ^{h} indicates aspiration. The symbol ⌐ following a consonant indicates that there is no audible release. Cantonese tones are not transcribed in the data sets as you do not need to consider tone for these exercises.)

Beginning Level

1. Table 12.1 contains a list of English words borrowed into Cantonese.
   a. How are the English voiced stops /b, d, g/ generally adapted into Cantonese when they appear in the original English words as the syllable onset?
   b. How are the English voiceless stops /p, t, k/ generally adapted into Cantonese when they appear in the original English words as the syllable onset? Are there any exceptions in this data set to the general rule?
   c. How are the English voiceless stops /p, t, k/ adapted into Cantonese when they appear in the original English words as the syllable coda?
   d. Keeping in mind that the way words are pronounced in the language that borrows them can tell us a lot about the phonology of that language, use your answers to (a)–(c) to respond to one more question: What generalizations can you make with regards to Cantonese stops? (Hint: To answer this question, pay attention to voicing, aspiration, release, and the syllable position in which the stops occur in the "Cantonese pronunciation" columns in the data set.)

TABLE 12.1 English words borrowed into Cantonese

English spelling	English pronunciation	Cantonese pronunciation	English spelling	English pronunciation	Cantonese pronunciation
donut	doʊ.nʌt	tʊŋ.let˥	pie	pʰaɪ	pʰei
guitar	gə.tʰar	ki:t˥.tʰa:	tips	tʰɪps	tʰi:p˥.si:
number	nʌm.bə˞	lɛm.pa:	cookie	kʰʊ.kʰi	kʰʊk˥.kʰei
soda	soʊ.də	sɔ:.ta:	copy	kʰa.pʰi	kʰɛp˥.pʰi:
stick	stɪk	si:.tɪk˥	cutlet	kʰʌt.lət	ket˥.li:t˥
cheap	t͡ʃʰip	tsʰi:p˥	guts	gʌts	ket˥.si:

Advanced Level

2. Table 12.2 contains more data on the borrowing of English words into Cantonese. Each of the words in the source language contains the consonant /l/.

TABLE 12.2 English words containing /l/ borrowed into Cantonese

English spelling	English pronunciation	Cantonese pronunciation
cutlet	kʰʌt.lət	ket˥.li:t˥
laser	leɪ.zɹ̩	ləi.sɛ:
volume	vɔ.ljəm	wɔ:.lɛm

a. Determine how /l/ is borrowed from the English source into Cantonese in this data set. (Hint: To answer this question, pay attention to whether /l/ occurs in the onset or coda position in the English source.)

b. Now examine additional data in Table 12.3 showing loanwords that in the English source words contain either coda-final /l/ or syllabic /l/ in unstressed syllables, indicated as [ḷ] (Table 12.3). Explain how coda-final /l/ and [ḷ] are borrowed from the English source into Cantonese. (Once again, you will need to pay attention to onset and coda position.)

TABLE 12.3 Additional English words containing /l/ borrowed into Cantonese

English spelling	English pronunciation	Cantonese pronunciation
call	kʰɔl	kʰɔː
foul	faʊl	fɐu
coil	kɔɪ.ḷ	kʰɔːi.lou
sample	sæm.pʰḷ	saːm.pʰou
social	soʊ.ʃḷ	sou.sou
fail	feɪ.ḷ	fei.lou

Classifiers

As was explained above, classifiers and measure words are often matched with the nouns they classify according to some (e.g., physical) characteristic of the noun. Sometimes the relationship between a classifier and a particular noun characteristic might be quite straightforward, but this is definitely not always the case. Students of Chinese, in the U.S. as well as in Chinese-speaking communities across Asia, must study classifier–noun correspondences and commit them to memory in order to master their use. In this section, you will be exploring the use of classifiers in Standard Mandarin Chinese.

Beginning Level

3. Consider the data in Table 12.4:

TABLE 12.4 Data on Mandarin Chinese classifiers

Classifier	Mandarin example	Gloss
bēi	zhè bēi chá	'this cup of tea'
bēi	yī bēi pútáojiǔ	'a cup of wine'
bēi	sān bēi shuǐ	'three cups of water'
běn	zhè běn bǐjìběn	'this notebook'
běn	yī běn rìjì	'a journal'
běn	sān běn shū	'three books'
gēn	zhè gēn guǎizhàng	'this walking cane'

Classifier	Mandarin example	Gloss
gēn	yī gēn tóufà	'a (strand of) hair'
gēn	sān gēn yān	'three cigarettes'
jiā	zhè jiā diànyǐngyuàn	'this movie theater'
jiā	yī jiā cānguǎn	'a restaurant'
jiā	sān jiā shāngdiàn	'three stores'
jiàn	zhè jiàn chènshān	'this shirt'
jiàn	yī jiàn máoyī	'a pullover/sweater'
jiàn	sān jiàn wàitào	'three coats'
tiáo	zhè tiáo kùzi	'these trousers'
tiáo	yī tiáo qúnzi	'a skirt'
tiáo	sān tiáo wéijīn	'three shawls'
zhī	zhè zhī gǒu	'this dog'
zhī	yī zhī māo	'a cat'
zhī	sān zhī niǎo	'three birds'
gè	zhè gè hànzì	'this Chinese word'
gè	yī gè lánqiú	'a basketball'
gè	yī gè rén	'a person'
gè	sān gè sānmíngzhì	'three sandwiches'
gè	zhè gè xiǎngfǎ	'this idea'
gè	yī gè xuéqī	'a school term'

a. What characteristic do you think is denoted by each of the eight classifiers?
b. Does there seem to be a "default" classifier or measure word, one that denotes a broader range of noun types than the others?

Advanced Level

4. What do the additional examples in Table 12.5 tell you about the range of nouns that can follow the classifiers *jiàn* and *tiáo*?

TABLE 12.5 Additional data on Mandarin Chinese classifiers

Classifier	Mandarin example	Gloss
jiàn	zhè jiàn gōngjù	'this tool'
jiàn	yī jiàn jiājù	'a piece of furniture'
jiàn	zhè jiàn shì	'this matter/affair'
jiàn	sān jiàn zhēnpǐn	'three treasures'
tiáo	liǎng tiáo tuǐ	'two legs'
tiáo	zhè tiáo lù	'this road'
tiáo	zhè tiáo yú	'this fish'

References

Bauer, Robert S., and Paul K. Benedict. 1997. *Modern Cantonese phonology*. Berlin: Mouton de Gruyter.

Chao, Theresa Hsu. 1997. *Chinese heritage community language schools in the United States*. *ERIC Digest*. Washington, DC: ERIC Clearinghouse on Languages and Linguistics.

Chen, Su-Chiao. 1992. Language maintenance and shift in the Chinese community of Greater Philadelphia. PhD diss., University of Pennsylvania, Philadelphia.

Cheng, Cindy I-Fen. 2006. Out of Chinatown and into the suburbs: Chinese Americans and the politics of cultural citizenship in early cold war America. *American Quarterly* 58.4: 1067–1090.

Chow, Willard T. 1977. *The reemergence of an inner city: The pivot of Chinese settlement in the East Bay region of the San Francisco Bay Area*. San Francisco, CA: R & E Research Associates.

Dong, Lorraine, and Marlon K. Hom. 1980. Chinatown Chinese: The San Francisco dialect. *Amerasia* 7.1: 1–29.

Fong, Timothy P. 2008. *The contemporary Asian American experience: Beyond the model minority*. Upper Saddle River, NJ: Pearson Education.

Hall-Lew, Lauren. 2013. 'Flip-flop' and mergers-in-progress. *English Language and Linguistics*, 17(2): 359-390.

Hall-Lew, Lauren. 2009. Ethnicity and phonetic variation in a San Francisco neighborhood. PhD diss., Stanford University, Stanford, CA.

Jia, Gisela. 2008. Heritage language development, maintenance, and attrition among recent Chinese immigrants in New York City. In Agnes Weiyun He and Yun Xiao, eds., *Chinese as a heritage language: Fostering rooted world citizenry*, 189–203. Honolulu: University of Hawai'i, National Foreign Language Resource Center.

Laguerre, Michel S. 2006. The globalization of a panethnopolis: Richmond district as the New Chinatown in San Francisco. *GeoJournal* 64: 41–49.

Lee, Rose H. 1949. Social institutions of a Rocky Mountain Chinatown. *Social Forces* 27.1: 1–11.

Lewis, M. Paul, ed. 2009. *Ethnologue: Languages of the world*. 16th ed. Dallas, TX: SIL International. http://www.ethnologue.com/

Li, Charles N., and Sandra A. Thompson. 1989. *Mandarin Chinese: A functional reference grammar*. Berkeley: University of California Press.

Li Wei. 2009. *Ethnoburb: The New Ethnic Community in Urban America*. Honolulu: University of Hawaii Press.

Li Wei. 2007. *Chinese*. In David Britain, ed. *Language in the British Isles*, 308–324. Cambridge, UK: Cambridge University Press. .

Li Yuming and Li Wei, eds. 2013. *The language situation in China*. Vol. 1. Berlin: De Gruyter.

Luo, Shiow-Huey, and Richard L. Wiseman. 2000. Ethnic language maintenance among Chinese immigrant children in the United States. *International Journal of Intercultural Relations* 24: 307–324.

Matthews, Stephen, and Virginia Yip. 1994. *Cantonese: A comprehensive grammar*. New York: Routledge.

Mouw, Ted, and Yu Xie. 1999. Bilingualism and the academic achievement of first- and second-generation Asian Americans: Accommodation with or without assimilation? *American Sociological Review* 64.2: 232–252.

Norman, Jerry. 1988. *Chinese*. Cambridge: Cambridge University Press.

Pan, Shiwen. 1997. Chinese in New York. In Ofelia Garciá and Joshua A. Fishman, eds., *The multilingual apple: Languages in New York City*, 231–255. Berlin: Mouton de Gruyter.

Schachter, Paul. 1985. Parts-of-speech systems. In Timothy Shopen, ed., *Language typology and syntactic description*, vol. 1, 3–61. Cambridge: Cambridge University Press.

Semple, Kirk. 2009. In Chinatown, sound of the future is Mandarin. *New York Times*, October 21. http://www.nytimes.com/2009/10/22/nyregion/22chinese.html

Senft, Gunter. 2000. *Systems of nominal classification*. Cambridge: Cambridge University Press.

Shinagawa, Larry Hajime, and Dae Young Kim. 2008. *A portrait of Chinese Americans*. Washington, DC, and College Park, MD: Organization of Chinese Americans and Asian American Studies Program, University of Maryland.

Starr, Rebecca. 2011. Acquisition of sociolinguistic knowledge in a Mandarin-English dual-immersion school. PhD diss., Stanford University, Stanford, CA.

U.S. Census Bureau. n.d. B16001: Language spoken at home by ability to speak English for the population 5 years and over: Universe: Population 5 years and over. *2008–2010 American Community Survey 3-Year Estimates*. http://factfinder2.census.gov/faces/tableser vices/jsf/pages/productview.xhtml?pid=ACS_10_3YR_B16001&prodType=table

Wang, L. Ling-Chi. 2007. Chinatown in transition. *Amerasia Journal* 33.1: 31–48.

Wiley, Terrence G., Gerda de Klerk, Mengying Li, Na Liu, Yun Teng, and Ping Yang. 2008. Attitudes toward Mandarin, heritage languages, and dialect diversity among Chinese immigrants and international students in the United States. In Agnes Weiyun He and Yun Xiao, eds., *Chinese as a heritage language: Fostering rooted world citizenry*, 67–87. Honolulu: University of Hawai'i, National Foreign Language Resource Center.

Williams, Ashley M. 2006. Bilingualism and the construction of ethnic identity among Chinese Americans in the San Francisco Bay Area (California). PhD diss., University of Michigan, Ann Arbor.

Wong, Amy Wing-mei. 2010. New York City English and second generation Chinese Americans. *English Today* 26.3: 3-11.

Wong, Amy Wing-mei. 2007. Two vernacular features in the English of four American-born Chinese. *University of Pennsylvania Working Papers in Linguistics: Selected Papers from NWAV 35* 13.2: 217–230.

Yung, Judy, and the Chinese Historical Society of America. 2006. *San Francisco's Chinatown: Images of America*. San Francisco, CA: Arcadia.

Zhou, Min, and Yang Sao Xiong. 2005. The multifaceted American experiences of the children of Asian immigrants: Lessons for segmented assimilation. *Ethnic and Racial Studies* 28.6: 1119–1152.

13

HAITIAN CREOLE

Arthur K. Spears

Introduction

Haitian Creole is also called Haitian, Haitian French Creole, and simply Creole when it is clear which of several languages called Creole is being discussed. Linguists usually call it Haitian, while the speakers themselves usually call it Creole (*kreyòl* in Haitian). It is spoken by all Haitians (over 9 million) in Haiti, the nation occupying the western third of the Caribbean island of Hispaniola. The Dominican Republic occupies the other part of the island.

It is also spoken by perhaps three-quarters of a million to a million Haitian immigrants in the U.S., primarily in the cities of New York, Boston, and Miami. There are also significant communities of speakers in the Dominican Republic. In addition, there are speakers in Canada as well as in France and some of its overseas departments (part of France): Guadeloupe, Martinique, and French Guiana. Speakers are also found in Francophone African countries and in Caribbean countries. Indeed, Haitians are the largest immigrant group on almost all of the Caribbean islands and in the Bahamas, which are nearby in the Atlantic Ocean.

Haitian is a language of the creole type. Most linguists consider creole languages a sociohistorical category, but a few believe that many or most creole languages can also be characterized grammatically. (See the chapter on language contact.) Creole languages emerged out of intense contact among peoples speaking different languages. It is estimated that Haitian Creole had its genesis in the period between 1680 and 1740 (Lefebvre 1998: 57).

Although all Haitians speak Haitian and very few speak French, Haitian has long been stigmatized, shunned in education and the halls of power. So it is important to stress that Haitian is not a corrupt form of French, as many people believe. It is a separate language governed by its own grammatical rules, just as French is separate from Latin, each with its own grammatical rules.

History

Haitian Creole's history shows important features in common with the histories of other creole languages in the Caribbean and nearby areas. Among those languages are the following, with the colonial language that is the source of most of their vocabulary in parentheses: Martinique Creole (French); Palenquero (Spanish), in Columbia; Belizean Creole (English), Central America; Louisiana Creole (French); and Jamaican Patwa (English). (See the chapter on Jamaican Creole and that on Louisiana Creole and Cajun French in this book.) Most of Haitian Creole's morphology and syntax appear to come from West African languages, more specifically the Benue-Kwa languages of the Niger-Congo language family, primarily Gbe languages (Ewe and Fongbe). These were the most widely spoken West African languages during the Haitian language's formative period. Other languages, especially Bantu languages such as Kikongo, may have significantly influenced Haitian grammar afterward, due to the great surge in Bantu language–speaking Africans in the latter eighteenth century (Spears 1993). Most of the vocabulary came from the vernacular French of the colonists.

Haitians have immigrated to what is now the U.S. since before American independence. Indeed, the founder of the city of Chicago (in the 1770s), Jean-Baptiste Point (also Pointe) du Sable, was a (nonwhite) Haitian immigrant. The first wave of Haitians to immigrate to the U.S. comprised colonists, free mulattoes, and slaves. They arrived primarily in Louisiana, which was then a colony of France, as was Haiti, then called Saint-Domingue. This wave began with the outbreak of the Haitian Revolution in 1791. The revolution began as a slave revolt, with enslaved and free blacks and mulattoes fighting and winning their independence from France in 1804. This slave revolt was the first recorded one that was permanently successful. That is, the slaves were not eventually re-enslaved or incorporated into another political entity.

With independence, Haiti became the second European colony in the Western Hemisphere, after the U.S., to gain independence. Haiti's slave revolt, in addition to wars in Europe, so frustrated Napoleon in his efforts to solidify a great French colony in North America that he sold French Louisiana to the U.S. in 1803. Louisiana at that time consisted of a third of what is now the continental U.S. Thus, the Louisiana Purchase was a crucial factor in the rise of the U.S. to world power status, partly by means of territorial expansion westward.

The second wave of Haitian immigration to the U.S. took place during and after the U.S. occupation of Haiti between 1915 and 1934, which caused many hardships and deaths. This wave, consisting mostly of businessmen, professionals, and politicians, settled primarily in Harlem (New York City) and integrated into the U.S. mainstream (Joseph 2010).

The third wave began immediately after François "Papa Doc" Duvalier, who was supported by the U.S. government, became president of Haiti in 1957 (he later became a dictator). At first, these immigrants, most fleeing Duvalier's brutal rule, were primarily members of the business and professional elite or political opponents of Duvalier. The majority settled in the New York City area, with smaller numbers in Miami, Chicago, Boston, and Philadelphia. Later, many more middle-class Haitians came.

After Duvalier's death in 1971 the fourth and fifth waves of Haitian immigration occurred. The fourth wave was the largest one and took place after Duvalier's death, when his young son, Jean-Claude "Baby Doc" Duvalier, was installed as president for life. Many were working class, often with few or no skills, fleeing poor economic conditions. Many risked their lives at sea to get to the U.S. Most settled in the Miami area, while others settled in the New York City metropolitan area and in nearby cities such as East Orange, Irvington, and Newark, New Jersey, and also in Stamford, Connecticut.

The fifth wave of immigration was caused by the coup in 1991 against Haitian president Jean-Bertrand Aristide and the widespread instability and insecurity stemming from political and economic turmoil. This wave began to lessen significantly in 2003 when the U.S. Coast Guard, along with state and local government agencies, began activities, including the deployment of vessels in the Caribbean, to deter illegal and unsafe immigration from Haiti and other locations. The sixth wave came in the wake of the horrific 2010 earthquake in Haiti, from which Haiti was still recovering several years afterwards. (See Fouron 2010; Zéphir 2010; and Joseph 2010 for more on Haitian history.)

Social Context

Haitian Creole has the largest number of speakers of any creole language in the Western Hemisphere. (Nigerian Pidgin English, spoken in West Africa, has over 100 million speakers, but we do not know how many speak it as a native language, making it a creole language in their case. As a creole, it probably has more speakers than Haitian.) Today, Haitian has an official orthography (Faraclas et al. 2010), and it has been recognized as the co-official language (along with French) since 1987.

Although French in Haiti has always been the de facto official language (de jure since the 1914 constitution), it is spoken by only a tiny bilingual elite. Perhaps 5% of the population is proficient in French. All Haitians speak Creole. Haiti is a classic example of **diglossia**. Diglossia occurs in a society where a high (H) language, largely used in formal and government domains (those normally requiring literacy), coexists with a low (L) language of the masses. The low language is largely restricted to informal interaction and smaller-scale undertakings of local scope. (See the chapter "Language Contact" in this volume.) Since the country has traditionally been diglossic, with a functional separation of the two languages, the great majority of Haitians are relegated to second-class citizenship by their lack of knowledge of French. Currently, diglossia is weakening, with Haitian coming to be used in contexts formerly reserved for French, especially in education (Spears and Joseph 2010). Its use in Haitian schools has been established. However, the school system still has inadequate resources, due in part to the political turmoil that Haiti has suffered during the recent past.

Already challenged by political problems, Haiti saw its overall situation worsen in the aftermath of the devastating earthquake in January 2010 and the political and general social upheaval resulting from it. Earthquake deaths are estimated at over 300,000 people, with another 300,000 injured, and a million made homeless.

As noted, Haiti is a (decreasingly) diglossic country but one in which there is little bilingualism. Haitians in the U.S. who are fluent in French were typically members of the very small middle and upper classes in Haiti, where knowledge of French is common. Since they usually have not been able to transfer their higher status to the U.S., where they often live in the same neighborhoods and have the same incomes and occupations as Haitians from humble backgrounds, they cling to French as a status marker. Thus, at their social gatherings, introductions are made and conversations with strangers begun in French. Only after some degree of social comfort has been established can a switch to Haitian Creole be triggered. Even among French speakers, Haitian is used in most social interaction by far. Indeed, among Haitian-French bilinguals in the U.S., there is no domain in which French is used exclusively (Zéphir 2010).

To a certain extent, the Haitian-French diglossic situation in Haiti has been recast in the U.S. It is becoming one involving Haitian and English, where English instead of French is the high language. Haitian American conferences, meetings, workshops, award ceremonies, and club meetings are mostly conducted in English, even though all or almost all of the participants are Haitians (Zéphir 2010).

In their search for some cultural signifier to distinguish them from African Americans and other blacks, U.S. Haitians value and promote Haitian as an emblem of their distinct ethnicity, since too few in the community are proficient enough in French to use it. Also, Haitian has a higher status among U.S. Haitians than it does among the population of Haiti, which makes it easier to adopt it as a badge of ethnicity in the U.S.

The Haitian language in the U.S. as spoken by most speakers shows significant lexical borrowing from English, although the borrowing of morphological and syntactic structures appears to be minimal or insignificant at present. Lexical borrowing largely involves terms for goods that are much more widely found in the U.S. than in Haiti, for example, *CD* (compact disc), *cell(phone)*, *SUV* (sport utility vehicle), *microwave*, and *flatscreen* (television) (St. Fort 2010). Codeswitching among Haitian, French, and English is common, perhaps the norm. (See the chapters on language contact, Southwest Spanish, Chicano English, and Cajun French and Louisiana Creole for more on codeswitching.)

Print media targeting Haitian Americans are mostly in French, typically with a few pages devoted to articles or columns in Haitian. However, the leading newspaper in the U.S., the *Haitian Times*, is written almost completely in English. Radio broadcasts use Haitian and French and sometimes have heavy codeswitching (Zéphir 2010).

Most of the published information that we have on Haitian-English bilingual education is for New York City, although programs have been initiated in other metropolitan areas, notably Miami-Dade County and Boston. It took a while for public school administrators to understand that the overwhelming majority of Haitian students speak Haitian, not French or a Haitian French but a completely different language. Now there are bilingual programs located in the three New York City boroughs of Manhattan, Brooklyn, and Queens.

For a number of years, the New York State Department of Education has funded the Haitian Bilingual/ESL Technical Assistance Center, which produces instructional materials, organizes programs, and has offered a Haitian Language Academy, with immersion courses for nonnative speaker educators and advanced courses for Haitian-speaking educators focusing on reading, writing, and teaching the language. Haitian is also taught in courses at universities, among them Kansas University; the University of Massachusetts, Boston; and Indiana University, whose Creole Institute has been the most active producer of Haitians with graduate degrees in linguistics. Some governmental agencies in New York City provide materials and service advertisements in Haitian, and all the major hospitals have Haitian-speaking volunteers serving as interpreters and offering comfort to patients who are fully comfortable only with Haitian (Joseph 2010).

Some Linguistic Features

Introduction

As pointed out above, Haitian is not a form of French, and it is certainly not a corrupt form of French. It is a language with its own grammar, which in many ways is quite different from French (and English, too). Moreover, Haitian is mutually intelligible with neither French nor any West African heritage language. In the grammar of Haitian, overall we note elements that can be traced to West African languages, to French, or to neither. In the last case, Haitian grammatical features developed independently of transfer from West African languages and French. Below I provide examples of elements traceable to the first two.

The Haitian Lexicon

Haitian has a strong relationship to French because French was one of the main languages that played a role in its formation in the later seventeenth through early eighteenth centuries, providing most of the words in Haitian. These words were "transferred" from French into Haitian. We use the term *transfer* instead of *borrowing* because French words came into Haitian during the process of language formation itself. The French words were not borrowings because words are borrowed into a language that already exists autonomously from other languages.

TABLE 13.1 Some Haitian words of French origin

	French		Haitian	
	orthography	*phonemic transcription*	*orthography*	*phonemic transcription*
(1)	morne 'knoll'	/mɔʁn/	mòn 'mountain, hill'	/mɔn/
(2)	forme 'form'	/fɔʁm/	fòm 'form'	/fɔm/
(3)	sortir 'go out'	/sɔʁtiʁ/	sòti 'go out'	/sɔti/
(4)	faire 'do'	/fɛʁ/	fè 'do'	/fɛ/
(5)	terre 'earth, ground'	/tɛʁ/	tè 'ground'	/tɛ/
(6)	(la) boue 'mud'	/labu/	labou 'mud'	/labu/
(7)	(l')idée 'idea'	/lide/	lide 'idea'	/lide/
(8)	(l')empereur 'emperor'	/lãpəʁœʁ/	lanpèrè 'emperor'	/lãpɛrɛ/
(9)	(l')état 'state'	/leta/	leta 'state'	/leta/

Words transferred into Haitian from French underwent various phonological and morphological processes that we commonly witness in the history of languages. Look over the data in Table 13.1, which are discussed below. Note that the French uvular *r* is represented by the International Phonetic Alphabet symbol [ʁ].

One process in the transfer of French words to Haitian was postvocalic *r* deletion, which occurred word-medially, as in examples (1)–(3), and word-finally, as in examples (3)–(5). Another process was the fusion of the preceding French definite determiner (or article) onto the front of the Haitian cognate, as shown in examples (6)–(9). The French determiner appears in parentheses. The determiner takes the orthographic form *l'* when its vowel precedes a vowel beginning the following word. The *l* or the full determiner is simply fused to the beginning of the Haitian word. Thus, the Haitian words in (6)–(9) are monomorphemic. The French determiner remnant, so to speak, is merely part of the Haitian single morpheme and has no meaning of its own. To the Haitian words in (6)–(9), one can add the postposed Haitian determiner, *a* in the case of these example words. (There are several phonologically conditioned allomorphs of the determiner.) The Haitian word in (7), when used with a determiner, would be *lide a* 'the idea'.

(There is an indefinite determiner in Haitian as well, *yon*, with several allomorphs; it precedes the noun.)

Tense-Mood-Aspect Marking

As already noted, the West Africans arriving in Haiti during the early years spoke mostly Gbe languages (Benue-Kwa group of the Niger-Congo language family). The tense, mood, and aspect (TMA) systems of these languages appear to have been transferred to Haitian also (see Lefebvre 1998). This transfer included only the basic structure of the TMA systems; it did not include the phonemic shapes of words from these closely related Gbe languages. Among the grammatical parallels between Haitian and the Gbe languages is the occurrence of clitics, called **preverbal markers** in Haitian grammar, before a verb to express tense, mood, and/ or aspect. (Clitics have a fixed position in the clause and show close phonological interaction with each other and with adjacent words. English has clitics, too, for example, *n't* and *'ll* in *don't* and *he'll*.)

Note the following Haitian sentence with a preverbal marker in bold:

(10) Li **ap** travay
3sg NONPUNCTUAL ASPECT work
'He/she works.' HABITUAL ASPECT
'He/she is working.' PROGRESSIVE ASPECT

First, observe that the Haitian third singular pronoun *li* can mean 'he' or 'she', a feature we find in a number of West African languages but also in other languages of the world. Second, observe that the **nonpunctual** aspect preverbal marker in a particular sentence may express progressive aspect or habitual aspect, as illustrated in the glosses for (2). (Nonpunctual is the name of this verb form in creole studies, which consists of a verb preceded by the nonpunctual marker.) The social or discourse context in which the sentence is uttered reveals which aspectual meaning is intended by the speaker.

Keep in mind that it is not unusual for one verb form in a language to express either progressive aspect or habitual aspect, depending on the social or discourse context of utterance. For example, the Spanish present tense (indicative mood) verb form does so in most dialects of Spanish:

(11) Juan trabaja.
'Juan works.' HABITUAL ASPECT
'Juan is working.' PROGRESSIVE ASPECT

Nonpunctual markers normally occur only with nonstative (i.e., active) verbs such as *run, play, write, talk*, and so forth. (I simply provide examples of active verbs rather than discussing a complicated definition.)

In some languages, such as English, tense marking is normally obligatory. For example, if you are talking about something that happened yesterday, you have to use the past tense form of the verb. As shown in the next example, followed by its Haitian gloss, in English this is done with the past tense suffix *-ed*, which has several allomorphs. The name of the verb form created by adding the past tense suffix to the bare infinitive (without *to*) is the simple past.

Now look at the Haitian version in (12) more closely:

(12)	English:	He	talked	with	John	yesterday.
	Haitian:	Li	pale	ak	Jan	yè.

In the Haitian, *pale* 'talk' is the bare form of the verb. In other words, it is not accompanied by any preverbal marker indicating TMA. In some cases, a speaker would use a preverbal marker in this sentence, but in most cases that speaker would not. The point is that the Haitian verb does not have to be marked as past. One knows the speaker is referring to the past by the social or discourse context—what the speaker is talking about or has said before, as well as all kinds of other background information that the speaker and her or his hearers share.

While English has only the one tense suffix, Haitian has several preverbal markers expressing tense. The preverbal marker, *te*, is a type of past marker, but it is not obligatorily present in most instances; it is usually optional. (In speaking of tense here, I am talking about the main meaning of the English suffix and the preverbal markers. They have secondary, much less frequent meanings too.)

Linguists call *te*, in example (13), an anterior marker rather than a past marker because it is a **relative tense marker**. Its use is usually optional, as noted. Most important, it marks a **situation** (action, event, or state of affairs) as anterior, in other words, as occurring at a time prior to that of another situation (i.e., past in relation to the time of another situation). The English simple past suffix is an **absolute tense marker**: it is usually obligatory, and its use marks any event or state of affairs as occurring in the absolute past, that is, before the moment one is speaking, not just before any time used as a reference point without regard to the moment of speaking.

(13)	M	te		rive	anvan	yo	pati.
	1sg	ANTERIOR		arrive	before	3pl	leave
	'I (had) arrived before they left.'						

The two Haitian TMA preverbal markers that I have discussed are two of the three markers in the TMA system that are regarded as having been transferred from the Gbe languages. There are nearly a dozen such preverbal markers in the entire Haitian Creole TMA system, making possible the nuanced expression of TMA meanings and relationships.

Further Reading

Fortunately, a recent, up-to-date book (2010) contains most of the information that a beginning student of Haitian Creole would want: *The Haitian Creole Language: History, Structure, Use, and Education*, edited by Arthur K. Spears and Carole M. Berotte Joseph. It covers many sociolinguistic topics, such as bilingualism, diglossia, codeswitching, proverbs and other communicative genres, and language in education. It also has chapters devoted to literature in Haitian Creole and French as well as Haitian history. The references in its chapters provide further readings for more advanced study.

This book does not have in-depth discussions of phonological processes, morphology, syntax, and semantics. There is a significant though small body of literature on these topics, all of it written for linguists; most of it is in the form of scholarly journal articles.

Problem Sets

The following problems will teach you some basic points about Haitian grammar. Remember that the language, as presented in these problems, has been somewhat simplified in order to create level-appropriate problems for beginning students. Since Haiti is the world's largest country with a creole language spoken throughout, it is not surprising that there are several dialects. The following problems deal mostly with a Haitian dialect spoken in and around the northern city of Port de Paix, a short distance west of Haiti's second largest city, Cape Haitian. (It is of course also spoken outside of Haiti by those from this area.) The problems also deal with the Cape Haitian variety and that of the capital, Port-au-Prince.

Phonology, Morphology, and Dialect Variation

Port de Paix and Cape Haitian are roughly 20 miles from each other, and a different dialect is spoken in each city. For example, in regular, everyday speech in Port de Paix we find the following:

(14) sè   –m
       sister   1sg
       'my sister'

In Cape Haitian it is as follows:

(15) sèr   –a   –m
       sister   to   1sg
       'my sister'

1. Compare the Haitian data in (14) and (15) with the French equivalents for 'my sister' in (16) and (17) and answer the questions below:

(16) *ma*   *soeur*
     1sg   sister
     'my sister'

(17) *une*   *soeur*   *à*   *moi* (somewhat limited pragmatically)
     DET sg sister   to   me
     'a sister of mine'

   a. What grapheme (orthographic letter or letters representing one sound) in Haitian is equivalent to the French grapheme <*oeu*> (/œ/) in *soeur*? (Note: The Haitian grapheme does *not* represent the same sound as in French. That French sound was changed when French words with this sound were incorporated into Haitian.)

   b. Which Haitian dialect's word for 'sister' is closer to the French word? Why?

2. Now note the data in Table 13.2 (Haitian words appear on the left in Haitian orthography, with the phonemic transcription to the right):

TABLE 13.2 Comparison of words in three Haitian varieties and in French

	Haitian			French
	Port de Paix	Cape Haitian	Port-au-Prince	
'sister'	sè / sɛ/	sèr /sɛʁ*/	sè /sɛ/	soeur /sœʁ/
'peace'	pè / pɛ/	pè /pɛ/	pè /pɛ/	paix /pɛ/
'priest'	pè / pɛ/	pèr /pɛʁ*/	pè /pɛ/	père /pɛʁ/

(The Haitian r is actually velar for many speakers, but it is transcribed with the symbol for the pho-netically similar uvular French r, since the IPA symbol for the Haitian r does not "look like" an r. The Cape Haitian data are based on Valdman 1977.)

Compare the phonemic representations of the words in the three Haitian dialects.

   a. Which of the dialects are most alike? Briefly state why.

   b. Which of the dialects are more likely to have homonyms, based on these data?

   c. Which of the dialects is closest to French, based on these data?

   d. In which of the three dialects would we find *pèr-a-m* 'my priest'?

3. In Haitian, a rule of regressive vowel nasalization often applies:

   I. A vowel preceding a nasal consonant is nasalized.

Transcribe phonetically the pronunciation of 'my priest' in Cape Haitian after the application of this rule. (Nasalized vowels are transcribed by placing a tilde, [~], over the vowel, e.g., [ẽ].)

4. In Haitian, when /a/ is nasalized, it is actually realized as a mid central lax vowel:

   II. The low back nasalized vowel /ã/ is phonetically realized as the mid central nasalized vowel [ʌ̃]. (Note that when this sound occurs in speech, it may be the nasalized vowel phoneme or the result of the application of the vowel nasalization rule in I.)

   In light of this additional phonetic detail, what would be the phonetic transcription of 'my priest' in the Cape Haitian variety?

5. Table 13.3 shows that Haitian has (a) full possessive adjectives in the form of postposed suffixes (morphemes meaning 'my', 'your', etc.), used in more formal contexts and for emphasis; (b) phonologically reduced possessive adjectives, also in the form of postposed suffixes, used in more informal contexts and where emphasis is not needed; and (c) other phonologically conditioned allomorphs of these suffixes that have their own rules of use. The inventory of allomorphs and the rules governing them vary across dialects and are quite complex, but let us consider some cases in the Port de Paix variety. After examining the data in the following table, answer the questions based on them.

   Note also that there is a rule of glide formation affecting possessive adjective suffixes:

   III. Word final i /i/ and ou /u/, when they follow a vowel, change into the corresponding glide, [j] or [w].

   Now, taking the data in Table 13.3 into account, fill in the phonetic, surface representation in the Port de Paix dialect of the items in Table 13.4 by completing the following steps:

   a. For each word, write the noun with the full form of the possessive suffix in the "Full Morphemes" column. (The first one is done for you as an example.)

TABLE 13.3 Some Haitian possessive adjective suffixes, Port de Paix dialect

Person and number	English gloss	Full form		Reduced form(s)	Another allomorph
1sg	'my'	-mwen	/mwẽ/	-m	[none]
2sg	'your (sg.)'	-ou	/u/	[none]	[none]
3sg	'his/her/its'	-li	/li/	-i	-ni
3pl	'their'	-yo	/jo/	[none]	[none]

Note: Some forms in Haitian orthography are followed by their phonemic transcription between slashes.

TABLE 13.4 Some nouns and possessive suffixes, Port de Paix dialect

English gloss	Full morphemes (phonemic)	Reduced morphemes (phonemic) (if there is one)	Surface phonetic representation (with all three rules applied)
'his sister'	/sɛ-li/	/sɛ-i/	[sɛ-j]
'your sister'			
'my sister'			

    b. Write the noun with the reduced form of the possessive suffix in the next column—if there is one. If not, proceed to (c).

    c. Apply all of the rules we have discussed so far (rules I, II, and III), then write the phonetic representation for each word in the last column.

6. Now consider the following rule for the Port de Paix dialect and the additional words in (18) and (19):

IV. If the noun ends in a nasal consonant,

    a. Only the full first person singular possessive suffix allomorph can appear.

    b. Only the third person singular possessive suffix allomorph *ni* can appear.

(18) chanm   / ʃãm/   'room'
(19) kwizin /kwizin/ 'kitchen'

Provide the phonetic representation of the following vocabulary items after applying all four of the rules presented so far:

    a. 'his room'   _____

    b. 'my kitchen'   _____

    c. 'their kitchen'   _____

Tense Marking

Above, the Haitian anterior marker, *te*, was discussed. One complication in its use is as follows: although *te* is usually optional for situations (states, actions, and events) that occurred in the past, for one subclass of verbs, *te* is obligatorily present or absent depending on the particulars of that situation. After examining the data in Table 13.5, paying close attention to what is and is not grammatical, answer the questions presented after the table.

Note on variation: In this dialect, the third singular pronoun is usually *i*, not *li*, which is normal in Port-au-Prince and some other areas; the same holds for *e* 'and', as opposed to Port-au-Prince *epi*. *Te* and *t* are allomorphs of the anterior preverbal marker in all dialects. Some of the other dialects variably attach a determiner to *isi* 'here' and pronounce it with a final /t/: *isit-la*. *La-a* in these examples = 'there' + determiner.

TABLE 13.5 Verbs requiring the presence or absence of *te* under certain conditions, Port de Paix dialect

Example sentences	English translation

(20) a. I   te vini oz Etazini men i   retounen lakay-li
       3sg   *come* *to* *U.S.*   *but* *3sg* *return*   *house-3sg*
     b. *I   vini oz Etazini men i   retounen lakay-li
	'He came to the U.S., but he went (back) home.'

(21) a. *I   te vini oz Etazini e   i   toujou isi
       3sg   *come* *to* *U.S.* *and* *3sg* *still* *here*
     b. I   vini oz Etazini e   i   toujou isi
	'He came to the U.S., and he's still here.'

(22) a. I   te viv an Ayiti men li   pa   viv   la-a   ankò
       3sg   *live* *in* *Haiti* *but* *3sg* *not* *live* *there* *anymore*
     b. *I   viv an Ayiti men li   pa   viv   la-a   ankò
	'He lived in Haiti, but he doesn't live there anymore.'

(23) a. I   t   ay oz Etazini lotane   men li   ja   retounen lakay-li
       3sg *TE* *go* *to* *U.S.* *last-year* *but* *3sg* *already* *return* *house-3sg*
     b. *L   ay oz Etazini lotane   men li   ja   retounen lakay-li
       3sg
	'He went to the U.S. last year, but he has already returned home.'

(24) a. *I   t   ay oz Etazini lotane   e   i   toujou la-a
       3sg *TE* *go* *to* *U.S.* *last-year* *and* *3sg* *still* *there*
     b. L   ay oz Etazini lotane   e   i   toujou la-a
       3sg   *go* *to* *U.S.* *last-year* *and* *3sg* *still* *there*
	'He went to the U.S. last year, and he's still there.'

(25)

a. I   te   rete   oz   Etazini   men   lotane   i   retounen
    3sg   stay   in   U.S.   but   last-year   3sg   return
    'He stayed in the U.S. (for a while), but last year he returned.'

b. *I   te   rete   oz   Etazini   men   lotane   i   retounen   toujou   la-a
    3sg   stay   in   U.S.   but   last-year   3sg   return   still   there

(26)

a. *I   te   rete   oz   Etazini   pandan   etid-li   e   li   toujou   la-a
    3sg   stay   in   U.S.   during   study-3sg   and   3sg   still   there
    'He stayed in the U.S. during his studies, and he's still there.'

b. I   te   rete   oz   Etazini   pandan   etid-li   e   li   toujou   la-a
    3sg   stay   in   U.S.   during   study-3sg   and   3sg   still   there

Note on variation: In this dialect, the third singular pronoun is usually *i*, not *li*, which is normal in Port-au-Prince and some other areas; the same holds for *e* 'and', as opposed to Port-au-Prince *epi*; *Te* and *t* are allomorphs of the anterior preverbal marker in all dialects. Some of the other dialects variably attach a determiner to *isi* 'here' and pronounce it with a final /t/: *isit-la*. *La-a* in these examples = 'there' + determiner

TABLE 13.6 The meanings of two verbs

Verb	Meaning

7. List all the verbs that occur with *te* in the examples (four in all). Provide the gloss for each.
8. Two of these verbs express motion in some kind of direction from one location to another. Which ones are they?
9. The other two verbs in these examples do not express motion, but they express something related to location (as do the motion verbs). Remember, we are interested in the meaning of these two verbs in the examples only. In Table 13.6, write in these two verbs and their meaning based on the sentences in Table 13.5. Include the word *location* in your statement of the meaning of each verb.
10. The first two verbs could appropriately be labeled as "motion verbs." What would be an appropriate label for the second two verbs, the meanings for which you just provided?
11. Provide a generalization, based on all of the examples in Table 13.5, stating the conditions under which *te* is obligatorily present and obligatorily absent in clauses with this subclass of verbs.

References

Faraclas, Nicholas, Arthur K. Spears, Elizabeth Barrows, and Mayra Cortes Piñeiro. 2010. Orthography. In Arthur K. Spears and Carole M. Berotte Joseph, eds., *The Haitian Creole language: History, structure, use, and education*, 83–105. Lanham, MD: Lexington Books.

Fouron, Georges E. 2010. The history of Haiti in brief. In Arthur K. Spears and Carole M. Berotte Joseph, eds., *The Haitian Creole language: History, structure, use, and education*, 23–54. Lanham, MD: Lexington Books.

Joseph, Carole M. Berotte. 2010. Haitians in the U.S.: Language, politics, and education. In Arthur K. Spears and Carole M. Berotte Joseph, eds., *The Haitian Creole language: History, structure, use, and education*, 229–247. Lanham, MD: Lexington Books.

Lefebvre, Claire. 1998. *Creole genesis and the acquisition of grammar: The case of Haitian Creole.* New York: Cambridge University Press.

Spears, Arthur K. 1993. Where did Haitian Creole come from? A discussion of Hazaël-Massieux's and Baker's papers. In Salikoko S. Mufwene, ed., *Africanisms in Afro-American language varieties*, 156–166. Athens: University of Georgia Press.

Spears, Arthur K., and Carole M. Berotte Joseph, eds. 2010. *The Haitian Creole language: History, structure, use, and education.* Lanham, MD: Lexington Books.

St. Fort, Hugues. 2010. Creole-English code-switching in New York City. In Arthur K. Spears and Carole M. Berotte Joseph, eds., *The Haitian Creole language: History, structure, use, and education*, 131–151. Lanham, MD: Lexington Books.

Valdman, Albert. 1977. Creolization: Elaboration in the development of Creole French dialects. In Albert Valdman, ed., *Pidgin and creole linguistics,* 155–189. Bloomington: Indiana University Press.

Zéphir, Flore. 2010. The languages of Haitians and the history of Creole: Haiti and its diaspora. In Arthur K. Spears and Carole M. Berotte Joseph, eds., *The Haitian Creole language: History, structure, use, and education*, 55–80. Lanham, MD: Lexington Books.

14

CAJUN FRENCH AND LOUISIANA CREOLE

Michael D. Picone

Introduction

Though it is endangered, the persistence of French in Louisiana three centuries after the initial colonization is remarkable. While Cajun music has recently given the French language of Louisiana a measure of public awareness, the rich and diverse history of French in that state is not well known. It includes not only the story of Cajun French but also the rise and fall of Plantation Society French and the creation of a French-lexifier creole language, generally referred to as Louisiana French Creole, Louisiana Creole, French Creole, or just Creole. A **creole** language is one that was formed under social conditions of intense contact among peoples speaking different languages, notably, in the case of the Americas, in plantation societies. (Note that there are French-lexifier creoles spoken around the globe that are called Creole by their speakers. Linguists usually add the place where the language emerged to the name in order to clarify which one is being discussed, for example, Haitian Creole. See the chapters on language contact, Jamaican, and Haitian Creole for more details on creole languages.)

The complete story of French in Louisiana, as diverse as it is, is in fact only part of a larger, unfolding drama of much linguistic diversity. In the following, a sociohistorical overview of ethnic and linguistic diversity in the region will be instructive and will allow French dialects to be situated in their proper context. Afterward, some remarks on the study of Cajun French and Louisiana Creole will be presented, followed by problem sets drawn from those languages that highlight certain language contact patterns stemming from generalized bilingualism in the Francophone and Creolophone populations of Louisiana.

History

The lower valley of the Mississippi River (present-day Louisiana and its environs) and the Caribbean, into which it empties, have a rich history of linguistic diversity, a history that, in some aspects, is unequaled anywhere else in the Americas. Nowhere else did the three great colonial powers vying for control of North America—Spain, France, and England—all come into contact with each other, resulting in alternating periods of confrontation and cooperation, with effects on regional language developments. Even before the arrival of the Europeans and the large population of bound African laborers that they brought into the region (Hall 1992), indigenous languages from a number of different families (Caddoan, Muskogean, Siouan) and isolates (Adai, Atakapa, Chitimacha, Natchesan, Tunican) occupied the lower Mississippi Valley and what is today the state of Louisiana (Kniffen, Gregory, and Stokes 1987; Munro forthcoming). Probably during the precolonial period, this linguistic diversity ushered in the widespread use of pidginized Mobilian Jargon as a trade language and a language of diplomacy among indigenous tribes, who were loath to use their own ancestral languages with outsiders. (See Drechsel 1997, but note that Crawford 1978 gives an alternate account and asserts that Mobilian Jargon did not take root until the arrival of the colonizers.) Today, only a few hundred speakers of the indigenous languages of Louisiana remain, primarily speaking Koasati and Choctaw (languages of the Muskogean family). All the other historic indigenous languages of Louisiana are now extinct, except for a small population of Caddo speakers (Caddoan family) subsisting in Oklahoma.

The earliest European explorers to set foot in the region were Spaniards (notably Hernando de Soto in 1542), but the Spanish language would not weave its way into the regional linguistic fabric until the eighteenth century and would never occupy the place of historical prominence that French was destined to assume. The first permanent European settlement in the region was indeed the enterprise of the French, first from New France (Canada) and then from France proper. Starting from Canada and then traveling down the Mississippi, the French explorer René Robert Cavelier de La Salle located the river's mouth in 1682 and claimed the entire Mississippi basin and all its tributaries as a possession of Louis XIV of France (hence, "la Louisiane"). French Canadians subsequently founded two fledgling colonies: one in 1699 at Biloxi (now in Mississippi) and another in 1701 at Mobile (now in Alabama).

French Canadian trappers (*voyageurs* and *coureurs des bois* 'woods runners') did not play the same role in the lower Mississippi Valley as they did farther north, but at least one renegade trader from Canada played a profound role in the development of the area. Situated on the inland border between French and Spanish claims in an area inhabited by a diversity of Native American groups, Natchitoches, founded in 1714 by the maverick Canadian trader Louis Antoine Juchereau de St. Denis, flourished as a trading post. It became the hub for the development of the entire Cane River area, located in what is today the lower northwestern part of Louisiana. The area eventually evolved into a prime location for slave-based plantation agriculture (mostly cotton), which provided the economic base for an elite "Creole" society, comprising both whites and Free People of Color (capitalized because it refers to a specific group of "mixed" people that was legally recognized in French Louisiana).

THE TERM *CREOLE*

To this day, some members of both white and nonwhite groups lay exclusive claim to the self-designation Creole. One important source of the contention is their reluctance to accept that *creole* has several different meanings. In the Cane River area, for example, some individuals having mixed African and European ancestry claim the denominator as their own. Others, however, use the term to refer to whites of European ancestry born and raised in Louisiana or elsewhere in the New World. Beginning in the nineteenth century, the adjective *creole* referring to any local produce or population has been common usage in Louisiana. Today, many African Americans use it to refer primarily to light-skinned Creoles of color. Linguists, on the other hand, use it to designate a type of language. As has been noted throughout this book, for linguists *creole* denotes a new language variety that often emerged in the type of language contact situation that arose in the plantation system of Louisiana. According to the most widely accepted view, creole languages emerged due to the massive importation of slaves who did not possess a common language and needed to communicate among themselves and with overseers, slave drivers, and sometimes with slave owners.

The first stable colony, established in 1701 at Mobile, was a joint venture involving French Canadian officers and colonizers from France, speaking various regional dialects of French. In 1718 France became more involved in the colonization of the region with the founding of la Nouvelle Orléans (New Orleans). The Louisiana colony foundered at first, partly because of a lack of supplies and infrastructure. Keeping French colonial soldiers from abandoning their forts and cohabiting with Native American women was a constant problem, one that certainly led to sustained contact between French and various American Indian languages. Recruitment of new civilian colonists was difficult. Many Germans and Swiss were recruited, and the prisons and brothels of Paris contributed a sizable number of forced recruits. Still struggling, the socially and dialectally diverse colony was eventually ceded to the Spanish. In due course, however, the invention of the cotton gin and technological improvements related to sugar extraction permitted an economic boom that had its initial thrust toward the close of the Spanish administration (1763–1800) and continued unabated after the establishment of the American administration (1803), through to statehood (1812), and right up to the Civil War (1861–65). In tandem with the robust growth of the plantation system, an elite Creole society, such as the one described above for the Cane River area, emerged in all the urban centers and in areas with the most arable land. The wealth of the Creole families allowed them to procure schooling for their offspring, either in France or in regional private institutions, where the prestige dialect of French was taught. For some, there were also relatively frequent trips to France. Thus arose the widespread use of Plantation Society French within Creole society during the nineteenth century, reinforced by the continual arrival of educated French immigrants drawn to the now-favorable conditions in Louisiana (Picone forthcoming).

This Creole society was composed of both Europeans (French and Spanish for the most part) and Free People of Color. The Spanish administrators, moreover, had consciously pursued policies that had led expressly to the expansion and the elevation of the class of Free People of Color, as a way of securing the cooperation and empowerment of an inside group, in order to better manage wary French colonists. The Spanish language had a significant presence during the time period of their administration (1763–1800). This was so even earlier in the Cane River region, bordering New Spain, where Spanish missions and a fort had been established at Los Adaes (in 1716, to counter the presence of the French at Natchitoches). Late in the eighteenth century, Spanish colonists from the Canary Islands were also recruited. A handful of their descendants, all elderly, still speak Isleño Spanish (Lipski 1990).

Nevertheless, even though the Spanish presence at Los Adaes lasted from 1716 to 1772 and the Spanish held administrative authority over the entire region for a period of four decades (1763–1800), French always remained the most prominent European language in use in the region until some time after the arrival of large numbers of Anglophone Americans after the U.S.'s Louisiana Purchase in 1803. This purchase was made possible by the black-led Haitian Revolution (1791–1804), which ejected the French from Haiti and caused them to give up on pursuing an American empire. It was during the Spanish administration, in fact, that the plantation system began to flourish, with French (not Spanish) serving as the lexifier for the creole language variety emerging among the burgeoning slave caste. Moreover, the Francophone and Creolophone populations in Louisiana even increased during the initial American administration. This increase was substantial due to the arrival of thousands of slaves with their masters, and others during and after the Haitian Revolution. The increase was also fed by a steady influx of new immigrants and refugees coming directly from France as a consequence of the economic boom in Louisiana and the upheavals accompanying the French Revolution and the ensuing Napoleonic Wars.

The steadily increasing population of Anglophone American planters from other parts of the Southeast created a new dynamic, however, that would eventually lead to the dominance of Anglophone networks and institutions at the expense of French ones. Moreover, the influx of Anglophone planters was paralleled by the prolific importation into Louisiana of slaves from Anglophone regions of the

Southeast. Many accompanied their transplanting Anglophone owners, but often Francophone planters needing additional labor had little recourse but to import slaves from Anglophone regions. The main condition that brought this about was the ban in 1808 on importing slaves from outside the U.S. Thus, there was considerable pressure on both the Creole overclass to switch from French to English, the new language of power in which many were formally schooled, and also the slave underclass to switch from the creole language variety to an English one. Observe that already by 1840 approximately 80,500 slaves had been imported into Louisiana from other southern states, comprising approximately 48% of the total slave population of Louisiana at that time (Picone 2003).

The above scenario explains the fact that the Plantation Society French acquired by the Creole elite was the first variety of French to undergo decline in Louisiana. This decline was greatly accelerated when the Civil War decimated the wealth of Creole society, with the result that there were no longer sufficient means to support schooling in France or at other Francophone institutions. The French-lexifier creole spoken primarily by liberated ex-slaves was also deprived of the main mechanism of its perpetuation, due to the loss of the plantation system that had generated and maintained it. As indicated, even prior to the Civil War, Creole was increasingly coming into competition with English. However, the presence of English, paradoxically, may have initially exercised a preserving force on Louisiana Creole dialects by shielding them from eventual decreolization and reabsorption into French. This, in addition to the isolated and impoverished social conditions of ex-slaves and their offspring, may explain why Louisiana French Creole has subsisted longer than the now-vanished Plantation Society French.

Social Context

It should be pointed out that in many situations during the antebellum period, whites also acquired Creole in Louisiana. Ample testimonies exist of white Creole planters being raised by bondswomen and learning Creole as their first language. This very dynamic, in fact, often fed the necessity of sending white children of the Creole population to France or private schools in order to wean them away from exclusive use of Creole. Laboring whites and small farmers probably also learned the Creole language in close proximity to the black slaves with whom they worked the land. White speakers of Louisiana Creole are particularly prevalent today in Pointe Coupee Parish. It is conjectured that there they not only worked side by side in previous generations but also raised their children together, creating optimal conditions for language transmission (Klingler 2003). Today the total population of Creole speakers in Pointe Coupee (all ethnicities combined) is a little less than 2,000 people, mostly elderly, making it one of the strongholds for the subsistence of Creole in Louisiana. According to the U.S. Census Bureau, there are 6,021 speakers of "French

Creole" in Louisiana (American Community Survey 2011a). Note, however, that this figure does not differentiate between speakers of Louisana Creole and more recently arrived speakers of Haitian Creole and their offspring.

Plantation Society French, on the other hand, as once spoken by the Creole elite, has all but completely vanished in Louisiana, unless one considers the school-acquired Standard French of some Louisianans to be—in form, if not in function or status—the direct descendant of this former prestige dialect. The French acquired naturally (outside the classroom) that has persisted until the present day in Louisiana is not that of former Creole society but primarily the French of the Acadian immigrants, who were exiled from their former Canadian homeland in 1755. Forced by the victorious English to depart from what was once known as Acadia (today known as the provinces of Nova Scotia, New Brunswick, and Prince Edward Island), they began arriving in Louisiana in 1765, during the Spanish administration. Most prime real estate had already been claimed by earlier colonists, but the Acadians were assigned arable lands in the outlying prairies and along certain bayous (which were then more farmable than they are today, as massive soil depletion has occurred in the former floodplain, caused by the erection of flood-control levees along the Mississippi and by the installation of an extensive system of navigation canals crisscrossing the marshes).

Residing in the interior and not being dependent on the plantation system (except for a minority who gentrified), the Acadians were more isolated from the dynamics that led first to the acquisition and then to the decline of Plantation Society French. However, the introduction of post–Civil War assimilationist laws during Reconstruction forbade the use of French for schooling and for official purposes. The proscription of French continued in force when post-Reconstruction constitutions were drawn up by the growing Anglophone majority in Louisiana. This, coupled with the arrival of compulsory education in 1916, eventually set the stage for the beginning of the decline of Acadian French, more commonly referred to as Cajun French in Louisiana.

Many scholars, however, prefer the ethnicity-neutral term *Louisiana French*. The history of the language is diverse, and although the Cajun population predominates in the majority of parishes, non-Cajun ethnic groups also speak French and have contributed to the overall profile of the language: in particular African Americans, including ones descended from Creoles of color; American Indians, especially Houma (who generally view their dialect of French as distinct from Cajun); and the descendants of the non-Acadian Francophone populations predominating in certain parishes (Avoyelles, Plaquemines, etc.).

Regardless of their ethnicity, most parents who in their youth had been castigated in school when they arrived on the first day of class knowing no English decided to stop speaking French with their own children, to spare them similar humiliation. Parents also knew that there was no way to circumvent the primacy of English as a prerequisite for social and economic advancement. Thus, abrupt language transmission failure occurred between one generation (those now in their late sixties and older) and the next. An extensive system of highways in the state and the onslaught of Anglophone mass media have added to the growing infrastructure that is greatly decreasing the isolation of Cajuns (and other Francophone ethnicities) and is consequently creating an obstacle to the maintenance of their French. Due to the unfavorable circumstances for the maintenance of French and due to the abrupt transmission failure that has taken place, French in Louisiana is definitely on the list of endangered varieties, despite the fact that the U.S. Census Bureau listed a combined total of 136,162 speakers of French in Louisiana (20,979 self-classified as speakers of "Cajun" and 115,183 as speakers of "French"; [American Community Survey 2011b, 2011c]).

To get an idea of the decline in speaker numbers, compare this figure with the 261,678 French and Creole speakers in the 1990 U.S. Census, where the two groups were lumped together. Note that the most recent figure actually exceeds the 126,727 figure arrived at in the 2000 U.S. Census. Rather than reflecting an actual increase in the number of French speakers, the higher figure is likely due to the destigmatization of French and the increased willingness on the part of its speakers in Louisiana to proudly self-identify. While this is a welcome development, all but the smallest percentage of these are elderly, which does not bode well for the natural transmission of Cajun French in the future. (It is interesting to note in passing, however, that Cajun English has replaced Cajun French as a mark of social identity for many Cajuns in Louisiana. Others, however, have conformed to the prevailing dialect of Southern American English.)

In fact, the population of children learning French in the rather extensive French immersion programs in Louisiana (instituted beginning in 1968, when the state underwent an about-face and decided to start promoting French-English bilingualism) probably greatly outnumbers the population of children acquiring French in natural settings. In 2002 there were 2,200 students enrolled in French immersion programs in the public schools in Louisiana, and the number has grown since then due to the popularity of these programs. Hence, some form of French is being maintained among a minority of young Louisianans in school, but by and large it is not Cajun French.

Nevertheless, the "Cajun Renaissance," beginning in the late 1960s, did serve to promote preservation. Some conscientious parents and grandparents returned to the practice of speaking French to their children and grandchildren. Many adolescent Cajuns with musical aspirations acquire a certain amount of French in the process of composing and performing Cajun songs, which have now garnered international popular appeal. Only the future will reveal how much French, and what kind of French, will be maintained in the state of Louisiana. As in the rest of the U.S., the immigration into Louisiana of Spanish-speaking people, a dynamic that accelerated due to rebuilding after the devastation of Hurricane Katrina in 2005, is destined to make Spanish the largest minority language in the state.

Some Linguistic Features

Cajun French and Language Contact

There are virtually no monolingual French speakers left in Louisiana. Today's fluent French speakers are also perfectly fluent English speakers. In such a bilingual setting, language contact phenomena are a fertile field for investigation.

There are some assimilated borrowings from English, the dominant language, into French: for example, *guimbler* [gẽble] 'to gamble', *improuver* [ẽpruve] 'to improve', and *récorder* [rekɔrde] 'to record'. Somewhat paradoxically, however, pervasive bilingualism seems ultimately to have led to less recourse to borrowing as a neological strategy (that is, a strategy for increasing vocabulary), because it is always possible to simply switch from French to English (that is, to engage in codeswitching) in order to insert a word, phrase, or sentence—and comprehension will never be compromised. As a result, the practice of codeswitching is very common in bilingual discourse in Louisiana. (See the chapters on language contact and Southwest Spanish for more discussion on codeswitching and borrowing.) For example, there is no need to invent a new expression in Cajun French to designate a new appliance, because the English term can be easily inserted into French discourse, and the term will be universally understood. Observe the following example, with a word-for-word translation for the French words under each line of the sentence (by common convention when transcribing, researchers of Louisiana French use small capital letters to designate codeswitched words inserted into French discourse):

(1) On   a   acheté   un   nouveau   MICROWAVE OVEN
     3pl   AUX   bought   Indef-DET   new
     à   l'ouvrage.
     at   work
     'They bought a new microwave oven at work.'

This kind of codeswitching may contribute to the neological impoverishment of French (and Creole) in Louisiana and may be a contributing factor in the process of language attrition and decline. But note, by way of comparison and contrast, that Spanish continues to thrive in most bilingual settings in the U.S., where similar codeswitching patterns are often observed (although the effects of neological impoverishment for some speakers cannot be ruled out). The difference is that various forces contributing to the maintenance of Spanish—a constant influx of new Spanish monolinguals, high population concentrations, fairly easy access to and consistent intercourse with Latin America, availability of Spanish media, and so on—have little or no parallel in connection with the use of French in Louisiana. Such factors either are absent or came too late to make a significant difference for the systematic maintenance of French.

Notice that codeswitched words, as opposed to borrowed words, do not assimilate to French pronunciation—as indicated, for example, by the English stress

patterns and the phonetic quality of the American English rhotic liquid consonant [ɹ] and [ɚ] in the word *trailer* [ˈtɹejlɚ] in (2). Note that for some speakers, the
word-final *r* would be absent altogether, replaced by a nonrhotic schwa, [ˈtɹejlə].
(Sometimes [ɚ] is transcribed as syllabic: [ɹ̩].)

> (2) On les a quitté le TRAILER.
> 'They left them the trailer.'

The morphological treatment of some codeswitched vocabulary in Cajun
French is of special interest. Some models of codeswitching assign every part of
every utterance to either one language or the other (e.g., Myers-Scotton 1993).
In the discourse of Louisiana bilinguals, however, there is evidence that code-
intermediate phenomena occur (that is, phenomena that are, strictly speaking,
neither French nor English) and that such code-intermediate phenomena remain
stable rather than constituting some kind of transitional phase leading to assimilation (see Picone 1994, 1997a for more discussion). Some of the problem sets
below provide an opportunity to reflect on aspects of this phenomenon.

Louisiana Creole Nouns and Verbs

Just as in Cajun French, codeswitching is very common in Louisiana Creole.
An examination of the examples from Louisiana Creole in the data sets below
will allow you to determine the kind of morphological treatment codeswitched
vocabulary is subject to.

Example sentences (3)–(5) provide instances of codeswitched nouns in contexts calling for plurality (Klingler 2003). Keep in mind that, just as in the case of
Cajun French, plurality in Louisiana Creole is represented by a preceding determiner or some other contextual clue, not by inflection of the noun itself. In (3)
and (4) the preceding determiner *de* [de] 'some' conveys plurality. In (5) no determiner is needed to correctly interpret the noun as being plural.

> (3) Ye   te   mèn   de   BAG
> they PAST bring some *bag*
> 'They used to bring bags.'

> (4) Li te   konnen di   de   bon   STORY.
> he PAST AUX-can tell some good *story*
> 'He could tell good stories.'

> (5) Mo te   konnen fe   QUILT.
> I   PAST AUX-can make *quilt*
> 'I used to be able to make quilts.'

As sentences (6)–(8) illustrate, Louisiana Creole, like virtually all creoles,
uses relatively little verbal inflection. Tense and aspect are usually designated by

preverbal markers. In (6), as in (3)–(5), the marker for the past is *te* [te], glossed as PAST$_1$.

(6) Li   te   travay.
     He   PAST$_1$ work
     'He worked.'

However, in the Pointe Coupee dialect of Louisiana Creole, as an alternative to the *te* preverbal marking, a long (inflected) form of the verb can also be used to indicate the past tense, glossed here as PAST$_2$:

(7) Li   travay   -e.
     He   work   PAST$_2$
     'He worked.'

In addition, Pointe Coupee also allows the preverbal marking to occur with the long (or inflected) form of the verb.

(8) Li   te   travay   -e.
     He   PAST$_1$ work   PAST$_2$
     'He worked.'

Further Reading

Both Cajun French and Louisiana Creole have suffered from relatively little scholarly attention until recently. Only one comprehensive treatment of Cajun French has been published to date: Conwell and Juilland 1963. It describes a dialect as it was spoken in Lafayette Parish in 1959, when there were still many monolingual French speakers alive. Almost four decades passed before another book-length treatment of Cajun French appeared: Rottet 2001 treats aspects of cross-generational linguistic phenomena accompanying language decline in Terrebonne and Lafourche parishes. The first book-length scholarly presentation (in English) of Louisiana Creole is also of recent vintage: Klingler 2003 comprises an extensive sociohistorical account of the probable genesis of Louisiana Creole followed by a linguistic description of the dialect spoken in Pointe Coupee Parish, as well as transcriptions of sample conversations in Creole with translations.

A compendium of recent research on both French and Creole in Louisiana was edited by Valdman (1997) and contains contributions from most of the active researchers in the field. Completed in 1998, the *Dictionary of Louisiana Creole* (edited by Valdman et al.) contains not only an extensive inventory of vocabulary but also a rich assortment of contextual examples, as does the recently completed companion volume *Dictionary of Louisiana French, as Spoken in Cajun, Creole, and*

American Indian Communities (Valdman et al. 2010). This same team of researchers also produced a CD-ROM on Cajun French, including many illustrative
transcriptions, sometimes accompanied by audio files (Rojas et al. 2003). Picone
(1997b) provides an overview of the use of Cajun French in its various registers
(that is, domains of daily living). Among the contributions to be found in *Language
Variety in the South: Historical and Contemporary Perspectives* (Picone and Davies
forthcoming), eight essays concentrate on the languages and dialects of Louisiana,
including French, Creole, English, American Sign Language, Caddo (Caddoan
family), and Ofo (Siouan family).

A very good sampling of authentic Cajun and Creole oral traditions, in the
form of transcriptions and facing translations, is available in *Cajun and Creole Folktales* (Ancelet 1994; see also Ancelet, Edwards, and Pitre 1991). Subsequent to the
cultural narratives of *Lâche pas la patate* (Reed 1976), there has also been a spate of
literary production in conjunction with the Cajun Renaissance and its aftermath.
Collections of poetry are the most common form of literary expression: *Cris sur
le bayou* (Ancelet 1980), *Acadie tropicale* (Ancelet 1983), *Voyage de nuit* (Richard
1987), and *Lait à mère* (Cheramie 1997), among others. Prose is not entirely absent:
C'est p'us pareil (Guidry 1982) and *Feux follets* (Cheramie 1998).

Problem Sets

For the purposes of the following problems, you may assume that all native French
forms, native Creole forms, and codeswitched English forms have morphologies
similar to what you see in these data. This is a necessary oversimplification for ease
of presentation; in reality, some of the morphological patterns shown here correspond to very strong tendencies but are not absolutely regular.

In all of the problem sets below, be sure to base your answer on the phonetic
transcription and not the orthography since the spelling may be misleading. For
example, the final -*s* or -*x* of plurality affixed to French nouns is an orthographic
convention only and is not pronounced. This is all the more important in the
context of the ancestral Francophone Cajun population of Louisiana, since, as
indicated above, very few of them have ever had the privilege of being schooled
in French and, consequently, are not literate in the language.

Cajun French Nouns and Pluralization

Now examine the following data, referring to the information provided in Table
14.1 as your key for understanding the behavior of the determiners. The same set
of nouns appears in the singular in the left-hand column and in the plural in the
right-hand column. Nouns and their preceding determiners are all underlined
for easy recognition and are immediately followed by their phonetic transcriptions (with a space added to each transcription to indicate the boundary between
the determiner and the following noun, and with a stress mark preceding each
stressed syllable in the accompanying phonetic transcription).

TABLE 14.1 French nouns

Singular forms	Plural forms
(9) a. la canne [la ˈkɔn] 'the cane'	b. Je connais les cannes [le ˈkɔn]. 'I know about sugarcane.'
(10) a. Le bateau [lə baˈto] était contre la maison [la meˈzõ]. 'The boat was up against the house.'	b. Les bateaux [le baˈto] étaient contre les maisons [le meˈzõ]. 'The boats were up against the houses.'
(11) a. Je pêche dans le bayou [lə baˈju]. 'I fish in the bayou.'	b. Je pêche dans les bayous [le baˈju]. 'I fish in the bayous.'
(12) a. la chevrette [la ʃəˈvrɛt] 'the shrimp'	b. les chevrettes [le ʃəˈvrɛt] 'the shrimp'
(13) a. la grive [la ˈgriv] 'the robin'	b. les grives [le ˈgriv] 'the robins'
(14) a. l'arbre [l arb] (masc.) 'the tree'	b. les arbres [lez ˈarb] 'the trees'
(15) a. l'affaire [l aˈfær] (fem.) 'the thing'	b. les affaires [lez aˈfær] comme ça 'things like that'
(16) a. l'écume [l eˈkym] (fem.) 'the foam'	b. Quand il était cuit un peu, fallait ôter les écumes [lez eˈkym]. 'When it was cooked for a little while, it was necessary to skim the foam.'

Notice that in examples (9)–(13), it is the preceding determiner that marks plurality due to a change in vowel quality from *le* [lə] (masculine singular) or *la* [la] (feminine singular) to *les* [le] (plural for both genders). Note also that if a singular determiner, whether masculine or feminine, is followed by a vowel or a semivowel (glide) at the beginning of the next French word, the determiner loses its own vowel, as in (14)–(16). This vowel loss is represented orthographically as a contraction: *l'* [l]. For the plural determiner before a vowel or a semivowel at the beginning of the next French word, sandhi (or *liaison*, the term used in French grammar) results in an additional phonological representation of plurality because, in that particular context, *les* is usually pronounced [lez], not [le].

Now answer the questions below concerning how codeswitched nouns (Table 14.2) are incorporated into Cajun French sentences:

TABLE 14.2 Codeswitched (English) nouns

Singular forms	Plural forms
(17) a. On les a quitté le TRAILER [lə ˈtɹejlɚ]. 'They left them the trailer.'	b. On les a quitté les TRAILER. [le ˈtɹejlɚ] 'They left them the trailers.'
(18) a. le SOYBEAN [lə ˈsɔjbin] 'the soybean'	b. Les SOYBEAN [le ˈsɔjbin] c'est une récolte qui existait pas trente ans passé. 'Soybeans, that's a crop that didn't exist thirty years ago.'
(19) a. le TANK TRUCK [lə ˈtejnk tɹʌk] 'the tank truck'	b. les TANK TRUCK [le ˈtejnk tɹʌk] 'the tank trucks'
(20) a. le WEEVIL [lə ˈwiv] 'the boll weevil'	b. Les WEEVIL [le ˈwiv], ils vont tous le manger. 'All the boll weevils are going to eat it up.'
(21) a. le ALLERGY [lə ˈæləɹdʒij] 'the allergy'	b. les ALLERGY [le ˈæləɹdʒij] 'the allergies'

1.   Do plural codeswitched nouns from English have the same inflectional mor-
     phology as plural French nouns? Explain your answer.

Cajun French Past Tense Verb Inflection

Now examine a second data set, where codeswitched verbs have been inserted
into Cajun French discourse. To analyze this data set, one must first be aware that
representation of the past tense in Cajun French is discontinuous. That is to say,
two noncontiguous components are normally present. This was also true for some
Creolophones in the Pointe Coupee area, as exemplified in (8) above. In the case
of Cajun French, however, discontinuous representation of the past involves (1)
the appropriate form of the auxiliary verb *avoir* 'to have' and (2) a suffixal inflection attached to the main verb to form the past participle, *-é*. For example, the
utterance *Il a travaillé* 'He worked' is analyzed as follows:

(22)   Il   a   travaill   -é.
       He   have-PAST₁   work   PAST₂
       'He worked.'

By way of comparison, the equivalent English past tense is represented by
verbal inflection alone, either by virtue of a suffix *-ed* (*He worked*) or by virtue of
vowel alternation (*She rode the horse*):

(23)   He   work   -ed.
            work   -PAST

(24)   She   rode   the horse.
             ride-PAST

Now consider the following data. Each actual French utterance appears above
a starred, ungrammatical utterance showing what would have occurred if French
inflectional morphology had been applied to the codeswitched verb from English
for that same utterance. But only the first utterance in each pair actually occurs.
Assume that the English words are pronounced as any native speaker of English
would pronounce them.

(25)   a.   Il   a   CONVINCE   sa   femme.
            he   have-PAST₁   his   wife
            'He convinced his wife.'
       b.   *Il   a   CONVINCE   -é   sa   femme.
            he   have-PAST₁   -PAST₂   his   wife

(26)   a.   Il   a   RETIRE.
            he   have-PAST₁
            'He retired.'

b. *Il   a   RETIRE   -é.
    he   have-PAST$_1$ PAST$_2$

(27) a. ça   a   PARK   le   char.
         they   have-PAST$_1$ the   car
         'They parked the car.'

   b. *ça   a   PARK   -é   le   char.
        they have-PAST$_1$ PAST$_2$ the   car

(28) a. ça   a   été   INVENT   avant   ça. (passive voice)
         that   have-PAST$_1$ be-PASS   before   that
         'That was invented before that.'

   b. *ça   a   été   INVENT   -é   avant   ça.
        that have-PAST$_1$ be-PASS   PAST$_2$ before   that

(29) a. Elle   a   RIDE   dessus   le   cheval.
         she   have-PAST$_1$ atop   the   horse
         'She rode on the horse.'

   b. *Elle   a   RIDE   -é   dessus   le   cheval.
        she   have-PAST$_1$ PAST$_2$ atop   the   horse

(30) a. On   a   DRIVE   en   ville.
         we   have-PAST$_1$ to   town
         'We drove to New Orleans.'

   b. *On   a   DRIVE   -é   en   ville.
        we   have-PAST$_1$ PAST$_2$ to   town

2. In the data above, do codeswitched verbs (in the real utterances, not in the ungrammatical utterances) conform completely to either the Cajun French or the English system of representation of the past tense? Explain your answer.

Cajun French and Louisiana Creole Verb Inflection with Other Tenses, with Aspect, and with Mood

A verb indicates an action or state of being (*eat, run, be, become*). Tense indicates the time when that action or state of being takes place (for example, past *we ate*, present *we eat*, and future *we will eat*). Aspect indicates the manner in which the action or state of being unfolds (for example, completed action, *we have eaten*; incomplete [or progressive] action, *we are eating*; beginning of action, *we start eating*; repetitive action, *we keep eating*; or some other temporal delimitation). Mood indicates the attitude of the speaker, usually regarding the reality, unreality, or potentiality of the action or state of being, in order to express possibility, uncertainty, or definiteness (using, for example, conditionals, *we would eat if . . .*; imperatives, *let's eat!*; and modal auxiliary verbs in English such as those in *we may eat, we might eat, we can eat, we could eat, we should eat*, etc.).

Cajun French Codeswitched Verbs

Now consider this additional set of data in Cajun French (Table 14.3). Compare the typical treatment of the codeswitched verb *drive* with the treatment of the Cajun French verb *travailler* 'to work'. (For ease of identification, inflectional verb endings are separated from the verb root by a hyphen.)

TABLE 14.3 Tense, mood, and aspect

PAST (TENSE):

with PRESENT AUX *a* 'has' (infinitive *avoir* 'to have')	(31) a. Il a travaill-é.	'He worked.'
	b. Il a DRIVE.	'He drove.'

FUTURE (TENSE):

PERIPHRASTIC FUTURE, with inflected PRESENT *va* (infinitive *aller* 'to go')	(32) a. Il va travaill-er.	'He will work.'
	b. Il va DRIVE.	'He will drive.'

or

SIMPLE FUTURE, with inflected main verb	(33) a. Il travaill-era.	'He will work.'
	b. *Il DRIVE-era.	'He will drive.'

INCHOATIVE (ASPECT):

with inflected AUX *est* 'is' (infinitive *être* 'to be') and PARTICIPIAL ADJECTIVE *parti* 'started'	(34) a. Il est parti travaill-er.	'He started to work.'
	b. Il est parti DRIVE.	'He started to drive.'

PRESENT PROGRESSIVE (ASPECT):

with inflected PRESENT AUX *est* 'is' (infinitive *être* 'to be') and ADVERB *après* 'in progress'	(35) a. Il est après travaill-er.	'He's working (right now).'
	b. Il est après DRIVE.	'He's driving (right now).'

PAST PROGRESSIVE (ASPECT):

with inflected IMPERFECT AUX *était* 'was' (infinitive *être* 'to be') and ADVERB *après* 'in progress'	(36) a. Il était après travaill-er.	'He was working.'
	b. Il était après DRIVE.	'He was driving.'

or

with inflected IMPERFECT main verb	(37) a. Il travaill-ait.	'He was working.'
	b. *Il DRIVE-ait.	'He was driving.'

CONDITIONAL (MOOD):

with inflected CONDITIONAL AUX *pourrait* 'could/would' (infinitive *pouvoir* 'to be able')	(38) a. Il pourrait travaill-er.	'He could/would work.'
	b. Il pourrait drive.	'He could/would drive.'

or

with inflected CONDITIONAL main verb	(39) a. Il travaill-erait.	'He could/would work.'
	b. *Il DRIVE-erait.	'He could/would drive.'

OBLIGATION (MOOD):

with inflected *a* 'has' (infinitive *avoir* 'to have') and PREPOSITION *pour* 'for'	(40) a. Il a pour travaill-er.	'He has to work.'
	b. Il a pour DRIVE.	'He has to drive.'

IMPERATIVE (MOOD):

1pl, with inflected PRESENT *allons* 'let's' (infinitive *aller* 'to go')	(41) a. Allons travaill-er!	'Let's work!'
	b. Allons DRIVE!	'Let's drive!'

or

2 sg, with inflected main verb	(42) a. Travaill-ez!	'Work!'
	b. *DRIVE-ez!	'Drive!'

3. Make a general statement about the inflectional morphology used on native Cajun French verbs as compared to that used on codeswitched English verbs.

Louisiana Creole Codeswitched Verbs

Now compare the morphological treatment of codeswitched verbs in Louisiana Creole (Klingler 2003). Each actual Creole utterance appears above a starred, ungrammatical utterance showing what would have occurred if inflectional morphology had been applied to the codeswitched verb from English for that same utterance. But only the first utterance in each pair actually occurs:

(43) a. La   lonmp, li   te   BLOW   li   OUT.
         Det   lamp   3sg   PAST$_1$ 3sg
         'The lamp, he blew it out.'
     b. *La   lonmp, li   te   BLOW   -e   li   OUT.
         Det   lamp   3sg   PAST$_1$ PAST$_2$ 3sg

(44) a. Li   di te   pa kapab mèt li   paski   li   te   pas QUALIFY.
         3sg say PAST$_1$ not able put 3sg because 3sg PAST$_1$ not
         'He said he couldn't put her [in office] because she didn't qualify.'
     b. *Li di te   pa kapab mèt li   paski   li   te   pas QUALIFY
         3sg say PAST$_1$ not able put 3sg because 3sg PAST$_1$ not
         -e.
         PAST$_2$
         'He said he couldn't put her [in office] because she didn't qualify.'

(45) a. Li   te   si   SHOCK.
         3sg   PAST$_1$ so
         'He was so shocked.' (Note that there is no verb meaning 'be' in Creole.)
     b. *Li   te   si   SHOCK   -e.
         3sg   PAST$_1$ so   -PAST$_2$

4. Review the morphology of Creole verbs as explained and exemplified in (6)–(8) and then answer the following question. How does the morphological treatment of English verbs codeswitched into Louisiana Creole compare to the treatment of Creole verbs?

5. How does the morphological treatment of vocabulary codeswitched into Louisiana Creole, both nouns and verbs, compare to what was observed for Cajun French?

General Questions about Language Varieties of Louisiana

6. Make a list of all the languages and language varieties named in this chapter. In cases in which enough information has been given, group them according to language families.

7. How is the linguistic history of Louisiana connected to the history of Haiti?

References

American Community Survey. 2011a. [U.S. Census data for French Creole] MLA Language Map Data Center. http://www.mla.org/map_data_results&mode=lang_tops& SRVY_YEAR=2010&lang_id=623

American Community Survey. 2011b. [U.S. Census data for "Cajun"]. MLA Language Map Data Center. http://www.mla.org/map_data_results&mode=lang_tops& SRVY_YEAR=2010&lang_id=624.

American Community Survey. 2011c. [U.S. Census data for French]. MLA Language Map Data Center. http://www.mla.org/map_data_results&mode=lang_tops& SRVY_YEAR=2010&lang_id=620

Ancelet, Barry Jean, ed. 1980. *Cris sur le bayou*. Montreal: Éditions Intermède.

Ancelet, Barry Jean, ed. 1983. *Acadie tropicale*. Lafayette: Center for Louisiana Studies, University of Southwestern Louisiana.

Ancelet, Barry Jean. 1994. *Cajun and Creole folktales: The French oral tradition of South Louisiana*. Jackson: University Press of Mississippi.

Ancelet, Barry Jean, Jay D. Edwards, and Glen Pitre. 1991. *Cajun country*. Jackson: University Press of Mississippi.

Cheramie, David. 1997. *Lait à mère*. Moncton: Éditions d'Acadie.

Cheramie, David, ed. 1998. *Feux follets: Anthologie de la nouvelle louisianaise*. Lafayette: Éditions de la Nouvelle Acadie.

Conwell, Marilyn, and Alphonse Juilland. 1963. *Louisiana French grammar*. The Hague: Mouton.

Crawford, James M. 1978. *The Mobilian Trade Language*. Knoxville: University of Tennessee Press.

Drechsel, Emanuel J. 1997. *Mobilian Jargon: Linguistic and sociohistorical aspects of a Native American pidgin*. Oxford: Clarendon.

Guidry, Richard. 1982. *C'est p'us pareil*. Lafayette: Center for Louisiana Studies, University of Southwestern Louisiana.

Hall, Gwendolyn Midlo. 1992. *Africans in colonial Louisiana: The development of Afro-Creole culture in the eighteenth century*. Baton Rouge: Louisiana State University Press.

Klingler, Thomas A. 2003. *If I could turn my tongue like that: The creole language of Pointe Coupee Parish, Louisiana*. Baton Rouge: Louisiana State University Press.

Kniffen, Fred B., Hiram F. Gregory, and George A. Stokes. 1987. *The historic Indian tribes of Louisiana: From 1542 to the present*. Baton Rouge: Louisiana State University Press.

Lipski, John M. 1990. *The language of the Isleños: Vestigial Spanish in Louisiana*. Baton Rouge: Louisiana State University Press.

Munro, Pamela. Forthcoming. American Indian languages of the Southeast: An introduction. In Michael D. Picone and Catherine Evans Davies, eds., *Language variety in the South: Historical and contemporary perspectives*. Tuscaloosa: University of Alabama Press.

Myers-Scotton, Carol. 1993. *Duelling languages: Grammatical structure in codeswitching*. Oxford: Oxford University Press.

Picone, Michael D. 1994. Code-intermediate phenomena in Louisiana French. In Katharine Beals, Jeannette Denton, Robert Knippen, Lynette Melnar, Hisam Suzuki, and Erica Zeinfeld, eds., *CLS 30-I: Papers from the Thirtieth Regional Meeting of the Chicago Linguistic Society*, Vol. 1, *The Main Session*, 320–334. Chicago: Chicago Linguistic Society.

Picone, Michael D. 1997a. Codeswitching and loss of inflection in Louisiana French. In Cynthia Bernstein, Tom Nunnally, and Robin Sabino, eds., *Language variety in the South revisited*, 152–162. Tuscaloosa: University of Alabama Press.

Picone, Michael D. 1997b. Enclave dialect contraction: An external overview of Louisiana French. *American Speech* 72: 117–153.

Picone, Michael D. 2003. Anglophone slaves in Francophone Louisiana. *American Speech* 78: 404–433.

Picone, Michael D. Forthcoming. French dialects of Louisiana: A revised typology. In Michael D. Picone and Catherine Evans Davies, eds., *Language variety in the South: Historical and contemporary perspectives.* Tuscaloosa: University of Alabama Press.

Picone, Michael D., and Catherine Evans Davies, eds. Forthcoming. *Language variety in the South: Historical and contemporary perspectives.* Tuscaloosa: University of Alabama Press.

Reed, Revon. 1976. *Lâche pas la patate: Portrait des Acadiens de la Louisiane.* Montreal: Éditions Parti pris.

Richard, Zachary. 1987. *Voyage de nuit: Cahier de poésie, 1975–79.* Lafayette: Éditions de la Nouvelle Acadie.

Rojas, David M., Deborah Piston-Hatlen, Kathryn Propst, Madeleine Gonin, and Tamara Lindner, eds. (Project Director: Albert Valdman, in collaboration with Barry Jean Ancelet, Amanda LaFleur, Michael D. Picone, Kevin J. Rottet and Dominique Ryon.) 2003. *A la découverte du français cadien à travers la parole/Discovering Cajun French through the spoken word.* Bloomington: Indiana University Creole Institute. CD-ROM.

Rottet, Kevin J. 2001. *Language shift in the coastal marshes of Louisiana.* New York: Peter Lang.

Valdman, Albert, ed. 1997. *French and Creole in Louisiana.* New York: Plenum.

Valdman, Albert, Thomas A. Klingler, Margaret M. Marshall, and Kevin J. Rottet. 1998. *Dictionary of Louisiana Creole.* Bloomington: Indiana University Press.

Valdman, Albert, Kevin J. Rottet, Barry Jean Ancelet, Amanda LaFleur, Richard Guidry, Thomas A. Klingler, Tamara Lindner, Michael D. Picone and Dominique Ryon. 2010. *Dictionary of Louisiana French: As spoken in Cajun, Creole, and American Indian communities.* Jackson: University Press of Mississippi.

CONTRIBUTORS

Barbara E. Bullock is Professor of Linguistics in the Department of French and Italian at the University of Texas. She specializes in the structural outcomes of the Romance languages in the American diaspora. Her research interests include linguistic change in its ecological context and the language of immigrant, heritage, and borderland speakers who have been isolated from the standardizing norms of literacy and education. Her research program has involved fieldwork in Frenchville, Pennsylvania, and the borderlands of the Dominican Republic and Haiti. Her laboratory research concentrates on bilingual and contact speech, including codeswitching and convergence. Most recently she has begun to explore the power of corpus linguistics and natural language processing as effective tools in research on language variation. She is the co-editor of *The Cambridge Handbook of Linguistic Code-switching* and *Formal Aspects of Romance Linguistics.* Her many articles and book chapters have covered phonology, bilingualism, language contact, and language change.

Marianna Di Paolo is Associate Professor of Anthropology, Director of the Shoshoni Language Project, and Adjunct Associate Professor of Linguistics at the University of Utah; and Research Associate at the National Museum of Natural History (the Smithsonian). In 2003 she chaired the Committee on Ethnic Diversity in Linguistics of the Linguistic Society of America. Her research focus is on sociophonetics and variation and change in English and Shoshoni, and on the documentation and revitalization of Shoshoni. Her recent publications include "The Peripatetic History of ME *ɛ:" (co-author, 2010) and *Sociophonetics: A Student's Guide* (co-edited, Routledge, 2011). The Shoshoni Language Project (SLP) includes the Shoshone/Goshute Language Apprenticeship Program; pre-K–12 and university-level Shoshoni curriculum and materials development; language teacher training; and the production of a 30,000-word electronic lexicon, a 3,000-word Talking Dictionary, children's picture books, and claymation films. The SLP received the William G. Demmert Cultural Freedom Award from the National Indian Education Association in 2013.

Dirk Elzinga is Associate Professor of Linguistics and English Language at Brigham Young University in Provo, Utah. His research interests include the sound structure of English and the documentation of the native languages of Utah and the Great Basin. Among his publications are "English Adjective Comparison and Analogy" (*Lingua* 116.6: 757–770), "Preaspiration and Gemination in Central Numic" (co-author, *International Journal of American Linguistics* 71.4: 413–444), and "Another Look at Shoshoni Taps and Spirants" in *Uto-Aztecan: Structural, Temporal and Geographical Perspectives*, edited by Eugene Casad and Thomas Willet (Universidad de Sonora, Hermosillo, Mexico).

Carmen Fought is Associate Professor of Linguistics at Pitzer College in Claremont, California. Her research focuses on the dialects of California, from those associated with Latinos and Latinas to the much-discussed "Valley Girl" way of speaking. Dr. Fought is also studying the representation of language in the media, including film, television, and commercials. She is the author of *Chicano English in Context* (Palgrave/Macmillan, 2003) and the editor of *Sociolinguistic Variation* (Oxford University Press, 2004).

MaryEllen Garcia is Associate Professor Emerita at the University of Texas at San Antonio. Her publications explore the linguistic repertoire of Mexican Americans, based primarily on her own fieldwork in El Paso and San Antonio, Texas. In addition to examining the syntax, semantics and discourse of bilingual Spanish speakers, she has recently investigated the slang style called Pachuco Caló. Dr. García has served on the editorial board of *Language Sciences* and the *Southwest Journal of Linguistics*. She was the first Chair of the Linguistic Society of America's Committee on Ethnic Diversity in Linguistics.

Lauren Hall-Lew is a Lecturer in Sociolinguistics at the University of Edinburgh. She specializes in phonetic variation in English and is particularly interested in the relationship between sound change and social meaning. She is a co-author of the language learning textbook *Let's Speak Twi: A Proficiency Course in Akan Language and Culture* (2010, CSLI Publications).

Mauricio J. Mixco is Professor Emeritus of Linguistics at the University of Utah. Born in El Salvador and educated in the San Francisco Bay Area, among other subjects, he has taught Ibero-Romance Linguistics, Historical Linguistics, Native American Linguistics, Field Methods, Language Maintenance and Revitalization.

Aside from Yuman and Siouan research and articles, he has also been working on Shoshoni (Numic, Uto-Aztecan) for the last decade or so, specifically, editing the traditional texts in the *Wick R. Miller Collection*. He is the author of *Kiliwa Dictionary, Kiliwa Texts: 'When I Have Donned My Crest of Stars', Cochimí and Proto-Yuman: Lexical and Syntactic Evidence for a New Language Family in Lower California, Kiliwa, Kiliwa del Arroyo León, Baja California (Archivo de Lenguas Indígenas de México), Mandan* and Lyle Campbell and Mauricio J. Mixco, *A Glossary of Historical Linguistics*. He has also translated two biographies from Spanish and a grammar from English to Spanish, Luis Nicolau D'Olwer, *Fray Bernardino de Sahagún 1499-1590*, Miguel de León-Portilla, *Bernardino de Sahagún, First Anthropologist,* and Lyle Campbell, *Gramática Pipil*.

Peter L. Patrick was born in New York City and grew up in Jamaica. He is Professor of Sociolinguistics at the University of Essex and a member of the Essex Human Rights Centre. His research interests include language variation, creole languages, applied sociolinguistics, language rights, and forensic linguistics. He is the author of *Urban Jamaican Creole: Variation in the Mesolect* (1999) and *Comparative Creole Syntax: Parallel Outlines of 18 Creole Grammars* (2007), with John A. Holm. As an expert on Creole languages, he has testified in U.S. and UK courts in civil and criminal cases and assisted in the development of Jamaican language programs in the UK's Further Education section. He has recently been working to challenge and refine the use of language as a tool for determining origins in asylum applications and has authored expert opinions in over 60 cases in the UK immigration and asylum tribunals. He is the convenor, with Monika Schmid and Karin Zwaan, of the Language and Asylum Research Group (http://www.essex.ac.uk/larg) and is co-author of the 2004 *Guidelines for the Use of Language Analysis in Relation to Questions of National Origin in Refugee Cases*.

Michael D. Picone is Professor of French and Linguistics at the University of Alabama. He is based in the Department of Modern Languages and Classics, which he formerly chaired. His publications and program of research encompass an assortment of lexicological, phonological, and language contact topics, as well as contemporary and historical profiles of language use in the Gulf South, especially in Louisiana and Alabama, and, more recently, language in relation to the visual arts. He is the author of *Anglicisms, Neologisms and Dynamic French* (1996, John Benjamins), a detailed study of borrowings and other types of lexical creativity in the French of France. He is co-editor of the *Dictionary of Louisiana French, as Spoken in Cajun, Creole, and American Indian Communities* (2010, University Press of Mississippi) and is co-editor of *Language Variety in the South: Historical and Contemporary Perspectives* (forthcoming, University of Alabama Press). For distinguished contributions involving French-related education and research, he was named Chevalier de l'Ordre des Palmes Académiques by the French National Ministry of Education.

Keren Rice is University Professor and Canada Research Chair in Linguistics and Aboriginal Studies at the University of Toronto, where she is currently chair of the Department of Linguistics. Her research is in the area of Athabaskan languages, phonology, morphology, and language revitalization. Her publications include the book *Morpheme Order and Semantic Scope: Word Formation in the Athapaskan Verb*, as well as the co-edited *Current Issues in Athapaskan Linguistics: Current Perspectives on a Language Family* and *Athabaskan Prosody*, as well as many articles on Athabaskan languages and phonology. Professor Rice won the 2013 National Achievement Award from the Canadian Linguistics Association for outstanding contributions to the field of linguistics, and received the Killam Prize in 2011 and the Molson Prize in 2012. She served as editor of the *International Journal of American Linguistics* for 11 years. Professor Rice served as President of the Linguistic Society of America in 2012 and President of the Canadian Linguistics Association from 1998 to 2000. She was elected a Fellow of the American Academy for the Advancement of Science in 2005 and of the Royal Society of Canada in 2012.

Arthur K. Spears is Presidential Professor at The City University of New York (in the Anthropology Department at The City College and in the Linguistics and Anthropology Programs at The Graduate Center). Professor Spears's research spans sociolinguistics, linguistic anthropology, pidgins/creoles and language contact, grammatical analysis, race and ethnicity, education, and ideology. His language specialties are African American English and Haitian Creole. He is the founder and first editor of *Transforming Anthropology* and was the President (2007–2009) of the Society for Pidgin and Creole Linguistics. Among Professor Spears's books are *The Haitian Creole Language* (co-editor, 2010); *Black Linguistics: Language, Society, and Politics in Africa and the Americas* (co-editor, 2003), *Race and Ideology* (editor, 1999); and *The Structure and Status of Pidgins and Creoles* (co-editor, 1997).

Almeida Jacqueline Toribio is Professor of Linguistics in the Department of Spanish and Portuguese at the University of Texas at Austin. Her research deals with U.S. and Dominican Spanish, with particular attention to language contact as implicated in phonology and morphosyntax; language ideologies as related to language maintenance and identity formation in borderland contexts (Haiti and the Dominican Republic); sociolinguistic variation in U.S. and Dominican Spanish; and, notably, codeswitching, demonstrating its importance for our understanding of clausal syntax. She co-edited *The Cambridge Handbook of Linguistic Codeswitching* and a special issue of *Bilingualism: Language and Cognition*, devoted to convergence; she edited a special issue of *Lingua* on the syntax of codeswitching.

Walt Wolfram is William C. Friday Distinguished University Professor at North Carolina State University, where he also directs the North Carolina Language and Life Project. He has pioneered research on social and ethnic dialects since the 1960s and published more than 20 books and over 300 articles on socioethnic and regional varieties. Professor Wolfram is particularly interested in the application of sociolinguistic information for public audiences, including the regular production of television documentaries, the construction of museum exhibits, and the development of innovative dialect awareness curricula for the North Carolina Department of Public Instruction. He received the Caldwell Humanities Laureate from the North Carolina Humanities Council; the Holladay Medal for lifetime achievement; and the Linguistics, Language and the Public Award from the Linguistic Society of America. He has also served as President of the Linguistic Society of America, the American Dialect Society, and the Southeastern Conference on Linguistics.

Amy Wing-mei Wong is a PhD candidate in the Linguistics Department at New York University. Her research focuses on the sociophonetics of regional and social variation in English, with particular interests in language and Chinese American identities. She has also worked on issues related to bilingualism, including codeswitching, language shift and maintenance, and contact varieties of English. She is a native speaker of Cantonese Chinese and has experience teaching Cantonese Chinese as a heritage language in the United States.

INDEX

Page numbers in *italics* indicate tables.

AAE *see* African American English (AAE)
AASE *see* African American Standard
  English (AASE)
AAVE *see* African American Vernacular
  English (AAVE)
absolute tense markers 187
accommodation 144
acrolectal varieties 127
African American English (AAE) 101–14;
  about 101; African Americans and their
  language varieties 103–4; *be* in semantics
  in 90–2; *be done* in 109–12, *110,
  111*; consonant cluster simplification
  99, *100*; defining 107–8; diaspora
  varieties 105; Ebonics controversy
  104–5; grammatical camouflage 106–7;
  history 102–3; language contact 10, 18;
  linguistic features 105–8; non-African
  American speakers of 103; phonology
  112–13, *113*; postvocalic word-final
  /l/ deletion 112–13, *113*; problem
  sets 90–92, 99–100, 109–13; regional
  varieties 105; semantics and pragmatics
  109–12, *110, 111*; social context 103–5;
  standard and vernacular 101–2
African American Language *see* African
  American English (AAE)
African Americans, defined 24, 101
African American Standard English
  (AASE) 101, 102, 105–6, 107; *see also*
  African American English (AAE)

African American Vernacular English
  (AAVE): about 101, 102; *be done* in
  109–12, *110, 111*; Ebonics controversy
  104; grammatical camouflage 106, 107;
  native speaker intuitions and 90–2,
  91; Remote Perfect tense 24; *see also*
  African American English (AAE)
agglutinating morphology 58–9, *59,* 73
American Indian languages in the U.S.
  16, 197; Mandan 69–81; Navajo 37–52;
  Shoshoni 53–68
analytic languages 171–2
Anglophone American planters 199–200
anthropology 5
Apache languages 37, 38, *38*
Appalachian Vernacular English 87–90, *88*
a- prefixing 87–90, *88*
argot 145
Arikara 70, 71
aspect, defined 91, 130
attrition, language 15–16

Bacon's Rebellion 31
Bajan 19
Barbados 19
barely, in Chicano English 120
basilectal varieties 127
be 90–92
be done, in AAE and AAVE 109–12, *110,
  111*
be regularization *96,* 96–7, *97*

bidialectalism 15
bilingual education 168–9, 183
bilingualism 13–15
BIN, in African American English 106–7
Black English *see* African American English (AAE)
borrowing 17, 42–3, 141–3, 203

Cajun French: about 196; borrowings 203; codeswitching 203–4, *207,* 209, *210,* 211; French nouns 206, 207, *207;* history 197–200; language contact 10, 14, 203–4; linguistic features 203–4; nouns and pluralization 206–8, *207;* past tense verb inflection 208–9; problem sets 206–11; social context 200–2; verbs, codeswitched 209, *210,* 211; *see also* Louisiana Creole
Caló 140, 145–6, *146*
calques 141
camouflage *see* grammatical camouflage
Cane River area 198, 199
Cape Haitian dialect of Haitian Creole 188, *189*
case 23
Charbonneau, Toussaint 55, 56
Chicano English 115–25; about 115–16; history 116; language contact 10, 115; linguistic features 118–20; myths about 116–18; phonology 118, *122,* 122–5, *124;* problem sets 121–5; real language data 121–2; reflexive pronouns 119; semantics 119–20; social context 116–18; syntax 119; verb forms 119
Chinese 163–79; about 163–4; classifiers 176–7, *176–7;* history 164–7; linguistic features 169–73; loanwords 174–6, *175, 176;* morphology, syntax, and word order 170–2; phonetics and phonology 169–70; phonology 174–6, *175, 176;* problem sets 174–7; social context 167–9; tones 170; varieties, regional 163–4; writing system 173
Chinese Exclusion Act (1882) 165, 166
Chinese immigration to the U.S. 164–5, 166
Clark, William 55, 56
class, socioeconomic 31–2
classificatory verbs 49
classifiers 49, 172, 176–7, *176–7*
codeshifting 16
codeswitching, defined 16, 117, 140, 143
code-talking, Navajo 50–1

codification 140
communicative events 16
consonant cluster simplification 99, *100*
contractions 140, 141
could, in Chicano English 120
creole continuum 19, 127–8
creoles 10, 18–19, 196, 198; *see also* Haitian Creole; Jamaican Creole; Louisiana Creole
creole substrate hypotheses 102, 103
creolisms 108
creolist hypotheses on African Ameerican English origins 102
Croatian 23
culture, development of 22

DBGF (distinctively black grammatical features) 107–8
deictic words 59
descriptive work 3
devoicing in vernacular dialects 98–9, *99*
dialect continuum 54
dialects: defined 11; languages *versus* 11–12; *see also specific dialects*
diglossia 15, 127–8, 167, 182–3
Diné bizaad *see* Navajo
diphthongization 140
directness, in African American English 109
discourse markers 144
distinctively black grammatical features (DBGF) 107–8
divergence: of African American English from other U.S. dialects 102
diverse, as term 25–6
diversity 21–33; about 5, 21–2; ethnicity 27–8; human equality and language equality 22–4; minority, as term 26–7; race 28–31; socioeconomic class 31–2; as term 25
Dominican immigration to the U.S. 152–3, 154
Dominican Spanish 151–62; about 151; dialects, regional *158;* double plural marking data *160;* history 152–3; language contact 10; linguistic features 154–7; morphology 160, *160;* phonology *158,* 158–9, *159;* problem sets 157–61; social context 153–4; sociolinguistics 157–8; syntax 160–1
Duvalier, François "Papa Doc" 181–2
dynamic verbs 132

Ebonics *see* African American English (AAE)
education 168–9, 183, 202
ello, in Dominican Spanish 160–1
English-lexified creole 126
equality: human 22–3; language 23–4
ethnic groups, defined 27
ethnicity 27–8

false cognates 142–3
first language (L1) 13
formulaic routines 144
Fort Berthold Reservation 69, 70, 71, 72
Free People of Color 198, 199

genetic descent, defined 128
grammatical, defined 86
grammatical camouflage 106–7
grammaticality: defined 85; social acceptability *versus* 92–3, *93*

habitual aspect 91, 131
Haitian Creole 180–95; about 180; dialect variation 188–9, *189*; Haitian lexicon 184–6, *185*; Haitian words of French origin 184–6, *185*; history 181–2; linguistic features 184–7; phonology, morphology, and dialect variation 188–91, *189, 190, 191*; possessive adjectives suffixes *190*; problem sets 188–94; social context 182–4; tense marking 191, *192–3,* 194; tense-mood-aspect marking 186–7
Haitian immigration to the U.S. 181–2
Haitian Revolution 181
Hanyu Pinyin 173
hiatus 140, 147–8, *148*
Hidatsa 55, 56, 69–70, 71, *71*
human equality 22–3
hypercorrection 158, *159*

identity 144
Immigration and Nationality Act (1965) 166
immigration to the U.S.: Chinese 164–5, 166; Dominican 152–3, 154; Haitian 181–2; Mexican 138–9
imperative 79
imperfect learning 18
inherent variation 128
interference, language 17–18; *see also* transfer, of linguistic features
interlanguages 116

intermediate creoles 19
internalized oppression 32, 104
intransitive verbs 76
intuitions, language 85, 90–2, *91*
isolating languages 170

Jamaican Creole 126–36; about 126; history 126–7; linguistic features 129–31; nouns and determiners 135; orthography 129; palatalization 129–30, *132,* 132–4; problem sets 131–5; social context 127–9; sociolinguistic situation 127–8; tense and aspect 130–1, 134–5; use 128–9

language attrition 15–16
language contact 9–20; about 5; language groups affected by 9–11; languages in contact, effects on 16–18; languages' survival, effects on 15–16; new languages 18–20; outcomes 13–20; speech community, changes in 13–15
language death 15–16
language equality 23–4
language family, defined 12
language intuitions 85, 90–2, *91*
languages: analytic 171–2; dialects *versus* 11–12; first 13; isolating 170; lexifier 18; native 13; new 9–10, 18–20; noninflectional 171–2; partially restructured 19–20; pidgin 9–10; second 13; substrate 19, 126; superstrate 18, 126; topic-comment 171; *see also* specific languages
language transfer 17–18
language use 13
language variety, defined 11
Lau v. Nichols (1974) 168
learning, imperfect 18
Lewis and Clark Expedition 54–6
lexifier language 18
lingua francas 55
Linguistic Subordination, Principle of 86–7
linguists, defined 3
loan translations 141
locatives 59
Los Angeles School District 117
Louisiana Creole: about 196; codeswitching 204, 211; history 197–200; linguistic features 204–5; nouns and verbs 204–5; preverbal markers 204–5; problem sets 209–11; social

context 200–2; verbs, codeswitched 211; *see also* Cajun French

Mandan 69–81; about 69; history 69–71, *71*; language contact 11; linguistic features 72–3; morphology 75–80, *76, 77, 78, 79, 80*; mystery suffixes 79–80, *80*; negation, inflection for 78, *78, 79*; phonology 73–5, *74, 75*; problem sets 73–80; representation and phonological rules, underling 74–5, *75*; social context 72; subject agreement 75–6, *76, 77*; subject and object agreement 77, *77–8*; tense, inflection for 78, *78*; vowel length 73, *74*; vowel nasalization 74, *74*; word order 72–3
Mandarin Chinese classifiers 176–7, *176–7*
measure words *see* classifiers
media 168, 183
mesolectal varieties 128
Mexican Americans *see* Chicano English; Southwest Spanish (SWS)
Mexican immigration to the U.S. 138–9
Mid-Atlantic coastal dialects *96*, 96–7, *97*
Miller, Wick R. 57, 58
minority, as term 26–7
Mississippi Valley subbranch of Siouan 71, *71*
modismos 145
monophthongization 140
mood, defined 24, 130
morphemes: portmanteau 79; zero (Ø) 76
morphology, agglutinating 58–9, *59, 73*

native language 13
Navajo 37–52; about 37; allophones *versus* phonemes 41; alternations, voicing 41–2; Apache languages *versus* 37, 38, *38*; borrowings 42–3; classificatory verbs 48–50; code-talking 50–1; consonant system 39, *39*; diphthongs 39, *40*; history 37–8, *38*; language contact 11; linguistic features *39*, 39–40, *40*; morphology 43–6; numbers 43; phonology 41–3; problem sets 41–51; semantics 48–50; social context 38–9; statistics 37; syllables 42; syntax 46–8; as term 37; tones 40; verb structure 44–6, *45*; vowels 39, *40*; *wh-* questions 48; word order 46–8
neologisms 146
new languages 9–10, 18–20
noninflectional languages 171–2

nonpunctual aspect preverbal markers 186
nonstative verbs 132
normative Spanish 142, 154–6
Numic languages 12, 54; *see also* Shoshoni

Oakland School Board 104
oppression, internalized 32, 104

Pachuco Caló 145–6, *146*
palatalization 129–30, *132*, 132–4
paradigms 140
partially restructured languages 19–20
people of color/person of color, as term 26
pidgin languages 9–10
pin-pen merger 97–8
Pinyin 173
Plantation Society French 199, 200, 201
Pocho Spanish *see* Southwest Spanish (SWS)
Pointe Coupee dialect of Louisiana Creole 200, 205
polyglossia 167
population (*versus* race), defined 30
Port-au-Prince dialect of Haitian Creole *189*
Port de Paix dialect of Haitian Creole 188, *189, 190, 191, 192–3*
portmanteau morphemes 79
postpositions 72
prescriptive work 3
preverbal markers 186–7
Principle of Linguistic Subordination 86–7
progressive aspect 130–1
prosody 118–19
Puerto Rican English 117–18

quantifiers 94–6

race 28–31
racial hierarchy 28
racialization 31
racism 28
regularization *96*, 96–7, *97*, 119
relative tense markers 187
Rom 145
Rough Rock Demonstration School 38
rules, defined 140

Sacagawea 54–6
Sakakawea, Lake 70, 72
say, as creolism in African American English 108

second language (L2) 13
semantic gap 144
serial verb constructions 172
Shoshone (people), as term 53
Shoshoni 53–68; about 53; agglutinating
   morphology 58–9, *59*; consonants 58;
   coronal stops and continuants *64*, 64–5,
   65; demonstratives and demonstrative
   pronouns 59, *59*; history 54–6; language
   contact 11; linguistic features 57–60,
   58, *59*; locatives *62*; morphophonology
   65, 65–7, *66–7*; noncoronal stops and
   continuants 63, *63*; phonology *63*,
   63–5, *64*, *65*; phrases *62*; place-names in
   Great Basin 54; problem sets 61–7; social
   context 56–7; statistics 53; syntax 61–2,
   62; vowels 57–8, *58*; word order 60
sickle-cell allele 30
Siouan-Catawba language family 69, 70,
   71, *71*; *see also* Mandan
social acceptability 86, 92–3, *93*
societal bilingualism 13, 14–15
socioeconomic class 31–2
sociolinguistics 4, 127–8, 157–8
sociolinguistic variation 4
Southern American English: dialects in
   97–8; quantifiers in 94–6
Southwest Spanish (SWS) 137–50;
   about 137; borrowings 141–3;
   codeswitching 143–5, 149–50;
   defined 137; diphthongization 140;
   fricative consonants, deletion of 141;
   hiatus, reducing 147–8, *148*; history
   137–8; lexicon 141–3, 148–9; linguistic
   features 140–6; loan translations 143;
   Pachuco Caló 145–6, *146*; phonology
   147–8, *148*; problem sets 147–50;
   pronunciations 140–1; social context
   138–40; vowel contraction 141
Spanglish *see* Southwest Spanish (SWS)
Spanish: language contact 14; normative/
   standard 142, 154–6
speech community 12–15
stable bilingualism 14
standard dialect, defined 11
Standard English (Standard American
   English) 101–2
Standard Jamaican English 127, 128–9; *see
   also* Jamaican Creole
Standard Spanish 142, 154–6
stative verbs 132
stativity 132
stem form 130

styleshifting 16–17
substrate languages 19, 126
superstrate languages 18, 126
suprasegmentals 118–19
SWS *see* Southwest Spanish (SWS)

Taíno 152
te: in Haitian Creole 187, 191, *192–3*; in
   Louisiana Creole 205
tell, in Chicano English 120
tense, defined 130
Tex-Mex *see* Southwest Spanish (SWS)
them, as creolism in African American
   English 108
TMA (tense mood aspect) particles 130
tones 40, 170
topic-comment languages 171
transfer, of linguistic features 17, 18, 129,
   184, 185, 186, 187; *see also* interference,
   language
transitive verbs 76

variants 16–17
variation, defined 128
variety, defined 11
verbs: classificatory 49; dynamic 132;
   intransitive 76; nonstative 132; serial
   constructions 172; stative 132; transitive
   76
verb transitivity 76
vernacular, defined 102, 139
vernacular dialects of English 85–100;
   about 85–6; *a-* prefixing 87–90, *88*, *be,*
   restructuring past tense *96*, 96–7, *97*;
   consonant cluster simplification 99,
   100; data sets 93–7, *96*, *97*; devoicing
   in 98–9, *99*; grammaticality *versus*
   social acceptability 92–3, *93*; language
   intuitions, grammaticality, and social
   acceptability 86–90; native speaker
   intuitions and African American
   Vernacular English 90–2, *91*; nouns,
   quantifiers, and morphological
   patterning 94–6; phonological data,
   analyzing 97–9; *pin-pen* merger 97–8; *see
   also* African American English (AAE),
   Chicano English, Southern American
   English
vocabulary, defined 140
voiceless vowels 58

was regularization 96, *96*
well-formedness 85, 86

were regularization 96, *97*
West African languages 103
white ethnics 27–8
Wick R. Miller Collection Shoshoni
 Language Project 57, 61
women, referred to as minority 26

word classes 132, *132*
word order, defined 46

Yale romanization 173

zero (Ø) morphemes 76